RIGHTEOUS DECEPTION

RIGHTEOUS DECEPTION

GERMAN OFFICERS AGAINST HITLER

DAVID ALAN JOHNSON

Westport, Connecticut
London

Library of Congress Cataloging-in-Publication Data

Johnson, David, 1950–
   Righteous deception : German officers against Hitler / by David Alan Johnson.
     p. cm.
   Includes bibliographical references and index.
   ISBN 0–275–96953–3 (alk. paper)
   1. World War, 1939–1945—Secret service—Germany. 2. Canaris, Wilhelm, 1887–
1945. 3. Roenne, Alexis, Freiherr von. 4. World War,
1939–1945—Campaigns—France—Normandy. I. Title.
D810.S7 J47 2001
940.54'88743—dc21   2001021185

British Library Cataloguing in Publication Data is available.

Library of Congress Catalog Card Number: 2001021185
ISBN: 0–275–96953–3

First published in 2001

Praeger Publishers, 88 Post Road West, Westport, CT 06881
An imprint of Greenwood Publishing Group, Inc.
www.praeger.com

Printed in the United States of America

The paper used in this book complies with the
Permanent Paper Standard issued by the National
Information Standards Organization (Z39.48–1984).

10 9 8 7 6 5 4 3 2 1

Copyright Acknowledgment

Grateful acknowledgment is given to HarperCollins Publishers, Inc., for permission to
reprint quoted material from Sefton Delmer, *The Counterfeit Spy* (New York: Harper & Row,
1974). Copyright © 1971 by Sefton Delmer.

To Laura—thanks for staying out of the way—again!

Contents

Photo essay follows page 124

Preface

I began thinking about this subject while I was at work on my previous book on German intelligence, *Germany's Spies and Saboteurs*, which dealt extensively with Admiral Wilhelm Canaris and the Abwehr. It troubled me that German intelligence had compiled enough information on the impending Allied landings at Normandy to have stopped it on the beaches but, inspite of this, Hitler did not send massive reinforcements to Normandy. Even after the Invasion had taken place, half of the German forces in northern France, the Fifteenth Army, remained in Calais while the Allied armies pushed their way inland. The usual explanation for this inactivity—that Hitler was a raving lunatic who refused to listen to his generals or to intelligence—struck me as being too pat and simple.

After doing some extensive research into the activities of Admiral Canaris and his colleagues in the Schwarze Kapelle, the reason for Hitler's confusion, and his reluctance to release the Fifteenth Army to the fighting in Normandy, became apparent. Canaris had begun to work against Hitler and the Nazi Party several years before the war began. From 1939 onward he repeatedly misled Hitler and his generals, giving them false information that led them to make incorrect, and sometimes disastrous, decisions. Canaris' most blatant deception took place in January 1944, when he informed his superiors that there was no possibility of an Allied amphibious landing against Italy at the very moment that the Invasion fleet was approaching the Italian coast at Anzio. This "inefficiency" discredited the reputation of the entire German Intelligence Service. Feldmarschall von Rundstedt, the commander of all German forces in the West, had absolutely no confidence in German intelligence and paid no attention to any reports on the Allies or their intentions.

Admiral Canaris' acquaintance and fellow conspirator, Colonel Alexis Baron von Roenne, was more subtle and circumspect in his deception scheme. As head of Fremde Heere West, the data evaluation branch of intelligence, von Roenne was in a position to alter intelligence reports that had been submitted by agents in the field and by other sources. By changing data and tampering with numbers, he was able to carry out his subterfuge without being detected. Among other things, von Roenne doubled the estimated number of troops in the British Isles, which gave the impression that the Allies had enough troops and equipment to launch two separate attacks: one in Normandy and another in Calais. Total bewilderment, not insanity, was the reason behind Hitler's refusal to send the Fifteenth Army's Panzer units to Normandy. Admiral Canaris confused Hitler, while von Roenne misled and misinformed him with outright lies.

Even though Hitler knew when and where the Invasion would take place, he did not know if this was *the* Invasion or only a diversion. And so he decided to keep the Fifteenth Army in Calais to wait for an invasion that never took place. Admiral Canaris and his co-conspirators, especially Colonel von Roenne, were as vital to the success of Operation Overlord, and the subsequent campaign in Normandy, as anything the Allies accomplished in the way of deception and misinformation.

The title *Righteous Deception* comes from a quotation by the Greek dramatist Aeschylus, who lived five hundred years before Christ and was one of the earliest creators of Greek tragedy. He also knew something about human nature. The phrase is taken from Aeschylus' "Fragment 162": "From righteous deception, God standeth not aloof." Admiral Canaris, who had the moral stamina to stand against Hitler and the Nazis as early as 1934, would have appreciated the sentiment.

Abbreviations

AP	Associated Press
BOAC	British Overseas Airways Corporation
CEMA	Council for the Encouragement of Music and the Arts
COSSAC	Chief of Staff, Supreme Allied Command
CSM	Committee of Special Means
ENSA	Entertainments National Service Organization (British equivalent of the American forces USO)
FHO	Fremde Heere Ost (department of German Intelligence concerned with the Eastern Front)
FHW	Fremde Heere West (department of German Intelligence concerned with the Western Allies)
FUSAG	First U.S. Army Group
LCS	London Controlling Section
LSTs	Landing Ship Tanks
NCO	Noncommissioned officer
OKW	Oberkommando der Wehrmacht
OSS	Office of Strategic Services
RAF	Royal Air Force
SD	Sicherheitsdienst (security service)
SHAEF	Supreme Headquarters, Allied Expeditionary Force
SIM	Italian Intelligence Service
SOE	Special Operations Executive

Spies and Counter-Spies

First Lieutenant John Murphy of the U.S. 4th Division was finally going to get what he wanted most in the world: two days' leave in London. At long last, he would be going to the city he had heard about all his life. His mother was born in London, and his father taught English literature. He was avidly looking forward to seeing The Tower, Westminster Abbey, and all the other places he had been told about.

But before he left, Murphy and everyone else in his unit had to sit through a lecture on security by the camp's intelligence officer; "Careless Talk Costs Lives" was the subject. It completely ruined his two days away from the base.

"I was so busy worrying what I *could* say, and what I *couldn't* say, and what I absolutely *must not* say, that all I did was worry," Murphy remembered. "I had the feeling that I was being followed by a German spy, and kept looking over my shoulder all the time. I was so damned worried about giving away some vital piece of information. I probably didn't even know any vital information, but that didn't keep me from being a nervous wreck. That was probably the most nervous couple of days in my life, even worse then when my wife had our first baby."[1]

First Lieutenant Murphy was not the only person in the British Isles who was nervous about security in the spring of 1944. Security, censorship, and "careless talk" had become an obsession. Everyone in Britain, soldier and civilian, was warned to be on strict guard against spreading rumors and was reminded over and again that "The Enemy Is Listening."

Senior Allied officers did their best to wall off the British Isles from the German-occupied Continent, if not from the rest of the world. Newspapers and radio broadcasts were censored strictly. Letters, telegrams, and even telephone calls made by men and women in uniform, were screened for "loose talk," accidental disclosures of information that might fall into enemy hands. General Dwight D. Eisenhower, Supreme Allied Commander, issued a warning about leaking military information, followed by a threat that he would see that "the most stringent disciplinary action is taken in all cases of the violation of security."[2]

The object of all this security, and all the tension, was obvious to everyone in the British Isles, but especially to those in southern England. Tanks and other military vehicles choked narrow country lanes. Men in uniform were everywhere; in some small towns in the south of England, soldiers in nearby camps far outnumbered civilians. The long-awaited invasion of the German-occupied Continent, D-Day, was close at hand. Anyone could see that. But, of course, no one knew exactly when the great event would be taking place. And everyone, soldier and civilian alike, was warned not to speculate—the enemy was indeed listening.

Senior Allied officers, British and American, were making every possible effort to keep as much information on the impending Invasion from the curious. Anyone who might have access to documents or official information was given a thorough background check and was liable to periodic checks even after being given security clearance. Allied planners were determined that the operation would remain as mysterious as humanly possible, with no leaks and no breaches of security.

But everyone connected with Overlord, from General Eisenhower down, realized that the Invasion could never be kept completely secret. The very size and scope of preparations for the landings made secrecy impossible. Britain was alive with troop movements, training exercises, supply build-ups, and all the other vital activities leading up to D-Day. And the enemy kept his eyes and ears trained on Britain constantly, watching to pick up any clue even remotely connected with the Invasion. Trying to keep anything as big as Overlord a secret would be like trying to conceal the phases of the moon or the positions of the planets.

So Allied intelligence decided to do just the opposite—instead of trying to keep Overlord a secret, they would release a flood of false and contradictory reports about the operation and its preparations. An array of false information was "leaked" to the enemy. Among the information that was allowed to fall into enemy hands were: communiqués on non-existent army units, a wide range of reports regarding the "genuine" site of the D-Day landings—naming landing areas as far removed as the coast of Norway to the Balkans and a wild range of landing dates and times. The object was to overwhelm the enemy with so much information that he would not recognize the truth if he happened to come across it.

An Anglo-American "deception unit" was formed to coordinate this campaign of trickery. This unit was given the wonderfully benign-sounding title The Committee of Special Means (CSM), which was part of the complex deception plan code-named Bodyguard.

Bodyguard was actually an overall plan to deceive the Germans, a sort of master committee to fool Hitler and his OKW (Oberkommando der Wehrmacht or German High Command) into thinking that the Allies were planning to launch their Invasion of the Continent somewhere other than Normandy. It was made up of a number of component operations, each one having its own specific purpose. Some of the main Bodyguard components were:

Fortitude North: A deception plan to convince the Germans that the Allies planned to launch their Invasion in German-occupied Norway

Fortitude South: A plan to deceive Hitler into believing that the main Allied Invasion would come in the Pas de Calais

Ironside: A plan to mislead the Germans into thinking that the D-Day Invasion would be on the Bay of Biscay coast

Vendetta: An operation to convince the Germans that a major landing would take place in the south of France, near Marseilles.[3]

By the spring of 1944, with the date of the Invasion drawing near, the main task of Bodyguard narrowed. By that time, its sole function was to convince the Germans that the Allied landings would take place in the Pas de Calais, and that the Normandy invasion was only a diversion.

The concept behind Bodyguard had its origins in the carnage of the First World War. Its purpose was to prevent the protracted killing matches of 1914–1918, such as the battles of Ypres, Arras, Passchendaele, and the Somme. In the Battle of the Somme, in July 1916, 2,000 British infantrymen were killed during the first hour of fighting. Bodyguard, it was hoped, would avert this sort of slaughter. Instead of trying to overpower the enemy, the strategy would be to trick him—fool the enemy into concentrating his weapons and reserves in one place—and then attack someplace else. Deception would not completely do away with the bloodshed, but it should keep it to a bare minimum.

This plan was not just the lofty idea of some armchair staff officer—by 1944, it had already been tried and proven. Bodyguard began its operational life as Plan Jael. Jael was the code name for a deception plot against Feldmarschall Erwin Rommel, the legendary Desert Fox, and his Afrika Korps.

Jael is a biblical name. Her disturbing story is in Judges 4:1–22 and involves the war between Israel and Canaan. When chapter 4 opens, Sisera, the commander of the Canaanite army that is oppressing Israel, is in flight after a defeat by the Israelite forces. In his flight, he arrives at the tent of Jael, the wife of Heber, an ally of the Israelite commander.

Jael invites Sisera into her tent, gives him milk to drink and a comfortable rug for sleeping. When he is fast asleep, Jael takes a sharp wooden tent peg and drives it into Sisera's brain. The Israelite commander, Barak, passes her tent in pursuit of Sisera; Jael proudly asks Barak to come inside and see what she had done. "So he went into her tent; and there lay Sisera with the tent peg in his temple." Jael represents not only deception, but also deadly trickery in war.

In the autumn of 1942, General Sir Bernard Montgomery was preparing for an attack against the Afrika Korps at El Alamein. In order to ensure the success of the operation, it was vital that these preparations be kept secret. If the Germans knew about Montgomery's planned offensive in advance, the outcome would have been a killing match of First World War proportions, and probably would have resulted in failure for Montgomery and his Eighth Army. Jael was concocted to keep the offensive, code-named Operation Lightfoot, hidden from the enemy until the last possible minute.

With the help of a film set designer, some experts on camouflage, and a few intelligence men, Plan Jael's leaders did just that—they successfully concealed the movements of Montgomery's entire Eighth Army. One thousand tanks, 150,000 men, about 1,000 artillery pieces, and several thousand supply and support vehicles crossed the flat desert terrain without the Germans knowing anything about it. Montgomery's masters of deception had completely fooled Rommel and his intelligence.

An officer who took part in the offensive referred to this deception plan as Operation Bertram instead of Plan Jael. This officer watched the plan as it was taking shape. The deception was accomplished by making dummy tanks and vehicles out of wood and canvas, which were left in plain sight and gave the impression of a concentration in the north. The armored units, meanwhile, slipped away to the south. The tanks moved at night, and covered up their tracks as they went. Radio operators stayed behind, sending meaningless messages to give the impression that no movement had taken place. The build-up in the south was kept under camouflage nets, which concealed all the elaborate preparations from German reconnaissance.[4]

When Operation Lightfoot was finally let loose, on 23 October 1942, the Afrika Korps was taken completely by surprise. On the following morning, the Germans still had no idea exactly what the situation was, or precisely where the main attack had occurred along a 40-mile front. By 5 November, the Afrika Korps was in full retreat. Rommel realized that his position in North Africa was beyond salvaging.

A year later, Plan Jael was renamed Plan Bodyguard. Senior officers hoped that it would be as successful in northern Europe as it had been in North Africa. New name or not, its function would be the same: confuse the enemy; deceive the enemy; fool the enemy; mislead the enemy into believing that D-Day would take place in the Pas de Calais instead of Normandy.

In addition to Bodyguard, Allied intelligence also had another extraordinarily effective, and experienced, deception unit: the Double-Cross Committee. Double-Cross, simply stated, turned German intelligence against itself. Whenever a German spy was captured by British intelligence or Scotland Yard, the unfortunate soul was given a choice: either go to work for British counterintelligence (MI-5), sending false information to their superiors in Germany, or be hanged as a spy. Most of them did not hesitate to choose the less painful of the two evils and were soon sending phony but genuine-sounding information across to Berlin or Hamburg.

The main objective of Double-Cross was to dominate the German espionage system. The Hungarian writer Ladislas Farago described the function of Double-Cross: "to utilize fallen agents in a systematic deception campaign aimed at their original employers." This meant controlling captured German agents, finding out the enemy's military intentions, especially concerning their defenses against a landing in northern France, and misleading the enemy regarding Allied intentions.

The last item was probably the most important. "Turned" agents would keep Hitler and the OKW off balance by sending a dizzying array of reports that were either misleading or totally false. Agents in the United States sent detailed reports on the movements of totally fictitious U.S. Army units, including dates and times of their departure for the British Isles. Contacts in Britain gave German intelligence "completely reliable information" that the D-Day landings had been planned for the Pas de Calais and would be preceded by a massive bombardment of the Calais area. None of these reports were true; they just sounded that way.

Bodyguard and Double-Cross very nicely complemented each other. Together, the two plans would keep German intelligence completely off balance regarding Allied strength for the D-Day landings, as well as where and when the Invasion would actually take place.

But in spite of the elaborate deception plans and the determination of Allied planners to keep all vital information regarding D-Day out of the hands of the Germans, information about the Invasion had a nasty habit of getting away from its keepers. By the spring of 1944, several secret documents and any number of important disclosures, including the meaning of the code name Overlord, had been discovered by the enemy. These discoveries caused no small amount of anxiety for both British and American intelligence, who did not really know how much damage they had done to the D-Day operation.

One major breach in Overlord security came in March 1944. A package of secret documents had been sent mysteriously to Chicago; the loosely wrapped envelope had broken open in a mail sorting room. Four U.S. Army sorters had seen the documents, along with the Chicago post office employees. All of these people had the chance to examine the papers, which had the name Overlord printed prominently in a number of places.

The secret papers divulged the day and date of the invasion, named Normandy as the object of the landings, and also revealed planned Allied movements in France after the Invasion had taken place. In short, all the details that Bodyguard and Double-Cross had been trying to keep secret all those months—dates, times, places, preparations—had literally been made public.

General Eisenhower's naval aide, Captain Harry C. Butcher, noted: "The G-2s are excited, particularly in Washington." (G-2 was the designation for U.S. Army intelligence.) Which proves that the British are not the only nationality that have the gift of understatement. The G-2s were not excited. The G-2s were panic-stricken. An entire envelope filled with top secret papers had been sent out of the country, practically right under their noses, and they had no idea who might have done it. Frantically, they set out to find out how such a violation of security possibly could have taken place.

It turned out that the documents had been sent by a sergeant named Thomas P. Kane, who was stationed in Ordinance Supply in London. He had sent the package to his sister, who lived in Chicago. Both Sergeant Kane and his sister were of German descent; the address to which the package had been sent was in a German-speaking neighborhood. This information served to heighten the panic of the G-2s.

When Sergeant Kane was confronted with the evidence, he said that he could not imagine how he could have sent the documents to his sister. His only explanation was that he had been preoccupied with her and her well-being in recent days, after he found out that she was seriously ill, and also that he had been very tired and under a great deal of strain.

After considering the facts of the incident, his superiors came to the conclusion that Sergeant Kane was telling the truth, and that he should not be brought up on charges of espionage. He was certainly careless and probably a bit dim, if not altogether stupid, but he was not a spy. Kane was very lucky; both G-2 and the FBI wanted his head on a silver platter. He was kept under virtual house arrest until after D-Day, however, and his telephone was tapped. His family in Chicago were also kept "under surveillance" by the FBI. In addition, the FBI monitored the postal sorters who had seen the Overlord documents.[5]

General Eisenhower's naval aide, Captain Butcher, noted that the incident was "just another worry for the supreme commander." For the supreme commander, and G-2, and MI-5, and the FBI, and everybody else connected with Overlord. No one had any real idea of how much information may have been leaked to the other side. No damage seemed to have been done, but nobody knew for certain.

Other indiscretions took place, as well, causing still more worry for the Overlord staff. Two such incidents, which involved loose talk and bad judgment, came at the hands of senior military officers.

One of the worst offenders was a naval aide to Admiral Harold R. "Betty" Stark. Admiral Stark was the commander in chief of U.S. naval forces in Europe. His aide, identified as Captain Edward M. Miles, had access to a great many confidential details of the impending Invasion. He also had a bit too much to drink at a party, and talked openly of what he knew about Overlord—including the date and place of the Invasion. And Captain Miles could speak with authority, since he had access to information regarding Neptune, one of the most closely guarded secrets of D-Day. Neptune was the code name for the amphibious phase of Overlord, the actual landings on the Normandy coast. Admiral Stark was one of Neptune's key planners.

General Eisenhower heard about Captain Miles' intoxicated disclosures from Air Chief Marshal Sir Trafford Leigh-Mallory, Neptune's Tactical Air Force commander. Leigh-Mallory made it quite clear that he was not at all happy about the American naval officer's behavior. Eisenhower informed Admiral Stark of the incident and told Stark to deal with Captain Miles quickly and effectively. Admiral Stark got the message. Miles was banished to the United States. He was later put back on active service, however, and took part in the invasion of Okinawa in April 1945.

This was not the first incident of its kind. Almost a month before, a U.S. Army major general was guilty of similar behavior. Major General Henry Miller, who was quartermaster of the U.S. Ninth Air Force and had access to top secret information regarding Overlord, attended a party at Claridge's in London. During the course of dinner conversation, he told a group of Red Cross nurses that the Invasion would take place before 15 June.

This was an extremely choice bit of gossip, the sort of thing that German intelligence was always on the lookout for. It was divulged in a public dining room in front of a group of people who would be sure to pass the news along to all of their friends.

Since Major General Miller was an officer in the U.S. Army, Eisenhower dealt with this incident himself. And he dealt with it, and with Miller, immediately and harshly, in spite of the fact that he and Miller had been classmates at West Point. Eisenhower sent Miller back to the United States in disgrace and broke him in rank from major general to lieutenant colonel—a reduction of three grades. This did not prevent any damage that might have been done by Miller's lapse of judgment, but it did serve as a warning that no one would be exempt from punishment where the security of Overlord was concerned.

During the tense weeks of the Overlord build-up, other scares also took place. The plans for Neptune were left in a London taxi by a British brigadier. Fortunately for the Allies, the taxi driver turned the plans over to lost property at Waterloo Station. Lost property notified its owner, who promptly claimed it.

The briefcase of another British officer disappeared in an air raid. It was thought that the briefcase, which contained documents relating to Neptune and one of its deception plans, was blown up by the same bomb that killed the officer carrying it. But no one knew for certain exactly what happened to it, and the deception plan was discontinued while the situation was analyzed.

Other incidents also attracted the attention of Allied intelligence. In the weeks leading up to the Invasion, MI-5 noticed something odd in the daily crossword puzzles of London's *Daily Telegraph*. Five highly secret code names connected with Overlord had appeared as answers to puzzle clues within a matter of a few weeks.

In 2 May 1944's puzzle, no. 17 across was, "One of the U.S." (4 letters). The answer was Utah, which was printed in the following day's edition. Utah was the code name for one of the American beaches on the Normandy coast. On 22 May, no. 3 down had this clue: "Red Indian on the Missouri (5)." Omaha was the answer—the code name for the second of two U.S. landing beaches.

Within the next few weeks, the odd situation became odder still. The puzzle of 30 May offered this for no. 11 across: "This bush is a centre for nursery revolutions (8)"—the solution was Mulberry, the name given to the two artificial harbors that would supply the Invasion forces after the landings. On 1 June, no. 15 down was, "Britannia and he hold to the same thing (7)"—this was Neptune, code name for the amphibious assault on the Normandy beaches. And on 27 May, Overlord was the correct response to the obscure clue for 11 across: "but some big-wig like this has stolen some of it at times (8)."

To MI-5, five code names in a month's time went beyond odd; it was bizarre and frightening. Investigators decided to pay a visit to the compilers of the puzzles, two schoolmasters, Leonard Sidney Dawe and Neville Jones, who lived in the suburbs of London.

Two intelligence men went to see Dawe at his home in Leatherhead, Surrey, and very politely asked how he came to use those five particular words in his puzzles. Dawe seemed surprised by the question and could not give a concrete reason. He went on to say that he could not even say when he and his friend Jones made up the puzzles—it could have been six months before. The only reason he could think of that the five top secret code words appeared in a month was, as Cornelius Ryan put it in *The Longest Day*, "fantastic coincidence."[6]

MI-5 had no proof that either Dawe or Jones was involved in espionage, and the matter of the bizarre crossword puzzles became a closed file. But in years following the war, the matter has been rethought. Writers and historians have suggested that the two puzzle makers could not possibly have been as innocent as they seemed and that the string of coincidences was far too fantastic to be believed. But there was no proof, one way or the other.[7]

One of the worst security breaches involving Overlord, probably *the* worst, involved British Prime Minister Winston Churchill. There was nothing either innocent or coincidental about it.

Prime Minister Churchill made many trans-Atlantic telephone calls to President Franklin D. Roosevelt, during which he discussed any number of important topics. Churchill made his phone calls without any fear of enemy eavesdropping. He always used his own private telephone booth at the war office, and his words, as well as President Roosevelt's, were scrambled, making the conversation sound like so much gibberish to anyone who might be trying to listen in.

The scrambler was actually a device called A-3, which had been developed by Bell Telephone. The A-3 device was kept in a guarded room in downtown Manhattan, at 47 Walker Street; its radio frequency was changed constantly by telephone operators who channeled the trans-Atlantic calls. Neither Churchill nor Roosevelt had any worries about the enemy tapping into their conversation. Even if German intelligence happened to intercept the telephone line, the Bell Telephone scrambler would render their intercept useless.

But German intelligence had indeed tapped their line. And they not only knew about the A-3 device; they also knew of a way to neutralize it—to unscramble the scrambler. Technicians at Philips Electronics in Eindhoven, Netherlands, discovered how A-3 worked, and how to manipulate it so that conversations could be heard without interference. They were even able to determine the frequency used by the device. With the help of the engineers at Phillips, the SD—Sicherheitsdienst; literally security service, the intelligence branch of the SS—had begun listening in on the Churchill-Roosevelt conversations in September 1941.

Via their telephone tap, the SD were able to learn any number of things about the Allies and their planned strategy, top secret information that gave them a vital edge over both British and American planners.

In 1943, Allied intelligence concocted another deception plan along the lines of Jael and Bodyguard. The plan was called Cockade; its purpose was to mislead the Germans into believing that an Allied invasion of France had been scheduled for 1943, which would keep German units tied up in France. Army units were not needed in France, but they were desperately needed elsewhere, especially in Russia and in Italy. In France, the Wehrmacht units would be safely out of the way; in Italy and Russia, they could cause no end of trouble for the Allies. There was a lot more to Cockade than this, including a ploy to wear down the Luftwaffe's fighter strength in northern France, but the main idea was to fool German intelligence, to convince them that an invasion of the Pas de Calais would take place in 1943.

In the course of one of his telephone conversations with Roosevelt, Churchill made mention of the fact that the invasion plans for 1943 were phony. The SD were listening, and reported the conversation. German intelligence had been suspicious of Cockade all along, for a number of reasons. Now they had their suspicions confirmed.

Since there was no need to keep their men in France, the German High Command was now free to transfer these units to other theaters—Italy, Sicily, Russia, and the Balkans. The failure of Cockade had another tragic result, as well. The Gestapo were able to round up members of the French resistance who came out of hiding to support the plan. Most of these *maquisards* were executed.

Throughout 1943, Churchill and Roosevelt continued their long-distance conversations, and the SD continued to listen and learn. Among the items picked up were the confirmations that the Allies would be launching their invasion of the Continent in 1944, and that the landing would take place in France. This information was much prized, especially considering its source.

As the year 1943 went on, however, the Americans began to lose faith in A-3. A series of tests had been run to check the device's immunity to tapping and enemy interference; A-3 turned out to be less secure than had been believed. These checks were not based upon any suspicion, either by G-2, British military intelligence, or by Bell Telephone. The timing was purely coincidental. As a result, a new security device was installed to replace A-3 at the very beginning of 1944. But by that time, a good deal of irreparable damage had already been done to Allied security. And eavesdropping on the Churchill-Roosevelt conversations would continue, despite Allied efforts.

Leaks in Allied security were certainly nothing new by 1944. Ominously, one of the worst failures of Allied intelligence to keep information out of enemy hands concerned Overlord's close cousin, Operation Jubilee, the Dieppe raid of August 1942.

Operation Jubilee was never meant to be an invasion of German-occupied France, at least not in the sense of anything large scale or permanent. Its objective was to seize a French Channel port, create as much damage and general mayhem as possible for a few hours, and withdraw. Orders for the Second Canadian Division, which made up the bulk of the assault troops, neatly summed up the purpose of the raid: "SEIZE

JUBILEE AND VICINITY. OCCUPY THE AREA UNTIL DEMOLITION AND EXPLOITATION TASKS ARE COMPLETED. RE-EMBARK AND RETURN TO ENGLAND." It would not be the Second Front that the Soviets had been demanding for nearly a year—far from it. But Jubilee should help to placate Josef Stalin, at least for a few days. It would also serve as a sort of dress rehearsal for the more ambitious, and much more involved, invasion of the Continent in time to come.

Preparations for Jubilee were carried out in strictest secrecy—"abnormal secrecy, even for those days," according to a British writer.[8] But in spite of all the secrecy, word of the impending Dieppe raid still got through the security net and reached German intelligence.

By the summer of 1942, it was evident to the German High Command that some sort of operation was imminent; intelligence had been given any number of clues. The presence of landing craft in English Channel ports was one definite tip-off. Also, the BBC European Division had suddenly increased its number of *messages personnels*, messages or instructions to units of the French underground, in the weeks immediately before Jubilee. Agents in France, including Frenchmen in collaboration with the Germans, also sent information indicating that a landing would take place on the coast of France. Some of the most useful reports were sent by an SD agent at large in England, who went under the code name of *der Druide*.

Der Druide, the Druid, was a Welshman named Gwyn Evans. Evans had been in Britain since the night of 10 May 1941, when he parachuted into Wales. He hated England and any ally of England, including the United States; he was a Welsh nationalist and saw the English as foreign invaders who occupied Wales and oppressed the Welsh people. Any enemy of England, including Adolf Hitler, was a friend of the Welsh nationalists.

As far as Evans was concerned, Adolf Hitler was not only a friend, but was also the would-be savior of Wales. If the Germans won the war, Evans was convinced that Hitler would give Wales its independence. And so Evans was determined to do everything he possibly could do to see that Hitler had every advantage.

Gwyn Evans had several advantages that would help him in Britain as an informer for the SD. He spoke Welsh fluently, which his father taught him, and had contacts among other pro-German Welsh nationalists. He also had a solid musical background, which would serve him well in Britain. Evans had formal training as a musician, and was an accomplished choral vocalist. Through connections, he landed a job as a concert organizer, arranging musical entertainment for Allied troops. The Council for the Encouragement of Music and the Arts (CEMA), was short of people who could arrange and schedule their shows and concerts for the men in the forces. They were glad to have someone with Evans' musical training and experience.

His first job with CEMA would be to organize a concert for the Second Canadian Division. The performers would be a string quartet made up of German refugees. Evans' job was twofold: to schedule a concert with the Canadian entertainment officer, and also to persuade the musicians to popularize their repertoire—to play Strauss waltzes and Gilbert and Sullivan selections instead of their usual Mozart and Beethoven.

As an official entertainment organizer for CEMA, Evans was issued a pass that allowed him to enter restricted areas and circulate among the Canadians. He was free to wander among the troops at will, with his eyes and ears open, picking up information on the impending raid wherever he could find it.

He was, in short, in the right place at exactly the right time, and he also had the perfect cover. He even had genuine papers and identification, issued by CEMA, in case anybody happened to get suspicious.

The refugee members of the string quartet were not all that happy about changing their repertoire; they thought of themselves as classically trained musicians, and did not like the idea of playing music that was beneath their concert hall standards. But the war made it impossible for them to earn a living by playing Mozart and the other works that they had performed in peacetime, so they went to work for CEMA. In the summer of 1942, they found themselves playing their new musical repertoire at open-air concerts throughout England, entertaining various church groups, musical societies, and army units. One of the military units was a regiment of the Second Canadian Division.

The Canadian troops plainly were not fans of chamber music. The reaction of the audience could be described most diplomatically as thin and unenthusiastic; their taste ran to entertainment that was a good deal more earthly and boisterous. Evans was not surprised by the response. After the concert, he left the music tent to find a drink someplace. He found what he was looking for at the temporary officers' club, which was equipped with a bar.

While he was having his drink, Evans was joined by a very young and more than slightly intoxicated lieutenant. The lieutenant was in an unhappy mood, somewhat the more morose for a couple of drinks, and was looking for someone to talk to. What he wanted to talk about was the upcoming raid, in which he would be taking part.

This particular lieutenant had either never been briefed concerning security and "careless talk," or else his tongue had been loosened by alcohol. He was full of chatter—he and his unit would be going ashore at Dieppe, on Midsummer's Day, 24 June, as part of Operation Rutter. He gave Evans full details of the impending landings, at least as much as he knew of them. He was drunk, afraid of what might happen to him, and happy to unburden his fears on any stranger who would listen. The possible consequences to his men, and to himself, apparently did not occur to him.

Evans pretended not to be particularly interested in what he was hearing, but listened very closely and tried to remember everything. That night, he reported his conversation with the Canadian lieutenant to his contact in Germany.

Actually, Evans' information had not been totally accurate. Operation Rutter was changed to Operation Jubilee for security reasons. And bad weather postponed the date of the raid, pushing it back almost two months. But his report alerted the OKW and the German defenses along the French coast.

When Allied forces came ashore at Dieppe on 19 August 1942—a small force of British Commandos and U.S. Army Rangers but mostly troops of the Second Canadian Division—the defending Germans were waiting. A murderous crossfire trapped the invading troops on the beaches, inflicting high casualties; a unit of the Royal Regiment lost 483 men and officers out of a force of 543. The intense machine gun fire made it impossible for the men to move off the beaches, let alone gain any sort of foothold.

The Canadians had begun landing at about 7:30 A.M. By 9:00, senior officers could see that the situation was already a near disaster and ordered a withdrawal. But getting the troops off the beaches proved to be as deadly as the landings had been. The evacuation took several hours and resulted in still more casualties.

Just over 6,000 troops had taken part in Operation Jubilee. Nearly half—over 2,800—were killed, wounded, or taken prisoner. Although the Allies tried to put on a brave face and contended that the operation served as a trial run for the yet unplanned invasion of the Continent, the raid itself was a disaster—50 percent casualties, with nothing much to show for it. An officer on the COSSAC staff (Chief of Staff, Supreme Allied Command; COSSAC was a predecessor of Overlord) flatly admitted, "everything that *could* go wrong went wrong with that operation."[9]

When Gwyn Evans read the newspaper accounts of Dieppe, he could take pride in the fact that he had played his own part in the Allies' setback. He was encouraged by his success and determined to do as much damage as possible to the hated English and their American allies.

British intelligence did not need newspaper articles to realize what had happened at Dieppe. They knew all too well that they had a problem, a dangerous security problem, on their hands.

The Double-Cross Committee was especially alarmed. They had claimed to have captured every German agent in Britain. It was embarrassing to discover that someone had penetrated the security that surrounded Jubilee, somebody operating in England. An unknown enemy agent managed to learn enough about the operation to alert the Germans and also was able to send his information across to his contact.

British counterintelligence was now determined to capture this elusive spy and to turn him into a double agent. They had two imperative motives for finding him: to stop the leaking of information to the enemy; and to save themselves further embarrassment.

No one knew anything at all about this mystery agent; they had no idea who he was or where he was getting his information. None of the Double-Cross agents—German agents now working for MI-5—had any information, either. Both British intelligence and G-2 were very much afraid. Unless the discovery of Jubilee had been a fluke, this unknown German agent might be able to uncover information about future operations, as well.[10]

The British and the American intelligence services had good reason to be afraid, as long as Gwyn Evans remained at large in Britain. He had a pass, which allowed him to travel anywhere in the country, good contacts in London, and a radio for sending his information to the SD. And he was determined to do as much damage to England and her allies as he possibly could. The coming months would give him ample opportunity to do just that.

Preparations for the Invasion of the French coast had been under discussion as early as January 1943. At the Casablanca Conference, a meeting attended by Winston Churchill, Franklin D. Roosevelt, and their chiefs of staff, the Invasion was diplomatically referred to as the "return to the Continent." The operation did not even have a code name as yet, but it was given a director—Lt. General Sir Frederick Morgan was nominated as COSSAC at Casablanca, and began working on the actual Invasion plans. Senior American officers wanted a cross-Channel invasion to take place in 1943. But Churchill remembered the casualties of the First World War. He feared losses from attacking the Channel coast and opposed any sort of landings on the French coast.

General Morgan was chosen for a number of reasons. For one thing, he had a reputation for being an able organizer and administrator: He knew how to get the job done, and was diplomatic toward both fellow officers and subordinates. For another, he liked Americans, and actually enjoyed their company—a rare trait among senior British officers! Morgan was also direct and plain-spoken, however; he often said what was on his mind regardless of who might be offended by it. This was sometimes a cause of irritation.

He sent the Foreign Office into a state of shock when he requested that foreign diplomats be stopped from sending information out of Britain via diplomatic pouch, at least for the duration of the war. Secret documents were a threat to security, Morgan insisted, and he went on to say that foreign diplomats were careless, at best, about information they sent out of the country. The Foreign Office icily overruled his request—foreign diplomats *must* be allowed to send secret documents, security notwithstanding. But General Morgan did have a point. Embassy employees and diplomatic staff would cause major problems for the Allies and their elaborate security precautions.[11]

Morgan had things to worry about besides security. From his headquarters at Norfolk House in London, he began making preparations for the great Invasion. Among the almost limitless details to be worked out were the number of troops to be landed, the number of transports needed to take them across the Channel, the amount of materiel needed to keep the invasion force supplied once ashore, the number and type of warships to support the landings with naval bombardment, and, most of all, the two main points of the landing—where would it take place, and when?

In September 1943, the Invasion was scheduled for the spring of 1944 and given the code name Overlord. Preparations for an amphibious operation of that size and scale would be overwhelming, especially from the standpoint of security. There were skeptics, on both sides of the Channel, who doubted that it could ever succeed. General Morgan had his hands more than full just with his own concerns. He could only hope that Anglo-American counterintelligence could keep Overlord a secret from the enemy's prying eyes.

Bodyguard and its various subbranches were in place; the war of deception was well under way. Colonel John Henry Bevan, the head of London Controlling Section (LCS) which arranged deception plots and stratagems in all theaters of operation in conjunction with Churchill's headquarters, informed General Eisenhower that his organization had already planted the seeds of deception to mislead and confuse Hitler and his OKW. If the plots succeeded, Colonel Bevan went on, Hitler would be completely thrown for a loss when trying to determine the exact time and place of D-Day; at the very moment when Allied troops were coming ashore at Normandy, the German army would be waiting for them in the Pas de Calais. All of Hitler's reactions and decisions would be based upon misinformation. This would lead to disaster for the Wehrmacht.

Eisenhower was impressed by what he heard. He appreciated the complexity of Bodyguard as well as the difficulty of making it work. After listening to Colonel Bevan, the Supreme Commander was convinced that Bodyguard probably would work, despite all of its subplots and complications, and that it had an excellent chance of accomplishing its goal— misleading Hitler regarding Overlord and its objectives.[12]

But German intelligence had a plan of its own—or, more accurately, counterplan—and were hard at work trying to penetrate Bodyguard's smokescreen. Hitler already realized that the Invasion would come sometime in the spring of 1944. Initially, he thought that the place would be Normandy, but had no specific information to back up his hunch. The SD, however, had its devices for finding this information, and for finding the all-important answers to the basic questions: where and when.

Collaborators in France were reporting on the activities of the *maquis*, the French underground. The SD was especially watchful for any increase in radio traffic, or in sabotage, in the Normandy and Calais areas. Gwyn Evans, the Druid, was still traveling throughout Britain, organizing concerts for the troops while keeping his eyes and ears open.

Also, the valet of the British ambassador in Ankara, Turkey, had been supplying the Germans with highly classified Allied documents since the autumn of 1943. The valet, named Elyesa Banza but operating under the code name Cicero, would continue to sell the Germans all the documents on Allied operations that he could get his hands on.[13]

Eisenhower's confidence in Bodyguard was not misplaced. It was just that he had no real idea what the Germans were up to on their side of the Channel.

Walter Bedell Smith, Eisenhower's Chief of Staff, gave Overlord only a fifty-fifty chance of succeeding. Had he known about Cicero, Gwyn Evans, and the other operatives working for German intelligence, he would have been a good deal less optimistic.

NOTES

1. Author interview.

2. From Eisenhower's letter to his commanders: Admiral Ramsey, Air Marshal Leigh-Mallory, Field Marshal Montgomery, and General Bradley, 23 February 1944, Eisenhower Library, Abilene, Kansas.

3. Bodyguard had two additional deception schemes involving operations in Western Europe: Overthrow, a plan to trick the Germans into believing that an invasion would take place in 1942; and Cockade, a similar plan involving an invasion deception for 1943. There were also some thirty-six subplans, as well as numerous—as many as fifty—subdivisions of these. The French resistance, the *maquis*, figured prominently in many of these subplans as saboteurs and as informants on German activities and troop movements. In addition, there were Bodyguard stratagems involving southern and eastern Europe.

4. The British officer who mentioned Operation Bertram was Cecil Ernest Lucas Phillips in his book *Alamein*.

5. The Chicago post office incident is cited in Butcher.

6. Ryan, p. 49.

7. British writer Anthony Cave Brown is of the opinion that the *Telegraph* puzzle clues were too much of a coincidence to be believed. Other writers also share this view. No one has been able to provide any evidence that the puzzle creators were actually engaged in passing information to the enemy, however.

8. The British writer is Anthony Cave Brown.

9. The officer on the COSSAC staff was Major Goronw Rees, quoted in *The World At War* (video series), vol. 17, "Morning."

10. British military intelligence would not confirm that *der Druide* even existed and also refused to acknowledge that any enemy agent operated in the British Isles during the Second World War.

11. An incident that may have prompted General Morgan's request relating to secret documents and diplomatic staff was the Tyler Kent case. Kent, an American, was an employee of the U.S. embassy in London. In 1940, he gave copies of hundreds of classified documents to a friend, Anna Wolkoff. Wolkoff sent them to Germany via the Italian diplomatic pouch. Kent's information gave German intelligence a great many insights into Anglo-American activities in the early part of the war.

12. General Eisenhower makes little mention of Allied espionage and counterespionage in his wartime memoirs, *Crusade in Europe*, in spite of his concern for security and in spite of the vital importance of intelligence in the success of Overlord. His naval aide, Captain Harry C. Butcher, mentions a number of security-related incidents in his diaries.

13. Cicero's activities remain highly controversial, as will be seen.

TWO

Old Fox

Although they did not know it, General Walter Bedell Smith, General Eisenhower, Field Marshal Montgomery, and all the other Allied planners had one tremendous advantage—the chief of German military intelligence, Admiral Wilhelm Canaris, was an enemy of the Nazi regime, and had been conspiring against Adolf Hitler since before the war had begun.

Mainly because of Canaris, Hitler had lost almost all confidence in the German Intelligence Services by 1943. This would prove to be a huge asset to the Allies in their campaign against Germany.

Hitler had been dissatisfied with German intelligence for some time. Both he himself and the OKW, the German High Command, had been misled too often by too many inaccurate—and sometimes totally wrong—reports about the Allies and their activities. Information from intelligence was not always wrong; agents in South America continued to send reliable sailing times of Allied convoys, which assisted U-boat captains in tracking down and sinking British and American ships in mid-Atlantic. But, just as often, desperately needed information regarding enemy plans, intentions, and troop movements turned out to be *dreck*, completely unreliable rubbish.

One of the worst of the intelligence blunders, at least to Hitler's mind, involved the defection of Italy to the Allies in September 1943. Italian dictator Benito Mussolini had been overthrown in July 1943; Hitler sent Admiral Canaris to Italy to determine the intentions of the new government. He feared that the Italians might try to surrender. If the new government, under Marshal Pietro Badoglio, tried to enter into negotiations with the Allies, Hitler threatened to occupy the country and destroy Rome.

Admiral Canaris met with his opposite number, General Cesare Ame, head of the Italian secret service, in Venice. When he returned to Germany, the admiral brought encouraging news: Italy would continue to be a dependable ally of Germany, just as she had been under Mussolini, and showed no signs at all of planning to go over to the Allies. Actually, General Ame had told Canaris just the opposite: Italy wanted to desert the German alliance and defect to the Allies, and wanted Canaris to help in carrying it off.

As the result of Canaris' information, Hitler did not carry out his threats to occupy Italy, arrest Marshal Badoglio, or destroy Rome. He remained suspicious of Badoglio, but Canaris' report reassured him. He decided to wait before taking any action. While he waited, Marshal Badoglio negotiated a surrender treaty with the Allies.

When Hitler learned about the Italian surrender, which was signed on 3 September, he launched into one of his famous temper tantrums. His chief of military intelligence had informed him that Italy would not change sides; a short time later, Italy changed sides. He was livid. Italy's conduct was "a gigantic example of swinishness," Hitler complained to Propaganda Minister Josef Goebbels.[1]

And when he found out that the Italian battle fleet had been turned over to the British at Malta—eight cruisers, eleven destroyers, and five battleships, minus the battleship *Roma*, which had been sunk by a radio-controlled German glider bomb—he had another fit. He had planned to capture the Italian warships himself, with the likelihood of transferring them to the Kriegsmarine. Now every one of those modern warships was in the hands of the British!

Hitler was not quite sure what to make of Admiral Canaris, the Abwehr, or the Intelligence Services in general. They seemed to have a knack for getting things wrong and for making mistakes—"mistakes" was the polite word for it. As far back as the Polish campaign, Hitler noted with no small amount of anger, Canaris had developed a habit of being wrong.

In September 1939, Canaris informed Hitler that the French were planning a massive offensive in the Saarbrücken area. Hitler was highly skeptical; he told the admiral that Saarbrücken was the strongest position in the German line. "Besides," he continued, "they would come up against a second and a third line which, if anything, are even more consolidated."[2]

Hitler guessed correctly; no massive French offensive took place. He had been right, and the Intelligence Services had been wrong. The significance of this meeting would become more pronounced with time, as the war went on and the Allies planned other offensives. Hitler would remember this particular incident whenever he heard anything about the invasion of France, and received reports regarding the possible time and place of the invasion.

These misgivings about German intelligence were reinforced six months later, just prior to the invasion of Norway in April 1940. Canaris sent reports that the British fleet was on the alert, and warned that the German transports would be decimated if a landing were attempted. Hitler read the reports, and went ahead with the invasion. The landings on 9 April 1940 received no interference from the British fleet, although a British destroyer flotilla sank several German ships off Narvk on the following day and returned to sink several more on 13 April.

Both the Abwehr and the SD had committed more than their share of blunders.[3] But the surrender of Italy, and the failure of intelligence to have picked up any inkling of Badoglio's plans, seemed to mark a new low point. Hitler wished that the German Intelligence Services could be more thorough and accurate—more like Britain's MI-6 or America's naval intelligence. He could not afford to be wrong about Allied intentions now and would be needing all the help he could get from his spy services. He was wary about putting too much trust in them, however, based upon how they had advised him in the past.

Hitler had no idea that most of the Abwehr's "mistakes" had been calculated moves—as had been the case with Badoglio and Italy's defection to the Allies. Canaris used his position as head of the Abwehr, along with his proximity to foreign intelligence, to mislead and misinform Hitler.

Admiral Canaris did not want the Nazis to win the war. On the day the Second World War began, 3 September 1939, he said that a victory for Hitler would be catastrophic. And when France surrendered in June 1940, and German fortunes were at high tide, he told an associate, "Should Hitler win, this will certainly be the end of us, and also the end of Germany. . . . And if Hitler loses, this will also be the end of Germany and ourselves, too, for having failed to get rid of him."[4]

Canaris had been appointed chief of the Abwehr on New Year's Day 1935, his forty-seventh birthday. From his new post, he had been able to watch Hitler's cold-blooded brutality from close quarters. Within a short time after his appointment, Canaris came to loathe Hitler, the Nazi Party, and everything they stood for.

When the Nazis first came to power in 1933, Canaris actually thought that they were just what Germany needed. Adolf Hitler wanted to rearm Germany and rebuild the German navy, two items that Canaris also favored. But after they began their campaign of murder and terror, he completely turned against Hitler and determined to do all he could to fight him.

The event that turned Canaris completely against the Nazis and changed his distrust to cold fury, was the so-called "Night of the Long Knives" on 30 June 1934, when Hitler ordered the killing of hundreds of political opponents. "Many were killed out of pure vengeance," according to William L. Shirer, "others were murdered apparently because they knew too much, and at least one because of mistaken identity."[5] Among those assassinated was Ernst Röhm, Hitler's chief of staff. Hitler was afraid that Röhm was ambitious for power within the Nazi Party, and that he might become a rival if something were not done. And so Hitler did something: He had Röhm murdered.

Canaris began his plan of subversion on the very day that the outbreak of war was planned. He was at Berchtesgaden on 22 August 1939, when Hitler announced his intention of invading Poland. Everyone present, including Luftwaffe commander Hermann Göring, realized that this would certainly mean war with Britain and France. Canaris was clear-sighted enough to know that Britain would somehow manage to bring the United States into the fighting, as well.

Although everyone had been expressly forbidden from taking notes, the admiral stood at the back and jotted down a summary of Hitler's remarks in pencil. As soon as the meeting broke up, Canaris drove straight to Munich; at the Hotel of the Four Seasons, he wrote down everything he could remember about Hitler's plans for the invasion of Poland—using his notes to refresh his memory.[6]

Canaris gave this summary to Colonel Hans Oster, who was the admiral's unofficial deputy at the Abwehr as well as a fellow anti-Hitler conspirator. Colonel Oster rewrote it, changing the wording to make Hitler's remarks seem even more crude and lurid. (A comment on the British and French heads of state became a charge that they were "cretins and imbeciles.") He then gave these documents to the Dutch military attaché in Berlin, Major G. J. Sas. Major Sas saw to it that representatives of both Britain and France received copies—including Major Francis Foley, who had been the British military intelligence representative in Berlin since 1920.

Forewarned by Admiral Canaris, both Britain and France placed their forces on full alert. Premier Edouard Daladier brought the Maginot Line defenses and all frontier troops to a war footing. In Britain, the army was mobilized, all leave was canceled, the navy was brought to full alert by the Admiralty, and all coastal defenses and antiaircraft commands came to readiness. In addition, both countries promised to come to Poland's assistance in the event of an attack by Germany.

Canaris had hoped that his warning would make Hitler change his mind about Poland, since an invasion would mean going to war with a fully alerted Britain and France. He even went so far as to hope that Hitler's generals might rebel at the thought of a two-front war against Poland in the east and France and Britain in the west.

But the admiral's intelligence coup only made Hitler postpone his attack. Furthermore, Mussolini had sent word that Italy would not come to Germany's aid in the attack on Poland. This also influenced Hitler's decision. The invasion of Poland, originally scheduled for 4:30 A.M. on 26 August, was pushed back to 1 September. At dawn on that Friday, the Luftwaffe attacked targets inside Poland; the Wehrmacht joined the attack a few hours later. Both Britain and France declared war on Germany two days later, on 3 September, as they had promised. And Admiral Canaris made a promise of his own: "Nothing should be omitted that would shorten the war."[7]

Within a week of the invasion, reports began arriving about the mass execution of Polish "undesirables"—Catholic priests who would not preach Nazi doctrine, intellectuals and university professors who would not conform to the New Order, Jews, members of the old aristocracy who refused to submit to German authority, anyone who was considered difficult. Hitler ordered his forces, "close your hearts to pity. Act brutally." The SS seemed to be taking Hitler's words to heart, and with a vengeance.[8]

Canaris lodged a protest with Feldmarschall Keitel, the chief of staff of the OKW. Keitel told Canaris that he had nothing to do with any atrocities; he would never have had the courage to relay such a protest to Hitler or any of the high-ranking Nazis. The murders and executions were the work of the SS and the SD, Keitel insisted. The head of the SD was Reinhard Heydrich, a ruthless, self-serving officer who would become known as the Butcher of Prague, and would also become Canaris' rival for power in German intelligence.

Keitel's dismissal of Canaris' protest, and the prosecution of the war in Poland generally, made the admiral more determined than ever to undermine Hitler and his war effort. He would leak German secrets to the Allies and use data gathered by the Abwehr to frustrate German intentions whenever possible. As head of the Abwehr, he had the authority to carry out any plan he thought necessary. He also had the determination to see his plan through until he was found out, or until Hitler was driven from Germany.

Wilhelm Canaris did not consider himself to be either unpatriotic or a traitor—although Reinhard Heydrich would have disagreed violently. Along with his friend and co-conspirator Colonel Hans Oster, Canaris would have considered himself a better German than anyone who followed Hitler. As evidence of his devotion to Germany, Canaris could have pointed to his service in the German navy, including his war record between 1914 and 1918.[9]

Wilhelm Canaris entered the naval service on 1 April 1905, as an 18-year-old cadet at the naval academy at Kiel. By the time war broke out in 1914, he was an officer on the light cruiser *Dresden*. The *Dresden* took part in the Battle of Coronel in November 1914, when the German China Squadron, under Admiral Graf von Spee, sank the British cruisers *Monmouth* and *Good Hope* off the coast of Chile.

Two months later, on 8 December, the British fleet had its revenge at the Battle of the Falkland Islands. *Dresden* managed to escape the relentless British squadron for nearly three months before being trapped off the coast of Chile, in Cumberland Bay. Shells from the British ships damaged the *Dresden*. The captain sent Lieutenant Canaris, the ship's flag lieutenant and intelligence officer, by boat to HMS *Glasgow* to lodge a protest: *Dresden* was in Chilean waters and, as such, should not be fired upon. The British commander rejected the protest.

The rejection was expected; the protest was only a ruse to buy time. While Lieutenant Canaris and the British captain were talking, the *Dresden*'s captain evacuated the crew and set demolition charges. When everyone had been put safely ashore, the *Dresden* was blown up, preventing capture by the British. This was Canaris' first act of duplicity in Anglo-German relations. It would not be his last.

Dresden's crew was interned on an island some 500 miles off the coast of Chile. But Canaris had no intention of remaining in quarantine for the rest of the war. He bribed the captain of a fishing boat to take him to the mainland. Once on shore, he made his way to the German embassy in Santiago, where he was issued a counterfeit Chilean passport in the name of Reed Rosas. By train and horseback, Canaris crossed the Andes mountains to Buenos Aires. From there, he sailed to Rotterdam on the Dutch steamer *Frisia*. The trip from Rotterdam to Berlin was the easiest part of his 7,000-mile journey.

When Lieutenant Canaris presented himself at the German Admiralstab on 17 September 1915, he was a physical wreck. The effects of malaria, exhaustion, and the grueling journey had all taken their toll. After being presented with the Iron Cross by Kaiser Wilhelm, Canaris was granted leave, for some much needed rest and recuperation.

After returning from leave, Canaris' first assignment was as an intelligence officer in Spain. He was to keep track of British shipping in the Mediterranean. Canaris spoke Spanish well (along with a smattering of French, Italian, and English) and seemed to have a natural flair for guile and deception.

He made good use of these talents in acquiring information from dock hands at the port of Cartagena, and passed all news along to U-boat commanders based at the Adriatic port of Pola. These reports proved to be both useful and informative. According to one source, "He blew up nine British ships from his base in Spain."[10]

But Canaris was not really a very hardy specimen and never really recovered from the effects of his exhausting journey from Chile. As one biographer put it, he "continued to weave his tangled web, but his heart was not in it."[11] He returned to Germany for an extended hospitalization. He finished out the war as a U-boat captain himself, and is credited with having sunk eighteen ships.

After Germany surrendered in November 1918, Canaris remained in the German navy, the small Reichsmarine, serving aboard the cruiser *Berlin* and the battleship *Schlesien*. In September 1934, just over a year and a half after Hitler came to power, Captain Canaris took command of the naval base at Swinemünde. He expected to remain at that post, which was considered a deadend job for an even reasonably ambitious naval officer, until he retired. But just a few weeks later came an opportunity—he was offered the post of Abwehr chief.

By 1935, Canaris could rightly claim to have gone gray in the service of his country. His hair was not gray, as a matter of fact, but totally white, which was probably a genetic trait rather than a symptom of premature aging. One of his nicknames was Old Whitehead. He was also known as the Old Man (*der Alte*), and *Kieker*, which translates roughly as "nosy." His office at 72–76 Tirpitz Ufer in Berlin was sometimes referred to as the Fox's Lair, and its inhabitant as the Old Fox.

Although Canaris may have been foxy and devious, he was also one of the most unmilitary officers in Germany. He seemed to go out of his way to be as unmilitary as possible. In January 1935, the Hungarian-born American writer Ladislas Farago met Canaris and admitted that he was not impressed. Canaris certainly did not look the part of a detective novel spy. For one thing, he was only about five feet, three inches tall. Also, he seemed dull, uninteresting, and not very bright. "I could not believe that this rumpled, tongue-tied absent-minded little man was the new chief of the Abwehr," Farago wrote.[12]

Canaris' unmilitary bearing had also earned him poor fitness reports from his superiors, most of whom were equally unimpressed. Senior officers had any number of complaints about Canaris. He did not seem particularly interested in military matters, and preferred foreign languages to naval tactics. He was vague to an irritating degree; he never seemed to give a straight "yes" or "no" answer and favored answering questions with a question. Also, there were his two dachshunds, Sabine and Seppel, which preoccupied him; he took them to the office every day, and even took them on official trips. Some senior officers could see no future at all for Canaris as a naval officer, and did not like him personally, either. Grossadmiral Erich Raeder, the head of the Kriegsmarine, was among those who did not have much use for Canaris.

It is characteristic of Canaris that he gave no formal explanation for the central event and turning point of his life: the rejection of Hitler and National Socialism, and the decision to risk his life to fight them. His transformation was certainly dramatic and complete enough to warrant at least some sort of explanation. In the First World War, he had an impressive combat record, proved himself a thorough and efficient intelligence agent, and was decorated with the Iron Cross. Yet in the Second World War, he dedicated himself to doing everything in his power to oppose Adolf Hitler, who had turned Germany into a formidable military power. Canaris' reasons for turning on Hitler can only be surmised.

Some find it incredible that the admiral acted from conscience. One motive that has been suggested is that Canaris was only following the attitude of his class toward National Socialism. But Canaris and his family were not members of the aristocracy or the officer class. None of his relatives had any connection at all with either the army or the navy. His father certainly could be described as wealthy, but he had made his money in the foundry business. The German aristocrats, nothing if not arrogant and conceited, would have turned up their noses at the Canaris clan and their furnaces and chimneys. Wilhelm Canaris and his aversion to Hitler and his regime had nothing to do with class snobbery.[13]

Another suggested motive has been ambition—if he could help to remove Hitler, Canaris would have a position of power and influence in the new German government. But if Canaris really wanted power and influence, he would have been better off backing Hitler instead of fighting him. A revolt against the Nazis was a chancy undertaking, at best; supporting them—especially in the 1930s, when Canaris first began his revolt—would have meant backing a sure thing.

The most solid clue given by Canaris himself was offered shortly after the invasion of Poland, after the admiral lodged his protest with Keitel regarding the organized mass murders by the SS and SD. Keitel's almost casual rejection of his protest revolted Canaris. "A war waged without regard to moral principles can never be won,"[14] he said. So according to this comment, at least, Canaris' objection was a moral one, rather than a personal or political motive. But, as Canaris realized, being a moral man in Hitler's Germany was not only discouraged; it was also dangerous.

One particular incident which shows Canaris' repugnance toward the Nazi regime, and their total disregard for morality and for human life, is the destruction of Belgrade in April 1941. A coup inside Yugoslavia had overturned the pro-German government; the new government leaders joined the Allies. When Hitler learned of the coup, he became almost incoherent with rage. As an act of revenge, he ordered a terror-bombing campaign against the Yugoslav capital, which he appropriately named Operation Retribution.

As soon as he heard about this new offensive, Canaris warned the Yugoslav government. But actually there was no need; within days of the beginning of the attack, the country had been overrun by the Wehrmacht. Belgrade was declared an open city.

But Hitler did not care if Belgrade was an open city or not; he was determined to go ahead with Operation Retribution. The city was bombed repeatedly between 6 April and 9 April. According to Winston Churchill, the Luftwaffe "blasted the city without mercy." By the end of the third day of bombing, over 17,000 civilians were dead, and Belgrade had been reduced to ruins.

Canaris himself went to Belgrade after German troops had moved in and declared the city secure. After a few hours of driving past smoking ruins and dazed inhabitants, he was on the verge of collapse. "I can't take any more of this," he said, and meant it. He was flown from Belgrade to Spain, where he suffered a nervous breakdown. A British writer said that Canaris "suffered a form of spiritual collapse from which he never recovered."[15]

Even many years after the war had ended, doubts about Canaris persisted. An American author described Canaris as "the quintessential intriguer whose cold heart, in the end, belonged to the Third Reich."[16] And although Canaris had begun his opposition to Hitler in 1934, over five years before the war began, there were many on the Allied side who did not fully trust him. Word of the admiral's anti-Nazi attitude had reached British intelligence—specifically Stuart Menzies, head of MI-6—but no one could be certain that it was not some sort of trick. It just seemed too good to be true—the chief of German military intelligence rebelling against his government, and showing willingness to betray German military secrets to the Allies! It had the smell of a German trap.

Canaris' credibility as an anti-Hitlerite was not helped by an incident that took place in September 1939. On the day that war was declared, the admiral sent a message to the British military attaché in Berlin, Colonel Dennis Daley; he wanted to reach Daley before he was recalled to London. The message consisted of a warning: Hitler was planning a full-scale air raid on London as a gesture of contempt and defiance. There was also a second part to the message: A group of anti-Hitler officers would try to communicate with MI-6 through the Vatican.

As it turned out, Canaris was wrong about the air raid; it had been called off. Hitler still entertained hopes of keeping Britain's role in the war as small as possible. He had no real plans for war against either Britain or the United States—and allowed himself to be talked out of it.

No one in London received any word that the raid had been canceled, however. Antiaircraft batteries were manned and ready all along the approaches to London that Sunday morning, but only one unidentified airplane showed up on British radar—an unarmed reconnaissance aircraft. General Menzies and MI-6 suspected that Canaris played an elaborate practical joke on them; it was just the sort of thing that might be expected from the Abwehr. So much for trusting Admiral Canaris.

But in the weeks following, contact was indeed made between MI-6 and German officers. Sir D'Arcy Osborne, British ambassador to the Vatican, received a message from a group of officers who said that they wanted to remove Hitler and discuss an armistice. The Foreign Secretary, Lord Halifax, gave approval to Sir D'Arcy to communicate with representatives of this group. It began to look as though there might be something to Canaris' story, after all.

This scheme was quickly discovered by SD Director Reinhard Heydrich. Canaris found out that Heydrich knew about his Vatican connection, and was able to defuse a possibly deadly situation before the SD could implicate Canaris or any of his associates. He would make other attempts to contact the British government through a representative, a Munich lawyer named Josef Müller.

There were other incidents that seemed to support the sincerity of Canaris' opposition to Hitler. One such incident took place toward the end of 1939. A heavy package was found on the doorstep of the British embassy in Oslo. The package contained technical drawings and documents written in German. The embassy staff did not quite know what to make of all the papers, but could see that some of the drawings looked like blueprints of torpedoes and other weapons. The entire parcel was sent to London via diplomatic pouch.

In London, all the diagrams and documents, soon to be known as the Oslo Report, were turned over to Dr. R. V. Jones, one of MI-6's scientific experts. When Dr. Jones first saw them, his eyes must have popped. He found himself looking at technical—and highly classified—information regarding some of Germany's most secret weapons programs. Among the drawings were plans for the Freya and Wurzburg radar sets, the X-Beams, a navigational aid that guided the Luftwaffe's bombers at night; a torpedo that homed in on the sound of the target ship's propellers; and a guided missile designated A-4, which would become known as the V-2 rocket.

The Oslo Report was extremely useful to the Allied cause. It was instrumental in helping British intelligence to "bend" the X-Beams, altering the radio beams to send the German night bombers off course. And reports on the V-2 rocket led to the photoreconnaissance of Peenemünde, the rocket testing base off Germany's Baltic coast, and to the devastating air raid of August 1943.

Although it has never been proven conclusively that Canaris himself delivered the Oslo Report—the package contained a note that was signed "a well-wishing German scientist," which was the only clue—it was beyond doubt sent by Canaris' co-conspirators in the so-called Schwarze Kapelle.[17] No German scientist, well-wishing or otherwise, would have had the means to do anything like this: to collect an entire package full of secret papers and drawings, smuggle them out of the country, and get them safely to Oslo. If the enclosed note did not have Canaris' signature, the package certainly had the mark of his handiwork.

The message was beginning to get through to MI-6: Admiral Canaris was what he said he was—a dedicated anti-Nazi working against Hitler.

The admiral's next move against Hitler took place in October 1940. It was a subtle act, but one that would have far-reaching effects. At that time, the Battle of Britain was winding down, and the night bombing of London, the Blitz, had just begun. Hitler was looking for a way of dealing Britain a damaging blow, perhaps a fatal one, without the complications of invading England. He would not be able to launch a landing in England until the spring of 1941, at the earliest. Hitler would have preferred to act sooner if something else could be arranged.

The something else that Hitler's advisors—including Hermann Göring and Alfred Jodl, the OKW's chief of operations—came up with was the invasion and capture of Gibraltar. With Gibraltar in German hands, his advisors insisted, Britain would be cut off both from her forces in Egypt and from the Suez Canal. The plan, simply stated, was "that Hitler's armies might march through Spain and seize Gibraltar, suffocating the Empire by cutting its Mediterranean lifeline."[18] On paper, at least, it looked fairly simple—anyway, a lot simpler than a full-scale amphibious invasion of southern England.

The Gibraltar problem was given the code name Operation Felix and put in the hands of Admiral Wilhelm Canaris. It was a logical choice. Canaris himself spoke fairly fluent Spanish, and the Abwehr had a number of active agents in Spain. Also, Canaris had enjoyed a friendly relationship with Francisco Franco, the Fascist dictator of Spain, since the 1930s. He had made arrangements for German assistance to the Fascists during the three-year civil war. Because of his influence in Spain, as well as his contacts among high-ranking officials, Canaris seemed the obvious man for the job.[19]

In July 1940, Canaris and a few subordinates left for Madrid, ostensibly for the purpose of evaluating the situation in Spain. After he and his group met with many Abwehr contacts, as well as people friendly with Canaris from the days of the civil war, the admiral sat down to write his report on the feasibility of Operation Felix.

At this stage, the German war machine was probably the most formidable since the German Army of 1914. The Wehrmacht, supported by the Luftwaffe, had just overrun France and the Low Countries in a matter of six weeks—something the Kaiser's armies had not been able to accomplish in over four years during the First World War. If Hitler had cared to march through Spain on his way to Gibraltar, nobody could have stopped him. Even if German forces could not have captured Gibraltar immediately—the Rock would likely have withstood "a long siege," to use Winston Churchill's words and opinion—they still would have been able to keep British ships from passing through the Straits of Gibraltar into the Mediterranean. This would have isolated the British army in Egypt and taken away its supply line.

Canaris realized all this, and also realized what a disaster it would mean if the Germans seized Gibraltar. He decided to do something about it.

Instead of reporting the facts and giving a true picture of the situation in Spain, Canaris did just the opposite. He told Hitler that Operation Felix would be a very long and hazardous campaign. For one thing, the admiral said, just moving troops through Spain would be slow and painstaking, even with the cooperation of the Spanish government. Good roads were few, and would not be wide enough to handle German motorized transport. And sending troops by train would not offer much of an improvement, since the gauge of Spanish rail lines was different from the French, which meant that all units would have to change trains when crossing the border.

Canaris did not become any more encouraging when he talked about Gibraltar itself. The British defenses, he said, would not be easily dislodged; machine gun and artillery positions were too well entrenched in the solid rock. Bombing would probably not be very successful for the same reason; also, antiaircraft batteries were numerous and had well-trained crews. If these defenses were not neutralized before attempting a landing, he could not offer much hope for success. Invading ground troops would be massacred by dug-in defenders, if they were not drowned in the heavily mined approaches on their way from the mainland.

The report concluded that Operation Felix represented a potential disaster. Canaris gave his report to Feldmarschall Wilhelm Keitel, who then gave it to Hitler. The admiral's conclusions tended to undermine Hitler's confidence in German intelligence even further. He disagreed totally with Canaris' account and his findings; he did not believe that Gibraltar was as impregnable as his Abwehr chief seemed to think it was.

Hitler was not easily dissuaded. Even at this stage of the war, he tended to ignore or play down the negative reports, although good news was always welcome. In spite of Canaris' opinion, he decided to press forward with Operation Felix. His first step would be to approach Generalissimo Franco for permission to attack Gibraltar by way of Spain.

But before Hitler could take any action, Canaris got in first. Dr. Josef Müller, Canaris' confidant, arranged to meet with Foreign Minister Serrano Suñer, who was also Franco's brother-in-law. Dr. Müller was now the Abwehr representative in Rome; Suñer happened to be in Rome on business.

Before he met with Dr. Müller, Suñer was expecting to hear a lecture on German military strength, German victories in France, and the impending victory against Britain, as well as on all the benefits that Spain could expect from an alliance with Germany. But what Dr. Müller actually told him came as a complete surprise, if not an outright shock.

"The Admiral asks you to tell Franco to hold Spain out of this game at all costs," Müller said. He went on to tell the astonished Suñer that Germany was not the military force he had been led to believe but that the situation was actually "desperate" and that Germany "had little hope of winning the war." And if Hitler should try to bully his way into Spain by threatening Franco with another Blitzkrieg, this was nothing but a bluff. "Franco may be assured that Hitler will not use the force of arms to enter Spain."[20]

When Suñer related this meeting to Franco, the generalissimo may also have been surprised at first. But this would soon have passed. Franco knew the little admiral, and knew that he would never have sent such a message if it had not been the truth.

Franco had no real interest either in helping Hitler dominate Europe or in a world empire. His only aim was to keep his grip on Spain, an iron grip that he maintained with an oppressive single-mindedness. The country had still not recovered from its three-year civil war. If Franco wanted to stay in power, he realized that he would have to concentrate on problems at home. He could not afford to be distracted by Hitler or his war with the British.

Hitler went to France on 23 October, to meet with Franco and state his case or, more accurately, make his demands. Thanks to Admiral Canaris, Franco already knew what Hitler was going to say, and he already had his answers prepared.

The two dictators met at the French border town of Hendaye. Hitler arrived first; Franco kept him waiting for two hours. When the generalissimo finally showed up, he was ready for what was to come.

Hitler did most of the talking. He regaled Franco with a nine-hour dramatic performance, during which he described German military successes in Poland, France, and the Low Countries; the U-boat war; the bombing of London. He also gave assurances that other successes would follow shortly. Through it all, Franco remained affable but unmoved. He refused to make any commitments but kept demanding concessions: He wanted huge shipments of grain in return for any assistance; he wanted large-calibre German artillery, which Hitler did not have (Canaris told him); and he demanded that Spanish troops, not German, capture Gibraltar.

Hitler tried everything to convince Franco to enter the fighting as an ally of the Greater German Reich, but Franco remained adamant: He intended to remain neutral, and would not allow German troops to cross Spain. Franco even disagreed with Hitler on the matter of who was winning the war at that stage. He told Hitler that even if German forces occupied the British Isles, Britain would carry on fighting from Canada with American help. Admiral Canaris' report had certainly had its effect.

After hours of badgering, bullying, pleading, and finally realizing that he was not going to get anywhere, Hitler gave up. It was the first time that his methods of bluster and intimidation had failed him, and he was thoroughly angry and frustrated. "I would rather have four teeth out than go through that again," he told Mussolini about the meeting.[21]

Hitler knew that he had been frustrated, but he did not realize that he had been dealt a major setback. Ian Colvin, Admiral Canaris' biographer, compared Hendaye with the German defeats at El Alamein, Stalingrad, and the Battle of Britain. And Canaris can be given full credit for the reversal.

If Franco had been persuaded—or bullied—into giving up Spanish neutrality, and if he had allowed German troops to attack Gibraltar from Spain, the course of the war would certainly have been much harder for Britain and for the United States. If Gibraltar had been in enemy hands, supplying the British Eighth Army in Egypt would have meant reaching the port of Tobruck, the main British port in the Mediterranean, by way of South Africa's Cape of Good Hope, and through the Suez Canal. This would have exposed the convoys to waiting U-boat patrols along thousands of additional sea miles. "How well Rommel might have fared if the Straits of Gibraltar had been closed by German guns and Stukas in 1941," one historian wrote. This advantage would very probably have allowed Rommel and his Afrika Korps to defeat the British Eighth Army and capture the Suez Canal.

Which means that before an assault on the coast of France could even have been attempted, the German troops occupying Gibraltar would have to have been dislodged. Otherwise, a well-entrenched enemy force would have been left behind the lines, always threatening. Neutralizing a German-held Gibraltar would have required a major military operation, which would have meant channeling men and resources away from Operation Overlord, and which probably would have meant postponing the Normandy landings beyond 1944.

And if Rommel had succeeded in driving the British out of North Africa, and in capturing the Suez Canal, Overlord may very well never have taken place. There would have been no point in invading northern France while the enemy still controlled the Mediterranean.

By deliberately misleading Hitler about the defenses of Gibraltar, and by warning Franco about Hitler's intentions, Admiral Canaris changed the course of the war. His acts of deception kept Gibraltar out of German hands and kept Spain out of the fighting. Canaris' dedication to the undermining of the Nazi regime certainly produced results at Hendaye, far-reaching results that even Canaris could not have imagined, even in his most optimistic moments.

Although Admiral Wilhelm Canaris used his position and influence to give the Western Allies every military advantage, this was not his only method of working against the Nazis. Canaris was deeply disturbed by Hitler's persecution of undesirables in Germany as well as in occupied countries. He was certain that "the Germans were committing the crime of the century and shouldering a burden of guilt of which no earthly power could acquit them."[22] And so, he devised a plan by which a few of these unfortunates—mostly Jews, but not exclusively—could be smuggled out of Nazi-controlled territory and away from the Gestapo. This gave Canaris the satisfaction of knowing that he was saving lives, while frustrating Hitler and his regime at the same time.

Canaris' plan was to smuggle these undesirables out of Germany under Abwehr protection, to give them cover as Abwehr agents and send them to Switzerland or overseas on assignment. Once safely out of the country, the refugees simply would not return. His first attempt was to move seven Jews to neutral Switzerland, under cover stories that they had been recruited for an operation against the United States, and so the plan was given the code name Operation Seven. Five more people were later added to the plot, but the name of the operation was not changed. Canaris' friend and fellow Schwarze Kapelle conspirator, Hans von Dohnanyi, organized the details.

Canaris managed to pull off his little ruse after a few complications regarding some bureaucratic red tape were dealt with. Von Dohnanyi, a lawyer, was able to take care of these details, including complications involving exit documents. The Gestapo had nothing at all to say about the operation, since—as Canaris was very much aware—the secret police had no jurisdiction over Abwehr personnel. Canaris' rival, Reinhard Heydrich of the SD, became suspicious over the fact that Jews had been employed by the Abwehr—Heydrich was always on the lookout for evidence to use against Canaris and his agency. But Heydrich's assassination in May 1942 put an end to any actions he might have been planning against Canaris and Operation Seven.

But other complications were not far off. Border guards stopped a Jewish family at the Czech/German frontier, and found a large amount of American currency in their luggage—thousands of American dollars. Foreign currency was strictly regulated; the guards wanted to know how they managed to acquire so many U.S. dollars. Their explanation was that the money had been given to them by Dr. Wilhelm Schmidhuber, the Portuguese counsel in Munich, who had asked them to hold it on account. Schmidhuber was also an associate of Admiral Canaris and Hans von Dohnanyi, and was involved in the scheme to smuggle Jews out of Germany as Abwehr agents.

The Gestapo were told about the incident. They, in turn, informed the SD. Walter Schellenberg had Schmidhuber arrested and brought to Munich, where he was beaten and threatened by the Gestapo. Under this pressure, Schmidhuber began talking—about Canaris and the Abwehr and a conspiracy to enter into secret negotiations with the Allies via the Vatican, and about Operation Seven. The Gestapo realized that they had a valuable prisoner and transferred Schmidhuber to Tegel prison in Berlin, which was beyond any possible attempt by Canaris to have him released.

A Gestapo commissioner and an investigator from the Wehrmacht, a Dr. Manfred Roeder, confronted Admiral Canaris with the charge that von Dohnanyi and Dietrich von Bonhoeffer, von Dohnanyi's brother-in-law, were guilty of plotting against the Nazi regime, and that von Dohnanyi was also guilty of accepting bribes for secreting Jews into Switzerland. Dr. Roeder then walked down the corridor to von Dohnanyi's office and, while Canaris looked on helplessly, made his arrest and searched the office safe.

Both Bonhoeffer and von Dohnanyi were prosecuted by Dr. Roeder. Bonhoeffer endured any number of appearances before Roeder; although he managed to escape the gallows, he remained in prison. But von Dohnanyi was able to maneuver his way out of his difficulties. He insisted that he knew nothing of any conspiracy, and that his "suspicious" activities in Rome were nothing more than official Abwehr business. As far as smuggling Jews out of Germany was concerned, he again insisted that he was only conducting routine Abwehr operations—the Abwehr had a need for many different kinds of agents. The bribery charges were fairly easy for Dohnanyi to repudiate, since Roeder had no evidence and there had never been any bribery to begin with.

Canaris also did his part to frustrate Roeder's case. Either Canaris himself or Judge Advocate General Karl Sack—who would be hanged on the same day as Canaris—complained to Feldmarschall Wilhelm Keitel that Roeder was deliberately slandering the good name of the Abwehr, the Wehrmacht, and the German High Command. Keitel opened his own investigation of Roeder's handling of the von Dohnanyi case, and reached the conclusion that Canaris had intended: Roeder had overstepped his authority. He ordered Roeder to stop prosecuting the political aspects of the dispute, including the charge of high treason.

Roeder was assigned to another case. His replacement did not have his drive or enthusiasm in pursuing von Dohnanyi, and the investigation "was less grimly pursued after that."[23] In the course of his investigation, Roeder had referred to the Abwehr's field unit, the Brandenburg Division, as nonsoldiers and shirkers. Canaris made a point of reporting this remark to the commander of the Brandenburgers. The commander cornered Roeder, slapped him across the face, and challenged him to a duel, which further discredited Roeder and his case against von Dohnanyi. Roeder's humiliation was also good for a grim laugh; it was not often that an army investigator got what was coming to him, especially not in public.[24]

Canaris and von Dohnanyi won that particular round, but the Gestapo were not easily discouraged and went ahead with their investigation in spite of Keitel's order. Following his trial, von Dohnanyi became seriously ill and had to be hospitalized. A Gestapo doctor came to the hospital and had von Dohnanyi removed to an SS clinic, where he was questioned by a member of the SD. The SD interrogator, an associate of Walter Schellenberg, pronounced that von Dohnanyi would be healthy enough to testify against Canaris within a week to ten days.

Von Dohnanyi realized that if the Gestapo got hold of him, he would be tortured into telling everything he knew about Canaris' connection with Operation Seven, as well as about the Schwarze Kapelle. In order to avoid this ordeal, he knew that he would have to attempt some drastic course of action. He managed to smuggle a request to his wife, a bizarre request that she obtain a diphtheria culture from a medical institute and send it to him in a food parcel. Frau von Dohnanyi sent the contaminated food, which had the desired result: Von Dohnanyi developed an acute case of diphtheria. He became so gravely ill that the Gestapo were not able to carry out their planned inquiry. His life was never in danger, but he was weak and debilitated enough to prevent him from being subjected to a prolonged questioning. He could not be moved, and was barely able to talk. The Gestapo were not able to examine von Dohnanyi, and Canaris, the Schwarze Kapelle, and Operation Seven were saved.

The Gestapo never did obtain their testimony from von Dohnanyi, and did not find out the story behind Operation Seven or acquire any of the information they needed to act against Canaris. Von Dohnanyi remained in custody, however, and was hanged in April 1945—apparently on the same day as Canaris, but at a different concentration camp.

Canaris' project for smuggling Jews out of Germany was unintentionally furthered by Hitler himself. In the summer of 1942, a sabotage operation was launched against the aluminum and light metals industry in the United States, code-named Operation Pastorius. Two four-man sabotage teams were taken across the Atlantic by U-boats and landed on the east coast of the United States: Four men came ashore in Florida, the other four landed on Long Island, New York. The eight men had been assigned the job of blowing up several large aluminum-producing factories in eastern and southern America. If these plants stopped producing their metal alloys, even for a short period, the American aircraft industry would have been severely affected. Without a steady supply of aluminum, the production of aircraft of all types was expected to fall off dramatically.

Whether or not the plan was a sound one was never determined; Operation Pastorius did not fail so much as it was never really tried. One of the eight saboteurs, George Dasch, was an anti-Nazi who had lived in the United States for many years, and had even served an enlistment in the U.S. Army. He had been recruited into the sabotage operation because of his familiarity with American ways and with the country itself. But Dasch was determined not to let the operation succeed, and made up his mind to ruin it at his first given opportunity.

Shortly after he landed on Long Island, Dasch persuaded another member of his four-man team to join his scheme. He got in touch with the FBI and told federal agents all about Operation Pastorius and its objectives—how they had been brought to the United States by U-boat, how they had been trained to place explosives inside an aluminum plant to inflict maximum damage, and where the other saboteurs might be found. With Dasch's help, the FBI rounded up all of the would-be saboteurs. As George Dasch had planned, Operation Pastorius had been stopped before it ever started.

George Dasch was never given any credit by the FBI for his central role in breaking up the sabotage operation. Bureau director J. Edgar Hoover made certain that he himself received full credit for capturing the Germans. The trial and execution of six of the saboteurs—George Dasch and his confidant, Ernest Burger, were given life sentences—were given full press coverage, which glorified Hoover and the FBI. When Hitler heard about the spectacular failure of Operation Pastorius, his reaction was predictable. Because it had been carried out under the auspices of the Abwehr, Hitler summoned Admiral Canaris to accuse him of incompetence—yet again.

Feldmarschall Keitel and Heinrich Himmler, Canaris' protector and probable blackmail victim, were also on hand to witness the proceedings. Hitler worked himself up to a fine fury. Among the charges he shouted at the admiral were that the lives of eight specially trained agents had been wasted on the Pastorius fiasco. Canaris explained that the eight men were not trained Abwehr agents, but were actually amateurs who were chosen because of their familiarity with America and that these eight men had been very quickly prepared for this particular job. Hitler was in no mood to be placated by Canaris' explanation. He shouted, "Why didn't you use Jews for that?" and continued in the same tone of voice until he finally ran out of charges and expletives.[25] Canaris and the others stood by without saying a word.

Hitler's outburst about using Jews gave Admiral Canaris an idea. He decided to take the remark literally, and to interpret it as an order. He would use this eruption of temper to justify his employment of Jews and other undesirables for operations outside the country. As far as Canaris was concerned, Hitler's tantrum had officially justified his plan. The fact that he gave his order in the presence of Keitel and Himmler made it even more convenient; Canaris had two high-ranking witnesses. If anyone in either the Gestapo or the SS questioned the nationality or religion of a suspicious Abwehr agent, Canaris would end the conversation by saying, "Orders from the Fuhrer."

No records exist that give the exact number of Jews and other refugees that Canaris helped in their escape from the Nazi regime. It was certainly many more than the dozen that left Berlin as part of Operation Seven.

In March 1941, the head of the Abwehr section in The Hague approached Canaris with an idea that would require some daring and courage. If Canaris would be willing to make use of his contacts in South America, a very large rescue operation involving hundreds of Jewish residents of the Netherlands might be undertaken. These people could be sent abroad, out of the Gestapo's clutches, as Abwehr agents to any number of places throughout Latin America. This would not be a smuggling operation of a dozen or so individuals, but a mass exodus from the Nazis and their Final Solution.

Admiral Canaris gave his approval. The operation was officially described as an "infiltration of agents into South America," which seemed perfectly logical; thousands of German agents were already operating in Uruguay, Argentina, Brazil, and in nearly every country in South America. Transportation of the Abwehr's new "agents" began in May, when about 500 Jews left the Netherlands for the other side of the Atlantic Ocean. They were first transported to Spain and sailed from a Spanish port. All of this was done under the auspices of Canaris, and with the knowledge of his friend from before the war, Generalissimo Franco.

Canaris was not able to smuggle every victim of the Nazis out of the country, but he tried to assist anyone who needed help. He also encouraged sympathetic Abwehr officers to aid Jews and refugees who were in trouble, and did his best to see that Jews and "half Jews"—those with one Jewish parent—were accepted into the Wehrmacht (or at least wore Wehrmacht uniforms) or were issued Abwehr identification. But in order to guarantee freedom from the long and persistent reach of the Gestapo, the only real solution was to maneuver victims and potential victims away from their influence, which usually meant getting them out of Germany.

Among those who left German-occupied territory with Canaris' assistance were Madame Czimanska, the wife of the Polish military attaché in Berlin; a rabbi from Warsaw, who was able to immigrate to New York thanks to the admiral; and the archbishop of Krakow. Hundreds of others were also given the necessary assistance to get away from Germany or its territories, or were put beyond the reach of the secret police by lying about their identity, their religion, their nationality, or by simply supplying them with Abwehr documents. While Himmler and the Gestapo waged Hitler's campaign against the clergy, intellectuals, Jews, and anyone else considered inconvenient by the Nazis, Canaris was doing all that he could to hinder their murderous campaign.

Not very much has been said about the Germans who protected Jews and other refugees during the Nazi era—the Good Germans. A Sunday news magazine article on the subject noted that for every Jew who survived, at least seven individuals must have acted to save that one person. The article goes on to say that these rescuers "came from all walks of life: pensioners and musicians, superintendents and nurses, prominent conductors, writers, clerics, religiously inspired individuals and atheists."[26] Their number also included one naval officer who was not afraid to use his rank and influence to help right a monstrous wrong, and really did have the courage of his convictions.

Allied intelligence was eventually getting the idea that Admiral Wilhelm Canaris was indeed working against Hitler, and that he could be trusted. An incident that took place early in 1942 confirmed Canaris' value to any remaining skeptics.

British agents in Gibraltar observed that Canaris made frequent trips to the Spanish town of Algeciras. The Abwehr had a post in Algeciras, which was just across the bay from Gibraltar. Canaris ostensibly went there on business, although it has also been suggested that he spent so much time in Spain to get away from Berlin and everybody in it.

One of the more ambitious agents on Gibraltar came up with a plan to kidnap Canaris and take him to London. The plan was approved by the governor of Gibraltar. Details were drawn up regarding the time and place of the abduction as well as particulars on taking him across to Gibraltar at gunpoint.

The plan might well have worked. But as soon as MI-6 heard about it, they ordered it called off. The communiqué from London did not say "Leave our man alone." According to Ian Colvin, the message was, "He is far more valuable where he is."[27]

London offered no explanation. Gibraltar was astounded by the order, but MI-6 was not about to spoil the situation. The officers in charge of MI-6 were shrewd enough to let the admiral alone, and to allow him to work in his own way without any interference.

In the autumn of 1942, OKW received a report from an agent in Britain concerning an upcoming Allied amphibious invasion. It had already been reported that an American general named Dwight David Eisenhower had arrived in Britain, and that he would be commanding some major operation. The report went on to say that this operation was code-named Operation Flama, Spanish for flame. Eisenhower looked to be its commander.

The agent in Britain actually got the name wrong. Operation Flama was actually Operation Torch, the planned invasion of French North Africa. Its commander was indeed General Dwight D. Eisenower.

This particular bit of information came from SD agent Gwyn Evans, code-named Druid. But other informants had also been at work. At the end of October 1942, naval intelligence sent word that an Atlantic troop convoy was underway, although its destination was not known. On 7 November, agents in Spain reported a procession of Allied troop ships and warships sailing through the Straits of Gibraltar into the Mediterranean.

Members of the German General Staff could only guess at the convoy's destination. Maybe it was bound for Sardinia or Sicily or possibly North Africa. Feldmarschall Albert Kesselring, commander of all German forces in the Mediterranean, could not offer any definite opinion; he could only say that it might be any of these three.

During the very early hours of Sunday 8 November, all the guessing ended. Three separate Allied landing forces, designated as the Western Task Force, Center Task Force, and Eastern Task Force, came ashore: at Casablanca, Oran, and Algiers. The troops were mostly American, although the Algiers force was made up of both British and American units. All three landings took the defenders completely unawares.

Allied deception plans were largely responsible for this overwhelming surprise, which succeeded beyond all expectations. Double agents leaked information that led some senior officers to believe that the landings would take place in Dakar, in French West Africa. Also, a tight security lid was placed on Operation Torch, which restricted leaks of genuine information and kept all talk to a minimum. But Admiral Canaris also contributed to the success of the operation, in his own subtle but highly effective way.

A German agent in Britain managed to discover that French North Africa was the true destination of those troop convoys. He sent his information across to Hamburg, which was the Abwehr's primary station for activities in Britain and the United States. This report was received by the station head, a Captain Herbert Wichmann, who claimed to have sent it on to the OKW under highest priority. But no one ever saw any trace of it. The report vanished into thin air.

When Canaris was asked about Captain Wichmann's report, he said that he never saw it. Captain Wichmann insisted that he indeed did send it, and that it *must* have gone on to someone in OKW. But Canaris calmly repeated that he had never seen any such report.

After the war, an Abwehr officer named Colonel Heinz remarked that Admiral Canaris deliberately downplayed all information pertaining to the North African landings. Officers in British intelligence came to the conclusion that Canaris had done just the opposite regarding British units in the Libyan desert. After reading captured intelligence reports, it became clear that Canaris consistently overrated British forces for the purpose of throwing Feldmarschall Rommel off balance.

"Canaris must have known how many—or how few—divisions we had in the Middle East at the time,"[28] said one British officer a few years after the war. He was right. Canaris knew. But he did not report what he knew; he told Hitler and the OKW what he wanted them to know.

With the Wichmann report, Canaris simply played a variation on a theme. Instead of submitting misleading reports about Operation Torch, he saw to it that a reliable report from the field did not reach its destination.

Hitler was becoming more than just a little annoyed with Admiral Canaris and his "inefficiency." General Jodl accused Canaris of being irrational and unstable. Hitler called the admiral a fool, and he must have seemed like one after what had happened with Operation Torch. The Allies had sneaked right up on the North African beaches, sailed right through the Straits of Gibraltar, and Canaris, the chief of military intelligence, apparently did not know anything about it. No one suggested that Canaris' failure was anything more ominous than incompetence. The High Command only knew that Canaris had fallen down on the job, this time with dire consequences.

Hitler and his generals had good reason to be upset about the North African landings, as well as with the failure of the Intelligence Services to give any warning of the impending Allied invasion. The success of Operation Torch effectively sealed the fate of Feldmarschall Rommel and his Afrika Korps, which were squeezed out of North Africa between the British Eighth Army in the east and the Anglo-American forces in the west. Not that Rommel went quietly—At Kasserine Pass in February 1943, he turned on the surprised Americans and inflicted heavy casualties. But he could not hope to hold out against the superior Allied forces for long. By the spring of 1943, all Axis forces had either surrendered or had been withdrawn.

Confidence in Canaris and the Abwehr had been diminishing for several months, even before the North African operation. On 27 February 1942, Hitler flew into another of his patented rages following a particularly brazen British commando raid. On that night, a group of paratroopers landed at Bruneval, on the French coast. Before the German defenders could do anything to stop them, the raiders physically removed vital parts from Bruneval's Würzburg radar unit, climbed down the 600-foot tall cliffs to the Channel, and were whisked back to England by waiting boats. The components of the Würzburg unit would be instrumental in helping Allied scientists learn the secrets of German radar, as well as its limitations.

When he heard about the Bruneval raid, Hitler sent for Canaris and demanded to know why the Abwehr could not stage similar raids in

Britain. For once, the admiral could not come up with a satisfactory answer, which served to increase Hitler's rage. He immediately removed all forms of technical and electronic espionage from the Abwehr's authority, including the acquisition of information about the enemy's radar and surveillance capabilities. From then on, Hitler decided, the SD would carry out these aspects—the SD being a reliable Nazi Party organization.

This was just what Reinhard Heydrich, the head of the SD, wanted to hear. He had been suspicious of Canaris for some time, but could not do anything—Canaris had evidence that Heydrich had Jewish ancestors,[29] and would give his evidence to SS chief Heinrich Himmler if Heydrich ever tried to make trouble for him or for the Abwehr.

But the directive from Hitler changed everything. If he took any authority away from Canaris now, Heydrich could truthfully say that he was only following orders.

Heydrich had an ambitious idea to unify the German Intelligence Services. Under his plan, the Abwehr and the SD would be combined—under his command. He never really liked or trusted Canaris, although he deferred to the admiral's rank and position. When he referred to Canaris as the Old Fox, he did not mean it in an affectionate or flattering way. The Bruneval raid, and Hitler's resulting anger with Canaris, gave him the excuse to approach Hitler and suggest that the SD take over *all* the Abwehr's functions, not just technical espionage, and replace the Abwehr as Germany's military intelligence organization.

As it turned out, Heydrich was not able to get everything he wanted. On 18 May 1942, Canaris met with Heydrich and Himmler at Hardcany Palace, Prague, to sign Implementation Directives. This document reduced the authority of the Abwehr, and made it subordinate to the SD. It did not, however, eliminate the Abwehr altogether, or allow the SD to absorb the Abwehr, which is what Heydrich really wanted.

Admiral Canaris knew all too well that Heydrich would not be satisfied with the concessions set down by the Implementation Directives, at least not for long. As Walter Schellenberg observed, Canaris knew that "Heydrich would attack again. The agreement offered no more than a breathing space."[30]

But things did not turn out the way Canaris expected, either. On the morning of 27 May, a group of Czech soldiers, trained in Britain and flown in from London, ambushed Heydrich. They waited for him as his Mercedes approached a sharp turning in the road to Hardcany Palace. One of the Czechs aimed at Heydrich at point-blank range, but the gun jammed; grass had jammed the breach mechanism. Heydrich drew his pistol, deciding to make a fight of it, which gave a second Czech the chance to throw a grenade. It missed its mark, exploding next to the car instead of inside of it. Heydrich was injured but was not killed outright.

At first, it appeared that Heydrich's wounds were not serious. But xrays showed that the explosion had broken one of his ribs, and also embedded fragments of the car's upholstery in his spleen. The top Nazi surgeon in Prague removed the fragments, but this did not prevent Heydrich's condition from worsening. He developed a severe infection, which resulted in a high fever and an eventual coma. Heydrich died on 4 June; the cause was given as "wound infection."[31]

In reprisal for Heydrich's assassination, the Czech village of Lidice was obliterated. All houses and buildings were burned; the ruins were bull-dozed by the German Labour Service, which spent many weeks making sure that no trace of Lidice remained. The SS executed 199 men of the village; 195 women and 85 children were sent to Ravensbrück concen-tration camp. Eight children were "Germanized" by being adopted by German families. Of those sent to Ravensbrück, most were either gassed, died of malnutrition, or simply disappeared.[32]

Heydrich's funeral was "the kind of barbaric display at which the Na-zis excelled."[33] The eulogy was given by Heinrich Himmler, who praised his colleague for his bravery, loyalty, and dedication to National Social-ism. He tactfully omitted mentioning Heydrich's deep-seated sadism and cold-blooded ruthlessness, which earned him the nickname The Butcher of Prague. Hitler also awarded Heydrich a decoration, which he called "the greatest honour which I can bestow."

Admiral Canaris was also at the funeral. He tearfully said that he had lost "a great man and a true friend in Reinhard Heydrich."[34] He certainly lost a dangerous rival, as well as a colleague that he could control by blackmail. Maybe he was crying tears of relief; maybe he knew that Hey-drich was getting close to the truth, and that even his evidence that might have proved Heydrich's Jewish ancestry would not have protected him for much longer.

Of all the carefully edited remarks made at the funeral, at least one of them was true: Heydrich was irreplaceable. No one else in the SD had Heydrich's ruthlessness, or his criminal aptitude for carrying out any campaign he set his mind to—including organizing the mass murder programs in the concentration camps and placing himself in charge of both the SD and the Abwehr. If this meant destroying Canaris, then he would also destroy Canaris. Heydrich had already begun to talk to Hitler about this, and had also begun high-level plotting against Canaris, at the time of his assassination.

Heydrich's replacement as head of the SD was Brigadeführer Walter Schellenberg. Schellenberg, 31 years old and the son of a piano manu-facturer, was not nearly as driven as Heydrich, and did not have Hey-drich's zeal for discrediting Admiral Canaris or for taking over the Abwehr. In short, Heydrich's assassination let Canaris off the hook.

Heydrich would almost certainly have succeeded in displacing Canaris as Abwehr director. With Canaris no longer in charge of military intelligence, information about the Wehrmacht and its intentions would no longer have been passed to the Allies. And, as in the case of the Wichmann report on Operation Torch, accounts of Allied intentions would no longer mysteriously disappear. Not only was Heydrich a ruthless professional, but he was also a dedicated Nazi.

With Heydrich as director of the newly combined Abwehr/SD, German intelligence would have been aggressive in obtaining information about the enemy. Any and all data pertaining to British and American troop movements, or Allied intentions, would have been passed efficiently along to the OKW, the Kriegsmarine, or whomever needed it most. All reports would ultimately have reached Adolf Hitler.

At the time of his assassination, Reinhard Heydrich was scheduled to leave Prague within a few days; his office and all his files had already been packed. He was to have gone to France to see to the elimination of undesirables in the West. If he had directed the Abwehr/SD from France, Heydrich certainly would have ordered a major crackdown against the French resistance, the *maquis*. This would have come as a serious setback to the planners of Operation Overlord; the resistance was a leading source of information about German activities in northern France. It would also have helped the German defenses immensely. Even though their sabotage operations against the railways and other objectives—including troop trains—were only sporadic, the *maquis* were a scourge to the Wehrmacht in occupied France.

Following the "inefficiency" of the Abwehr under Admiral Canaris, the new competence of Heydrich's combined Intelligence Services would have come as no small relief to Hitler and his generals. There would have been few complaints about Heydrich's inefficiency. Hitler would have had new confidence in reports submitted by German intelligence and would have believed them—including the increasing amount of information he was receiving about Allied preparations for a cross-Channel invasion.

But Heydrich's assassination left Canaris in charge of the Abwehr, and put Walter Schellenberg at the head of the SD. Schellenberg would keep a wary eye on the admiral—Heydrich had warned him that he was suspicious of Canaris—but he did not have his predecessor's killer instinct. He was no Butcher of Prague. The Allies had kept a friend in Canaris, and had lost a determined enemy in Reinhard Heydrich.

And with Canaris remaining at his post, Hitler continued to lose faith in his intelligence organization—including the SD. Canaris continued to be "wrong" too often to suit Hitler and his generals, and the image of incompetence rubbed off on Schellenberg's group. This would prove invaluable to British and American commanders in the planning of future operations, including, if not especially, planning and preparing for the Normandy landings.

The killing of Reinhard Heydrich proved to be a reprieve not only for Wilhelm Canaris but for the Allies, as well. If Canaris had been removed as head of the Abwehr in 1942 or 1943, the outcome of Operation Overlord, the invasion of Normandy, might have had quite a different outcome.

NOTES

1. Shirer, p. 1002.
2. Höhne, p. 381.
3. According to David Kahn in *Hitler's Spies*, the word "Abwehr" is related to the word "Wehrmacht." *Wehr* means defense, and the prefix *ab* equates to *of*. Abwehr, then, means warding off, or keeping at bay. Wehrmacht, literally making a defense, is beautifully euphemistic in the same way that the U.S. Department of War became the Department of Defense.
4. Manvell, p. 90.
5. Shirer, p. 223.
6. Rewording of Canaris' notes in Höhne, p. 348.
7. Colvin, p. 95.
8. Höhne, p. 347.
9. Canaris' biographical information came from a number of sources, including Höhne, Colvin, Kahn, Brown, and Waller. Colvin's account is one of the most useful, and also the most interesting, since it comes from a British point of view and was written by a journalist who actually knew many of Canaris' co-conspirators.
10. Colvin, p. 17.
11. Höhne, p. 42.
12. Farago, *Foxes*, 10.
13. Attitude of Canaris toward the Nazis in Wheal et al., p. 83. Canaris' turning against Hitler is mentioned in every biography, although the motives given by each of his biographers do not always agree.
14. Buchheit, p. 219.
15. Colvin, p. 161.
16. Persico, p. 49.
17. The Schwarze Kapelle, or Black Orchestra, consisted of a group of officers who secretly conspired against Hitler and the Nazi Party. Among its members were General Ludwig Beck, chief of staff of the army; Colonel Hans Oster, Canaris' aide; and General Enwin von Witzleben, Eric Hoppner, and a number of other high-ranking officers. Canaris was the group's founder. One of their goals was to supply the Allies with military, technical, and scientific information.
18. Waller, p. 152.
19. I learned about Canaris' role in derailing Operation Felix while researching my book *Germany's Spies and Saboteurs*, and I came across it again while writing about Franco's reaction to Hitler's air campaign against Britain in *The Battle of Britain*.
20. Colvin, p. 149.
21. Ibid., p. 152.

22. Höhne, p. 462.

23. Brissaud, p. 304.

24. The Brandenburg Division, which had been at regimental strength until the autumn of 1942, were part of Abwehr II and were trained in sabotage and sedition. The Brandenburgers took part in the invasion of the Low Countries in May 1940 and were able to capture a number of strategic bridges and other objectives. But later in the war they were most often employed as ordinary infantry. They were transferred to Russia and suffered heavy casualties in 1942 and 1943.

25. Johnson, *Germany's Spies and Saboteurs*, p. 124.

26. Schneider, p. 95.

27. Suggested plan to kidnap Canaris in Colvin, p. 187.

28. Ibid., p. 186.

29. Heydrich's biographer, Callum McDonald, only mentions "rumours about his Jewish origins," while Ian Colvin states that Heydrich's father, Bruno, was half Jewish. One reason behind Heydrich's campaign against the Jews was possibly to prove that he was not one of them himself.

30. Schellenberg, p. 405.

31. Callum MacDonald, p. 182.

32. Statistics on the destruction of Lidice, Bauer et al., p. 688.

33. Callum MacDonald, p. 182.

34. Colvin, p. 182.

THREE

Bits and Fragments

By the end of 1943, as the Third Reich unravelled on all fronts, Hitler was already facing disaster. In Italy, Naples had been taken by the U.S. Fifth Army in October 1943; in Russia, the Red Army had driven the Germans out of Kiev in November. The Battle of the Atlantic had already been lost, as Allied tactics and technology put an end to the U-boat offensive, and the Afrika Korps no longer existed. "Germany had passed the peak of her military strength," noted Lt. General Hans Speidel in a masterpiece of German understatement. But in spite of the failure and calamity that threatened from all directions, the main topic among Hitler and his senior officers was the impending Anglo-American landings in France.

Feldmarschall Erwin Rommel, who had been assigned to inspect the Western Wall fortifications beginning in November 1943, told Hitler that the success or failure of the landings would decide the outcome of the war. If the Allied forces were stopped on the beaches, "it would surely be some time before the Anglo-Americans would recover from the setback and try again," said one of Rommel's biographers.[1]

In short, there was only one hope for Nazi Germany: repel the invasion. For once in his life, Hitler did not dispute the obvious.

At this stage, Hitler's competence as a military commander might be questioned—and often has been, at length. But he was not the borderline lunatic, sitting in his bunker and completely isolated from reality, of popular legend. Although he definitely preferred not to hear bad news or to face unpleasant facts, and was beginning to put too much faith in German secret weapons programs—including the V-2 rocket—he had a better grasp of the situation than some of his senior generals. He realized all too well that the Allies were planning a massive invasion of the Continent. Although he had no real idea where or, just as important, when this operation would take place, Hitler had narrowed down the possibilities to either Calais or Normandy, and to those days when the tides and weather were favorable. He had his suspicions, but no actual facts to back them up.

On 3 November 1943, in his Directive 51, Hitler warned, "All signs point to an offensive against the Western Front of Europe no later than spring, and perhaps earlier." He went on to say, "I have therefore decided to strengthen the defenses of the West, particularly at places from which we shall launch our long-range war against England"—meaning the V-1 Flying Bomb campaign and V-2 rocket launchings. "For these are the very points at which the enemy will and must attack." He also ordered the strengthening of the Atlantic Wall fortifications and concluded, "There, unless all indications are misleading, will be fought the decisive invasion battle."[2]

Hitler's generals agreed that the *Grossinvasion* would be decisive, although they did not always agree on how it should be dealt with. Feldmarschall von Rundstedt, overall commander in the West, did not put much faith in the fixed defenses of the Atlantic Wall. He favored a mobile reserve, kept behind the coastal defenses, to deliver a knockout blow to the invaders as they moved inland.

Feldmarschall Rommel thought otherwise. At the end of January 1944, he became commander of Army Group B, which was made up of all German forces from the Netherlands to the river Loire, including Normandy. Rommel held the very strong opinion that the invaders should be stopped on the landing beaches, before they had the chance to move inland.

"The enemy is at his weakest just after landing," Rommel said. "The troops are unsure, and possibly even seasick. They are unfamiliar with the terrain. Heavy weapons are not yet available in sufficient quantity. That is the moment to strike them and defeat them."[3]

There was also a difference of opinion over where the invasion would take place. The two most obvious destinations for an assault that would be launched from southern England were the Pas de Calais and the Calvados coast of Normandy. Each of these sites had its advantages as a landing area. No one could agree which was the most likely point for the *Grossinvasion*.

The primary advantage of Calais as the invasion site becomes obvious just from looking at a map: It is only about twenty miles across the Straits of Dover from England. Calais would mean the shortest possible route for the invading armies, and would also put the Allied invaders in an excellent position to make a concerted drive on Germany.

As far as geography alone was concerned, Calais made a lot more sense than Normandy. Once they had consolidated their forces, the Anglo-American armies could make a broad swing to the east, through Belgium and Luxembourg and into Germany itself. This made perfect tactical sense, and was, in fact, the reversal of the route taken by the Wehrmacht in May 1940 (and would take again in December 1944, during the Battle of the Bulge).

Also the Pas de Calais had the harbors of Boulogne and Calais nearby—a primary consideration, since an adjacent port would be essential for keeping the invasion forces supplied and reinforced. And the area's closeness to England meant that the landing beaches would be within range of the maximum number of British and American fighters and fighter-bombers, which would give increased air support to the invasion. The majority of Hitler's generals favored Calais as the most likely site of the impending invasion. They were not alone in their thinking; U.S. general George S. Patton also favored Calais over Normandy as the site for Operation Overlord.

But Normandy could not be ignored. Although the beaches of the Calvados coast were three times farther from England, they also had several advantages over Calais. First, they were flat and almost entirely without cliffs. They were mainly made up of sand, with a minimum of clay. This made them well suited for landing troops and supplies; the absence of cliffs would allow troops and vehicles to move inland without interference from natural obstacles. Also, the port of Cherbourg was near enough to the landing zone to be used for supplying the invaders, as soon as they were able to capture it. The Calvados beaches would also be protected from the open sea by the Cotentin peninsula and—a vital point—were a lot less strongly fortified than Calais. Normandy had a number of points to recommend it as the invasion site.

It seemed that every general and field marshal in the Wehrmacht had his own opinion on where the Allied armies would come ashore. General Erich Marcks, commander of the 84th Corps and considered to be "one of the finest generals in Normandy,"[4] felt certain that the landings would take place in the Bay of the Seine. Crusty old von Rundstedt did not agree; he thought Calais would be the most likely spot.

Rommel also tended toward Calais. After making his inspection of the Atlantic Wall, he reported to Hitler, "It is quite likely that the enemy's main effort will be directed against the sector between Boulogne and the north of the Somme, and on either side of Calais. . . . His chief objective will almost certainly be to obtain possession as quickly as possible of ports capable of accommodating large numbers of ships."[5] Rommel did not rule out Normandy altogether, however.

Hitler himself thought that Normandy would be the landing area. But he wanted a lot more information before he made his final decision. Hitler hoped that, for once, his Intelligence Services would tell him something reliable, something that would end all the mystery. Canaris and his "little outfit," as Hitler sometimes called the Abwehr, had not been of much use up to now, but maybe this time Canaris would rise to the occasion. If Canaris' help was ever needed, it was now, in the early part of 1944.

As it happened, help regarding the impending landings came from a totally unexpected quarter. At the end of October 1943, the valet of the British ambassador in Ankara, Turkey, approached the German minister in Ankara. The valet said that he had possession of photos of secret British documents, photos that he had taken himself. He asked the German minister if he might be interested in buying the film.

The valet's name was Elyesa Bazna, a 39-year-old Turk with a somewhat shady background.[6] (Actually, Yugoslavia did not yet exist when Bazna was born in 1904; the town in which he was born, Pristina, was still a part of the Ottoman Empire.) Bazna had joined the embassy staff as valet of the British ambassador, Sir Hughe Montgomery Knatchbull-Hugessen, only a few weeks before. He noticed that Sir Hughe brought many of his diplomatic papers home every night, and that these documents were kept locked in dispatch boxes: The more important papers were kept in a red leather box, while the less pressing documents were locked in a black box. Always on the lookout for an opportunity, however dubious, Bazna made a wax impression of the key to these boxes, and had his own personal key made from the impression.

Sometime in mid-October 1943, Bazna used his new key to open the dispatch boxes. He took the papers to his room, where he photographed them with his Leica 35 mm camera. He then returned the papers to the boxes in Sir Hughe's room and relocked the boxes.

About a week later, Bazna approached the German minister in Ankara, Albert Jenke, and asked him to buy the photos of the secret British documents. Jenke and Bazna already knew each other; Bazna had worked as Jenke's valet before he went to Sir Hughe. Jenke did not like Bazna very much, and trusted him even less. He strongly suspected that his former valet was actually a trained espionage agent, and was using his position as manservant as a cover. He also suspected that Bazna had been sent by the enemy to set a trap for him.

But Jenke listened to Bazna's proposal. When he heard the price of the film—Bazna wanted $80,000 (£20,000) for the first roll and $60,000 (£15,000) for each succeeding roll—he was taken completely aback, to put it mildly. He said that he would need clearance from a superior, since he did not have the authority to approve such a large expense.

Jenke contacted the head of the SD in Turkey, Ludwig Moyzisch. Moyzisch, in turn, asked German ambassador Franz von Papen for permission to make a payment to Bazna. Von Papen authorized Moyzisch to pay the $80,000 if the photos seemed genuine. On the night of 30 October, Bazna went to the German embassy to turn his film over to Moyzisch. While he waited, Moyzisch had the film processed in a room in the embassy garden.

Bazna's motives for selling his employer's highly classified documents were, according to one version of the story, revenge and hatred. He said that he hated the British because his father had been shot and killed by a Briton in a hunting accident, and also because he himself had been sent to prison for vehicle theft. But after the war, he gave his own reasons: "my obsessional greed for money, my compulsive craving for the daily thrill—and my fear."

He described himself as "a short, thickset man, beginning to grow bald." Bazna was also vain, conceited, arrogant, greedy, and completely without scruples. He would do anything for money. He was a *kavass*, a servant in a foreign embassy. "A *kavass* is an insignificant nobody," Bazna said, "and I have always hated being a nobody." Now, he was in a position to do something about it.

When Moyzisch saw Bazna's photographs, he was literally speechless with astonishment. "Here, on my desk, were the most carefully guarded secrets of the enemy, both political and military and of incalculable value." The documents that Bazna had photographed were all highly classified. They consisted of communiqués between the British Embassy in Ankara and the Foreign Office in London. All of them had been sent during the past two weeks.

"There could be no shadow of a doubt that these were the real thing," Moyzisch rambled on in his excitement. "Out of the blue, there had dropped into our laps the sort of papers a secret agent might dream about for a lifetime without believing that he could ever get hold of them." He could be forgiven for letting his enthusiasm get the better of him; the photos he was looking at were of vital importance to Britain and the Allied war effort, and they were indeed the real thing.

Moyzisch paid Bazna his $80,000 in cash, which was wrapped in the French-language Turkish newspaper *La Republique*. "His price had not been exorbitant," Moyzisch thought. Franz von Papen felt the same way and gave Bazna the code name Cicero—"the name of a Roman famous for his eloquence," Bazna noted. "Herr von Papen thought that the documents with which I acquainted him were very eloquent, too."[7]

Ambassador von Papen sent Bazna's photos to Berlin for examination. When SD chief Walter Schellenberg saw them, what he felt was a lot closer to uneasiness than amazement. It seemed to him that their new-found fount of knowledge must be a British plant. Even though the photographed documents looked genuine, he was sure that they must be false. No simple valet could have done what Bazna said he did: broke into the British ambassador's dispatch boxes, photographed highly sensitive documents with speed and efficiency, and returned the papers a few minutes later—all without getting caught. And the quality of the photography was much better than a valet or any other amateur photographer should have been able to produce. Schellenberg did not know exactly what was wrong, but the entire episode concerning Bazna/Cicero made him suspicious.

Bazna's story was checked and rechecked. Ludwig Moyzisch asked Bazna to come to his office and explain exactly how he took his pictures. Bazna willingly obliged—unaware that his interview was being taped. He told Moyzisch, step by step, how he went to the ambassador's room, removed the documents to his own room, photographed them, and returned the papers to the dispatch boxes—all within three minutes. Moyzisch was especially interested in hearing Bazna explain that the only equipment he used was his 35 mm Leica, a small tripod, and a 100-watt bulb.

A professional photographer also examined Bazna's photos and agreed with Walter Schellenberg: They were too impressive to have been taken by anyone with Bazna's limited experience with a camera. Bazna's claim that he did the job with only a small, unstable tripod and a bare 100-watt light made his story even more unbelievable. And Moyzisch discovered that Bazna's knowledge of English was a good deal more limited than he acknowledged, which meant that either his choice of documents to photograph was done by the lucky dip method, or else he was working with someone else.

In short, the evidence seemed to support Schellenberg's suspicions. The SD were not sure what to make of Bazna/Cicero. Schellenberg decided to keep dealing with him, but also to keep a wary eye both on him and on the documents he sent.

The British also had their suspicions concerning Bazna. When he first came to the embassy as Sir Hughe's valet, a routine security check was run on the new employee. The background check was done by the assistant military attaché, Lt. Col. Montague Chidson. Chidson very quickly discovered that Bazna had previously been employed by the German embassy as Albert Jenke's valet. Taken by surprise, Chidson decided to do a more thorough investigation.

As the details of Bazna's recent history began to come in, Chidson's surprise quickly turned to alarm. It was evident that Bazna was no ordinary servant: Chidson found out that Sir Hughe's new manservant had been trained in intelligence methods by the Italian Intelligence Service (SIM). It looked as though the British ambassador in Ankara had an enemy agent, either German or Italian, as a valet.

Following the security check and the more detailed investigation, Bazna may have been confronted by Chidson and turned—given the options of sending falsified and useless documents to his German contact, or going to jail. Or Chidson may have laid a trap for Bazna and placed useless or misleading documents in Sir Hughe's dispatch boxes for Bazna to photograph. Or maybe neither of these possibilities took place.

It is definitely known that both British intelligence and the American Office of Strategic Services (OSS) discovered that a spy called Cicero worked at the British embassy, but it is not known exactly when this discovery was made. Bazna might not have been found out until shortly before he resigned as Sir Hughe's valet in April 1944. The SD kept in contact with Bazna until Easter week of 1944 and kept buying his film at $60,000 per roll. At that point, he feared that he was going to get caught and also thought that he already had enough money to leave the spy business for a more relaxed way of life.

But if Bazna was turned by Lieutenant Colonel Chidson, he managed to send a lot of information before anybody grew wise to him and his scheme. One of the items he turned over to the SD was the code name Overlord, as well as its meaning.

Toward the end of November 1943, during the time of the Teheran conference among Churchill, Rooosevelt, and Stalin, Bazna photographed a document that mentioned Overlord. It was a telegram: "IF TURKEY CAME IN ON OUR SIDE IT WOULD FREE THE ESCORT VESSELS WE NEED SO URGENTLY FOR OVERLORD." At about the same time, Stalin was giving the Western leaders his approval for the invasion of France.

Bazna came across other references to Overlord in Sir Hughe's dispatch boxes. "The word 'Overlord' kept cropping up in the documents I photographed," he said. At first, he had no idea what it meant. It was obviously a code word, but he had no way of knowing exactly what connection it had with Allied operations. It gradually occurred to him that "this could refer only to the second front that the Russians were demanding of their allies. . . . Whenever the Russians reiterated their demand, the phrase duly made its appearance in the telegrams."

Bazna photographed all the telegrams, and passed the film on to Ludwig Moyzisch. Thanks to Bazna, the SD had the code word Operation Overlord as early as November 1943. "Later I found out that it was I who first brought the phrase to the knowledge of the Germans," he proudly recalled.

In spite of his success, both financial and professional (if espionage can be considered a profession), Bazna was not entirely happy with his situation. By the spring of 1944, his main concern was that he was going to get caught, a possibility that was becoming more of a worry to him with each day that passed. The job was no longer as exciting as it had been at first, and he thought it might be time for him to stop taking risks and lead a more peaceful existence.

Bazna took stock of his career as a spy. He had made a great deal of money as Cicero—the result of selling numerous rolls of film to the Germans at $60,000 per roll. (He was always paid in cash, and kept the money under the carpet in his room at the embassy.) He was no longer an "insignificant nobody." He had sold enough military secrets to calm his alleged hatred of the British, and had taken enough chances in passing these secrets along to the Germans to satisfy his craving for thrills and excitement. Cicero decided that it was time to retire, to quit while he was still ahead.

For a while, Bazna "lived the life of a wealthy idler" in Ankara with his Greek mistress, a cabaret singer who had "a first-class figure but a third-class voice." He followed the war news very carefully, knowing that he had a hand in shaping it. When he heard the news of the invasion of France, he told his Greek singer, "This is Operation Overlord." He was more impressed by the announcement than she was.

After the war, Bazna used his Cicero money to become a partner in a construction firm. One of his more ambitious projects was to build a luxury spa hotel in the Turkish town of Bursa, "the future pride of the Turkish tourist industry." It was to be called the Celik Palace, a smart hotel for the rich, and just the place for a former *kavass* who had become filthy rich by outsmarting his employers.

One day, while Bazna was discussing construction details with his architect, the telephone rang. His partner was on the other end of the line, and he had very bad news: The firm's assets had been confiscated by the police and the authorities. A banker had become suspicious about all the British currency that their firm had deposited, and had the notes taken out of the vault and examined by Swiss banks and by the Bank of England. These tests showed that all the money that Bazna had deposited, the money that he had invested as his partnership in the construction firm and that had been used to finance the Celik Palace, was counterfeit. This was also the money that Moyzisch and the SD had paid him for photos of Sir Hughe's documents. When he heard the news, Bazna fainted.

Bazna thought that he was a millionaire. But, in fact, all he owned was a pile of expertly forged Bank of England notes. All of the money that he had received as payment for photographing secret Allied documents had been top quality forgeries. As Bazna himself put it, "The bank notes that I hoarded so jealously were not worth even the price of the Turkish linen out of which they had been manufactured."

The SD paid Bazna with counterfeit money for two reasons. They wanted to devalue the British pound on the international currency market, and hoped to cause a crisis for the British currency. Also, they needed to save on operating expenses; Moyzisch's department was short of currency, so they printed their own. Bazna complained that "the Germans had deceived me as grossly as I had deceived Sir Hughe." When his Greek mistress discovered that Bazna did not have any money, she immediately walked out on him.

Elyesa Bazna died in 1971, not much mourned and something of a comic figure. Up to the end, he was still trying to recover at least some money from the West German government. The Germans refused to take any action whatever on his claim, or even to acknowledge that he had a claim. His last years were spent in "a little side street remote from the metropolitan bustle of Istanbul," where he lived on the miserable edge of poverty.

A few years after the war, Bazna and his second wife made a visit to Bursa. They stopped at the Celik Palace, the luxury hotel that Bazna himself hoped to build. Their stay was very brief. They did not order anything from the dining room or take a room for the night; it was a very exclusive hotel, and Bazna could not afford the prices.

British intelligence tends to downplay Cicero's activities, including the selling of the code name Operation Overlord to the Germans. They insist that this was only one small bit of information, and was only one code word out of dozens, perhaps hundreds. But it was also one more piece to the puzzle that Hitler and his FHW (Fremde Heere West, the department of German intelligence concerned with the Western Allies and their intentions), were trying to put together involving the *Grossinvasion*.

The Cicero story is worth mentioning mainly because it shows how information is gathered, particularly regarding an operation as extensive as Overlord. Such information rarely comes in a flood. Usually, it comes in bits and fragments—a location here, a code name there, sometimes the name of a commander that might have been linked to a particular unit in the past. Bazna/Cicero may not have been a very sympathetic character, but he did a good job for the SD. Acquiring the name Overlord was a huge advantage for FHW; in the future, any names, units, or locations that appeared in conjunction with Overlord could be linked directly to the pending invasion.

There were still a lot of pieces missing. But the SD was trying to find as many of them as possible concerning Overlord, including the time and place of the impending landings. They had their agents at work in France, as well as in the British Isles, looking for other fragments of the puzzle. The officer in charge of FHW, Colonel Alexis Baron von Roenne, referred to this as piecing together a *feindbild*, a picture of the enemy.

While the SD, along with the FHW, was at work piecing together details concerning Overlord, its leader was trying to put together a case against Admiral Canaris and the Abwehr. Walter Schellenberg, Heydrich's successor as head of the SD, had been steadily collecting evidence on Canaris' collaboration with General Cesare Ame, specifically his joining forces with Ame to mislead Hitler concerning Italy's defection to the

Allies. He managed to put together quite a file against Canaris, proof that he hoped would put the admiral in a concentration camp or, better still, on the gallows. [8]

Schellenberg had his own personal spies in Rome, agents who worked for him and reported directly to him. He assigned two of his contacts to keep a close watch on General Ame, mainly to find out anything they could about Ame's association with Canaris. At that stage, Schellenberg suspected Ame and Italian military intelligence as much as he mistrusted Canaris; he thought that Ame was unreliable, at best, and was probably a traitor to the Italian alliance with Nazi Germany.

Schellenberg's personal agents managed to find out that Ame's two chauffeurs were homosexual. They used this bit of information, which would have landed the chauffeurs in prison in Fascist Italy, as blackmail; Ame's drivers were coerced into telling everything they knew about General Ame and his conversations with Canaris. Since Canaris and Ame held their discussions in the back seat of Ame's limousine, the chauffeurs had a great deal to tell.

As the result of his spies and their blackmail, Schellenberg found out all about Canaris' part in Italy's changing sides, and about his lying to Hitler about Ame's intentions. He made up a full report on Canaris, which gave all details of the Canaris-Ame intrigue.

Schellenberg now had what he considered absolute proof of Canaris' treachery. He personally handed his report to Reichsführer Heinrich Himmler, confident that he finally had all the evidence he needed to hang Canaris. The next step would be for Himmler to take the report to Adolf Hitler. When Hitler read what Schellenberg had to say about Canaris and General Ame, that would be the end of Canaris.

Schellenberg thought he had enough on Canaris to put a rope around his neck, and he was probably right. But Himmler did absolutely nothing at all with the report except promise to give it to Hitler "when the opportunity arose."[9]

At first, Schellenberg was surprised by Himmler's refusal to act on his behalf; then he was annoyed. He kept asking about the report but, every time he did, all he got was the same vague promise. He finally realized that Himmler never had any intention of giving the Canaris file to Hitler, and that the opportunity would never arise. Himmler was afraid, but Schellenberg had no idea why.

The only conclusion Schellenberg could reach was that Canaris had something on Himmler, some sort of incriminating evidence that made him afraid to cross the admiral. Himmler kept Schellenberg's evidence to himself, in his personal possession. No one besides Himmler and Schellenberg knew it existed. Schellenberg's scheme had fallen short, and Canaris—along with British and American intelligence—had another reprieve.

Exactly what kind of evidence Canaris held against Himmler has been a matter of question and controversy since about 1942. Several episodes in Himmler's life might well have been used by Canaris, who would not have hesitated to resort to blackmail if it would keep Himmler and the SS at bay. The admiral may have mentioned details of his evidence in a diary he kept, but that diary disappeared before the war ended.

One item was a rumored homosexual relationship between Himmler and Reinhard Heydrich. A good deal of gossip had been circulating about the two men since the late 1930s. The OSS office in Berne, Switzerland, heard stories that Himmler and Heydrich had been involved with each other. If the OSS knew about it, Canaris also knew; he had contacts among the OSS in Berne, and if he had not heard it from Berne, he would have heard about it someplace else.

If Hitler ever found out that the head of his elite SS was a homosexual, the results would have been predictable for Himmler—and not very happy. At the very least, it would have meant the loss of his position and public humiliation.

Another possible subject for blackmail was Himmler's own plot against Hitler, which dates to 1942 and the failure of the German offensive at Stalingrad. When the German position at Stalingrad became untenable in December, which resulted in the complete isolation of all German forces in the city and their surrender a few weeks later, Himmler realized that the war no longer could be won. More than 147,000 German troops had died in the Stalingrad pocket, and 90,000 more had been taken prisoner. Himmler was farsighted enough to see what this meant for the German army, not only in Russia but for the fighting on all fronts.

The Stalingrad defeat made Himmler see the true situation for Germany: Hitler was leading the country steadily toward destruction and total failure. Himmler secretly made contact with the Americans—again via the OSS, this time in Sweden—in an attempt to begin negotiations. His plan was fairly simple and straightforward: remove Hitler from power and take over the office of Führer himself.[10]

This move on Himmler's part was not just a flash in the pan; his plotting went on for the next several months. In August 1943, he even went so far as to meet with a member of the German anti-Nazi resistance, a Prussian named Johannes Popitz.

Nothing came of these talks, for several reasons. The main problem was that resistance members, particularly General Ludwig Beck, did not trust either Himmler or the SS. This 'plot' sounded like an SS trap. But even if Himmler were sincere about his desire to overthrow Hitler— which Beck held in serious doubt—most resistance members did not see Himmler as much of an improvement over Hitler. They preferred to wait for their chance to remove every one of the Nazi mob, including Himmler.

Admiral Canaris had eyes and ears everywhere. He knew all about Himmler's OSS contact, and was well informed of the Reichsführer's conversation with Johannes Popitz. He realized that either of these two incidents would mean a slow, painful death if Hitler ever found out about Himmler's contacts with anti-Nazi conspirators. (Hitler did eventually find out about Himmler's negotiations with the Allies, but not until the spring of 1945. He immediately issued a warrant for Himmler's arrest and execution. But by that time, the Third Reich was being overrun by both the Western Allies and the Russians. Himmler was captured by the British before Hitler could catch him, and he committed suicide.)

And so, Schellenberg was absolutely correct in his assumption. Canaris did indeed have something on Reichsführer Himmler—more than one something, in fact—which is why he did not dare take Schellenberg's carefully compiled and researched dossier to Hitler. But Schellenberg could only guess at the reason.

In spite of the efforts of Admiral Canaris and his fellow conspirators in the Schwarze Kapelle, FHW still received many and various accurate reports concerning Operation Overlord. This information came from a number of sources. Although some of it was sketchy and incomplete, these reports provided vital fragments of news from the other side of the Channel on Invasion preparations.

The Luftwaffe used to be a primary source for this sort of information. During the Battle of Britain and the Blitz, photoreconnaissance airplanes took pictures of targets as far inland as London and beyond. But the Luftwaffe was only a ghost of what it had been in 1940 and 1941. British and American fighters made reconnaissance flights over southern England a hazardous undertaking, at best.[11]

Reconnaissance flights were still being sent to photograph objectives in southern England, but there were a lot fewer of them these days. Enemy fighters were simply making the cost of aerial reconnaissance too high. Most of the pilots managed to bring their pictures home, although they frequently landed with bullets in wings and fuselage, and with hydraulic systems shot away.

The airplanes most often used for these extremely risky assignments were specially modified Messerschmitt Bf 109 fighters. These fighters were altered to give them maximum speed and altitude. All armor and excess weight were removed, including all guns. Their Daimler-Benz engines were very carefully tuned to give them maximum performance. Leading edges of wings and stabilizers were polished to a high gloss to reduce drag. Because they had no guns, they had to be able to outrun intercepting enemy fighters. The job of the reconnaissance pilots was to fly high and fast, to take their pictures and get away before the Spitfires or Mustangs could get them.

Even with their special modifications, the photoreconnaissance Messerschmitts did not always return. But the information they supplied was vital, so the risk had to be taken. They were sent out on irregular schedules, so that the enemy would not know when to expect them. Usually, only three or four flights per week were sent across the Channel; sending more would have meant tempting the fates, as well as the enemy's highly aggressive fighter pilots.

Photoreconnaissance pilots were usually assigned to photograph harbors on the south coast of England, and sometimes road and rail traffic leading to the coast. Their pictures allowed intelligence to keep track of ships in Channel ports, including the number of landing craft, as well as the amount of men and equipment on the move toward the coast—information which would help FHW evaluate when and where the Invasion would take place.

During the late winter and early spring of 1944, photoreconnaissance indicated that changes in Channel port traffic were gradual—meaning that the Invasion was not imminent. Most activity was in Ramsgate and Dover, just across the Straits of Dover from Calais. There was not enough shipping in any of the harbors to draw any conclusions about Overlord's probable destination, however.

Luftwaffe records do not give very much information about these reconnaissance sorties—sometimes just time of takeoff and time of landing. Some entries specify the objective of the flight—"Southampton," or "Dover area." Intelligence would have preferred more than just three or four flights per week. But the photos that the pilots were bringing back added more pieces to the Overlord puzzle.

Radio intelligence did not have to worry about enemy fighters and, so, could afford to be more persistent than the Luftwaffe. The radio reconnaissance unit responsible for monitoring broadcasts in both Britain and the United States was Communications Reconnaissance Regiment 5. Battalion 13 of Regiment 5 monitored radio traffic in the British Isles, including Northern Ireland, as well as in Canada. Battalion 12 kept track of American radio traffic, both internal and overseas broadcasts.

By listening in on talk between army radio operators, these two reconnaissance battalions did an excellent job of following the movements of individual army units. Battalion 12 was able to keep informed of which units were in training, which were scheduled to be transferred to another camp, and which units were being sent overseas. The installation at Euskirchen, designated Post No. 3, handled most of the American radio messages, and was able to trace most, if not all, troop movements in the United States. Once a particular unit arrived in Britain, another radio battalion took over.

Of course, the operators sometimes got things wrong. American geography was a mystery to most Germans; place names such as Iowa,

Idaho, and Ohio sounded alike to the German ear, and were often confused with one another. Exotic sounding places such as Chatahoochie, or even Mississippi, could be the cause of total bedlam. Also, monitors sometimes fell into the trap of reporting the activities of units that did not exist, divisions that were created by American intelligence to deceive the Germans. Two such units were the 49th and the 59th Divisions, which existed only to mislead the Germans as to American troop strength. The U.S. Army Signal Corps kept up a steady stream of messages regarding these purely fictitious units, solely for the benefit of eavesdroppers in Germany or elsewhere.

But Battalions No. 12 and 13 also gathered a great deal of accurate information on units that would play a key role in Overlord. The U.S. 1st and 4th Divisions, as well as the Second Armored Division, were discovered in Britain by Battalion No. 13, along with just about every other U.S. Army unit stationed in the British Isles during the Overlord build-up. British units were also tracked by the radio listeners. The famous 50th and 51st Infantry Divisions, veterans who had fought Rommel in North Africa, were discovered in the British Isles in the early spring of 1944. Radio reconnaissance kept FHW well informed of what the British and American armies were up to.

German agents in Britain and the United States also contributed their share of pieces to the intelligence puzzle, although their efforts were usually a lot more indirect than either radio intelligence or the Luftwaffe. These spies got their information out of the country and back to Germany by ways that, necessarily, were secret and circumspect. But they always managed to stay in touch with their contacts.

One such agent was a Dutchman named Walter Koehler, also known as Albert van Loop. Koehler entered the United States late in 1942, by way of Spain. At the American vice consul's office in Madrid, he confessed that he was an employee of the Abwehr, and also requested political asylum. He did not want to spy for the Germans, Koehler said, and wanted to enter the United States as a refugee; he actually was Dutch, which gave him a perfect cover story.[12]

To prove that he really was a German spy, Koehler produced all of his Abwehr issue equipment: a radio operator's manual, a prayer book that contained the codes he would use to send his reports, chemicals used to make invisible ink, a document written in invisible ink, and the $6,200 he was given by the Abwehr. He wanted to stay in the United States to escape the Nazis—life as an anti-Nazi Roman Catholic in occupied Holland did not offer much of a future, he explained—and would work for American counterintelligence against the Germans.

The director of the Federal Bureau of Investigation, J. Edgar Hoover, saw the opportunity in Koehler's arrival. Here was a ready-made double agent who agreed to cooperate fully with the bureau. Hoover made sure that Koehler would cooperate with him, and would do exactly as he was told.

Hoover gave his new double agent his own radio station on Long Island. The station was set up in a large house; guard dogs patrolled the expansive grounds to discourage visitors. But Koehler did not send any messages to Germany; Hoover did not trust him.

Koehler's radio station was run by a team of FBI agents; the operators were fluent in German and had also learned Koehler's "fist," his unique touch on the Morse key. When the first signal was across to Germany on 7 February 1943, Koehler was not even there, nor would he be for any subsequent messages. The FBI agents sent a steady stream of messages on the weather, on shipping arrivals and departures, and on troop movements. All information had been cleared by the War Department. The reports either were doctored to alter the facts, or were completely useless.

J. Edgar Hoover was absolutely delighted that his little ruse seemed to be working so well, better than he ever could have hoped. German intelligence believed every report that was sent, and had absolutely no idea that Koehler was working for the FBI. He congratulated himself for having used Koehler to fool the Germans for so long—right up to the end of the war.

Many years after the war ended, however, an American writer discovered that Koehler had not been double-crossing German intelligence; he had been triple-crossing Hoover and the FBI. Koehler's entire double-agent cover had been prearranged. He was not a Dutch refugee, but an active German agent who requested political asylum as a ruse go get him into the United States. While the FBI was sending falsified reports across to Germany, Koehler was sending genuine reports to Paris.

Koehler did not send his information out of the country by radio; he used couriers, most of whom crossed the Atlantic to Spain or Portugal on ships flying a neutral flag. After reaching their destination, the couriers would take Koehler's information by train to Paris. If there was something that was too urgent for the steamer, Koehler had a contact in Rochester, New York, who could send the data via a secret radio transmitter. When Koehler made contact, his friend would come to Manhattan to pick up his information, and would send it off to Paris as soon as he returned to Rochester. This radio contact was only used for news that was considered too vital to be sent via the slower, but safer, courier method.

Koehler continued with his secret communiqués until April 1945. When Paris was evacuated by the Germans in August 1944, he sent his reports to Hamburg. This subterfuge went on for more than two years. And the FBI never knew a thing about it.

Another item that the FBI never knew about was Koehler's source of income. Although he turned $6,000 over to the U.S. authorities when he defected, he had been given $16,000 before he left Germany. His portly wife wore the other $10,000 under her girdle, and walked right past federal agents with it. Agents who kept the Koehlers under observation suspected that they had more money than they should have had, but could never prove anything.

Walter Schellenberg considered Koehler to be one of his top agents, but Walter Koehler was not the only German agent at work in the United States. Nine senior agents also operated in the country, mostly in the east, but there were lesser agents, as well, along with dedicated amateurs who belonged to the German American Bund and the Irish Republican Army. The official FBI line on German spies is that none existed in the United States—that is to say, all spies and saboteurs were quickly arrested by the bureau before they could send any information back to Germany or perform any mischief. But records discovered after the war in Germany proved otherwise.

An event similar to the Koehler/FBI incident took place in Britain. The German agent in this case went by the name of Hans Hansen. Hansen landed by parachute just outside Salisbury in September 1940, along with an accomplice, a Swede named Goesta Caroli. Caroli was captured soon after he arrived in England and was given the two choices usually offered to captured German spies—go to work for MI-5, sending genuine-sounding reports to Germany that contained false or totally misleading information, or have his neck snapped by the hangman. Caroli gave the usual reply: He decided to go to work for MI-5.

Hans Hansen was also discovered by MI-5, and was also given the usual two options. Like his partner, he also opted for the less final of the two choices. But Hansen had a trick or two up his own sleeve, and he used them to outwit MI-5.

While he was sending his bogus reports to Hamburg, Hansen was also sending accurate information that MI-5 never suspected. No fault was ever found with any of the reports he sent to Germany; his contacts checked and rechecked all of his reports. Hansen decided that he was going to try to double-cross the Double-Cross Committee, and managed to get away with it.

Hansen's reports were so good—both timely and accurate—that a special panel was formed to examine them. This panel was made up of some experienced and highly skeptical individuals—both civilian and military—including a psychiatrist. These people went over Hansen's reports for any sign of irregularities or contradictions, and could not find any.

It is highly likely that Hansen got past his British observers by sending "flowers," accurate bits buried within the phony messages he made up for British intelligence. This method would have appealed to his devious nature, and would also explain his instant transformation from German spy to British informer. Hansen had been a confirmed Nazi in his native Denmark, a storm trooper so dedicated to Hitler and the party that he had to flee to Germany for his own safety. It does not seem very likely that he would have gone to work for the enemy without a great deal more persuasion than MI-5 appears to have used on him. Hansen gave in to MI-5 so easily because he had a way of getting around them, and getting messages across to Germany in spite of them.

Hans Hansen kept up his traffic to Hamburg from September 1940 until May 1945. He frequently was allowed to send his own reports, just to add to the authenticity (with an MI-5 operator sitting close by), which made it fairly easy for him to slip in a flower when needed. Among the flowers he sent were reports on Overlord which, by the Spring of 1944, was the most pressing item on everyone's mind. He also sent messages on other matters of interest, including British airfields. All the while, MI-5 thought they were putting one over on German intelligence.

German agents were also at work in neutral countries, picking up bits and pieces of useful information where they could find them. The German consulate in Geneva often sent messages of military interest to Hamburg, or to other contacts in Germany. Agent Ricardo in Lisbon also kept in touch, along with his counterpart in Sweden. All were on the lookout for any clues as to the probable date of the Invasion, as well as for any information on its probable destination.

Gwyn Evans, agent Druid, was still at large in England, and was still looking for news. He was still using his job as an entertainment organizer to travel throughout the British Isles, touring military bases around the country as the manager of a string quartet. The chamber group was made up of refugees from the Netherlands; they performed a pops repertoire, Strauss waltzes and selections from Gilbert and Sullivan instead of Mozart and Beethoven, for the troops. It is difficult to say which side found these concerts drearier, the musicians or the audience. But the musical programs served their purpose: They allowed Druid to visit military bases and other restricted areas as much as he wanted.

In 1942, Evans had been able to find out the date and objective of Operation Jubilee, the Dieppe raid. Now, the SD and OKW hoped that he would be able to do the same with Operation Overlord. He certainly had the means to do the job, and was in the right place for it.

Popular wisdom on German intelligence insists that reports on Overlord were sporadic, at best, and that any information that actually was received tended to be inaccurate and generally useless. This is not even close to the truth. Although FHW and the High Command would have preferred more information from all intelligence sources, particularly from Luftwaffe reconnaissance units based in northern France, reports relating to the Allied build-up arrived in Germany at a steady rate during the spring of 1944. Radio monitoring, agents in the field, contacts in neutral countries, and aerial reconnaissance, kept FHW well informed of Allied preparations. How successfully all this information would be employed by Hitler and OKW was largely dependent upon FHW. Fremde Heere West had the task of sorting through and evaluating this mountain of intelligence.

As hard as the various participants of the intelligence network tried to keep OKW informed of Allied activities, Admiral Wilhelm Canaris and his co-conspirators were doing their equal best to keep Hitler and OKW in the dark. Canaris and his colleagues in the Schwarze Kapelle were not concerned just with Overlord and its preparations. They were actively involved with any sort of deception that would confuse and mislead the High Command and their leader, and would help shorten the war.

In January 1944, Canaris was given another opportunity. On 21 January, he was asked to present himself at the headquarters of Feldmarschall Albert Kesselring, commander of all German forces in the Mediterranean. The SD had been hearing about impending Allied landings on the coast of Italy, near the town of Civitavecchia. Canaris was to give his views of the enemy's intentions toward Italy, as well as what he knew about any impending landings.

Canaris immediately put everybody's mind at ease. He did not go into any detail, but he told everyone present that there was no need to fear an Allied landing anytime in the near future. General Westphal, a member of Feldmarschall Rommel's staff, asked him if he knew where the British battleships were.

"We are looking after them—don't you worry," Canaris reassured him. Although he gave no specifics as to their whereabouts, the entire tone of Canaris' briefing was confident: There was nothing to fear from the enemy; he would be making no offensive moves.

At that precise moment, while Canaris was telling the meeting that the enemy had no plans for an amphibious landing, about 250 Allied ships were approaching the Italian coast. At dawn on 22 January 1944, 50,000 men and 5,200 vehicles of the U.S. Third Division and British First Division came ashore at Anzio, in one of the largest amphibious operations of the war. It was the beginning of a murderous battle of attrition between German and Allied forces that would go on for the next several months.[13]

Once again, Admiral Canaris had lulled everyone to sleep while the enemy was preparing a major operation, just as he had done prior to Operation Torch. But this time, he was not able to talk his way out of it.

Hitler was already annoyed and extremely dissatisfied with Canaris because of past intelligence shortcomings: his failure to give any advance warning of Operation Torch; his part in the failure of Operation Felix, the planned German takeover of Gibraltar; and, most recently, his starkly realistic appraisal of the disastrous military situation in Russia, which Hitler saw as evidence of Canaris' "pessimism." Also, Abwehr agents in neutral countries—in Turkey, in Switzerland, and in Portugal—began defecting to the Allied side,[14] which reflected badly on Canaris. Hitler had already had just about enough of the "little admiral" and his constant inefficiency, not to mention his pessimism about Russia. This latest disaster served as the final nail in his coffin.

If Hitler was angry because of Anzio, Walter Schellenberg, head of the SD, was relieved. He realized that he finally had his opening to take over the Abwehr and place the agency under his own control. None other than Heinrich Himmler approached Hitler with the suggestion that a single intelligence service be formed, and placed in the hands of a reliable Party man, namely Walter Schellenberg. Himmler realized that he could no longer go on protecting Canaris, which is why he took this purely expedient action on Schellenberg's behalf. Hitler listened to Himmler's proposal and agreed. He removed Wilhelm Canaris as head of the Abwehr, and unified the Abwehr and the SD under Schellenberg's direction.

Himmler saw to it that Canaris' removal was done gently; he was aware that the admiral still had a file full of damaging evidence against him. Canaris was dismissed from the service on 18 February 1944, after having been awarded the German Cross. He did not argue or put up any kind of a fight. As a sort of consolation prize, he was made director of the Economic Warfare Department, which was nothing more than a make-work desk job. Canaris accepted both the decoration and the demotion.

Friends and colleagues urged Canaris to get away, to go to Spain. Generalissimo Franco would certainly give him asylum, he was assured, and he would be away from Hitler and Berlin and everything he detested about them. But Canaris would not leave Germany. "I want to share the fate of Germany," he told his wife. He would come closer to getting his wish than he ever could have realized.

The Abwehr was finally dissolved in a decree signed by Adolf Hitler.

1. A uniform German intelligence service is to be established;

2. I put the Reichsführer SS in charge of this German Intelligence Service; and

3. Insofar as this affects the military intelligence and counterespionage services, the Reichsführer SS and the chief of the OKW are to take necessary steps after due consultation.[15]

Germany's Intelligence Services were now in the hands of the party—Himmler of the SS and Schellenberg of the SD.

Canaris remained in Germany, as he wanted. He lived a solitary life with his wife and his beloved pet dachshunds in a secluded fourteenth-century castle in Franconia, Burg Lauenstein. The castle's commandant—Burg Lauenstein was used by the Abwehr for intelligence experts who specialized in creating forged passports and microfilming secret documents—was instructed to keep the admiral comfortable but as far away from the outside world as possible.

Admiral Canaris was now retired from the service and out of the way, as Walter Schellenberg wanted. But Canaris had already accomplished much of what he set out to do—damage the credibility of the Intelligence Services to the point where Hitler was skeptical about any report received from any intelligence agency. Hitler and OKW second-guessed all such reports, and were more inclined to believe their own hunches than any information submitted by German intelligence even though all intelligence was now under control of the Nazi Party. This would be critical during the approach to D-Day.

(There has also been speculation that some of these hunches were based upon transcripts of the Churchill/Roosevelt telephone conversations.)

Although Canaris had now been removed, his fellow conspirators of the Schwarze Kapelle were still actively plotting against both Hitler and his Nazi Party. Among the conspirators were the military governors of two occupied countries, General Alexander von Falkenhausen of Belgium and General Karl Heinrich von Stuelpnagel of France. More important to the military situation in France were General Heinrich von Lüttwitz, commander of the 2nd Panzer Division, and General Gerhardt von Schwerin, commander of the 116th Panzer Division. Also prominent in the Schwarze Kapelle was General Hans Speidel, Rommel's chief of staff and, according to one British historian, "a dedicated veteran member of the conspiracy."[16] These officers, along with their colleagues, would make their influence—as well as Admiral Canaris'—felt during the coming critical months.

NOTES

1. Fraser, p. 453.
2. Comments on Directive 51 in Ruge, p. 4.
3. Carell, p. 8.
4. Ryan, p. 118.
5. Perrault, p. 178.
6. Elyesa Bazna's story exists in any number of versions. Some show him as a fool, others as a villain, and still others as a victim of the wily Nazis. The details of his career as an espionage agent are taken from his own memoirs, which seemed the most reliable source on the subject.

7. Moyzisch, p. 54.

8. Walter Schellenberg's efforts to trap Admiral Canaris come from Colvin, Schellenberg, Höhne, and Brown.

9. Schellenberg, p. 407.

10. Details of Himmler's attempts to contact the Western Allies in Padfield, Abshagen, Höhne, and Brissaud. Himmler was certainly one of the more interesting characters of the Nazi regime—or odd, depending upon one's point of view. He did not seem to trust anyone, and let few people get close to him, which is why each biography gives a different picture of him and his personality.

11. Most of the information on reconnaissance of southern England and the United States came from the Bundesarchiv in Freiburg.

12. I had uncovered the story of Walter Koehler and J. Edgar Hoover while doing research for my *Germany's Spies and Saboteurs*. It is also mentioned prominently in Farago's *Game of the Foxes*. The FBI still will not acknowledge that Koehler was actually triple-crossing Hoover and the bureau. I also learned about Hans Hansen while researching *Germany's Spies and Saboteurs*.

13. Admiral Canaris and his failure to report the Anzio landings in Colvin, Höhne, Farago, and Padfield.

14. In his book *The Game of the Foxes*, Ladislas Farago compares this defection with rats leaving a sinking ship.

15. Hitler's decree merging the Abwehr and SD in Gehlen, p. 94.

16. Brown, p. 654.

FOUR

"To Outwit the Enemy with Complicated Schemes..."

The Overlord deception planners realized that it would be impossible to keep such an operation secret. It was simply too big an undertaking to hide—there were too many troops, too many supply vehicles, too many ships, too much of everything that would be required for the great Invasion. Anyone in southern England could see evidence of the preparations for themselves. A British writer recalls that "the skies were seldom silent, and the once empty roads of Kent, Surrey, Hampshire, Dorset, and Devon were crowded with seemingly endless convoys of lorries, tanks, and bulldozers, all headed south or west towards the invasion ports."[1]

Because it was impossible to hide the Overlord build-up, senior British and American intelligence officers decided to take the opposite approach—give the enemy something easy to find, something that would satisfy his curiosity and also mislead him concerning the date and destination of Overlord. To convince German intelligence that the main landings would take place at Calais, Allied planners let them find an army in southeast England, just across the Straits of Dover from Calais. And so, intelligence planners invented a deception operation code-named Quicksilver, which was designed to mislead German intelligence into believing that Calais was the destination for Overlord. The main component of Quicksilver was the First U.S. Army Group (FUSAG), a mainly fictitious concentration of troops stationed in Kent and Sussex.

FUSAG was, in the words of a former U.S. Army officer who was stationed in London in 1944, "so devious that only the British could have thought it up."[2] (This retired officer married a British girl and stayed married to her for fifty years, which may account for his point of view.)

In order to trick the Germans into thinking that a main force was billeted just opposite Calais, an elaborate deception scheme was set in place in the quiet green fields of southeastern England. Entire camps were built, but nobody lived in them—tent cities made up of empty tents. Radio operators reported the movements of troops that did not exist; the troops consisted of two radiomen, one receiving and one sending, describing what nonexistent units were doing, or were planning to do.

Armored units attached to FUSAG had tanks and vehicles that were made of inflatable rubber. One of these dummy Sherman tanks could be picked up and moved by two men, but looked realistic even at close quarters. The squeaking noises of tank tracks had been previously recorded, and were played back on loudspeakers; listeners in France picked them up and believed them to be tanks on the move.

The finishing touch for the FUSAG deception was the appointment of General George S. Patton as its commander. Both German intelligence and OKW were of the opinion that Patton would be one of Overlord's main commanders—if not the principal Allied field commander, then surely as leader of the first assault. "The Germans had long feared Patton as the most able battlefield commander on the Allied side," according to one biographer, "and the most likely candidate to command the invasion force."[3] Because of his brilliance in North Africa and Sicily, Patton was admired as well as feared by many German officers; he might be called the American Rommel, only with more flamboyance and a great deal less discretion.

General Patton's presence in England as FUSAG's commander was no secret, although his appointment as commander of the U.S. Third Army was. The unpredictable general was under strict orders from General Eisenhower to behave with dignity and decorum, which is rather like telling a 5-year-old that he must never put ink in his water pistol. As could have been predicted, and as Eisenhower undoubtedly guessed, Patton did just the opposite of what he was told.

Instead of showing caution and keeping a low profile, Patton seemed to go out of his way to make his presence known in the most public way possible. Patton's behavior was one of the most reliable components in the early FUSAG plans. He went to the theater in London; he visited Eisenhower's headquarters in Grosvenor Square regularly, making sure that everyone knew he was there; he met the *Queen Mary* at Greenock and was seen by the thousands of GIs on board. Any time he made one of his "secret" visits, Patton was sure to tell everyone present, "I am not here," or "You have not seen me." Which, again, had just the opposite effect; everyone present could not wait to pass the word that they had seen "Ol' Blood and Guts" in person while he was on a top secret visit.

German intelligence very quickly discovered that General Patton was in England, as Eisenhower and his senior officers knew would happen.

SHAEF (Supreme Headquarters, Allied Expeditionary Force), the successor of COSSAC, wanted the Germans to know Patton's whereabouts. They did not want them to know that Patton was commanding Third Army, however, Eisenhower put up with Patton and his self-publicizing because the flamboyant three-star general was serving Quicksilver's purposes. Also, he realized that Patton could not act with discretion if he tried.

Patton strongly suspected that SHAEF did not want him to keep quiet. He also suspected that his movements were being made public deliberately, for the purpose of informing the enemy that he was in Britain. He was correct in both of his assumptions, as was shown in the so-called Knutsford incident in April 1944.[4]

A Welcome Club for U.S. servicemen had been organized by the residents of the town of Knutsford, in Cheshire. Because General Patton had his headquarters in Knutsford, he was asked to give a speech at the official opening of the club. Patton was under explicit orders to give no public speeches. But because he was assured that no reporters or photographers would be present, Patton decided to make an appearance at the opening just the same.

When he showed up at the club, Patton found a crowd, a band, a group of British servicewomen, and several photographers. He asked the photographers not to take any pictures; they agreed. He also was informed that no reporters were present, which put his mind at rest. After a brief introduction, the general took the podium.

Patton's speech was meant to be a humorous mix of belligerence and levity. He told the gathering, most of whom were women, that the only experience he had with welcoming to date was to welcome Germans to the "infernal regions." He went on to say that such welcome clubs served a real purpose because he believed, along with George Bernard Shaw, "that the British and Americans are two people separated by a common language. Since it seems to be the destiny of America, Great Britain, and Russia to rule the world, the better we know each other, the better off we will be." He concluded by telling the audience that when American women found out how lovely British ladies are, they would force the war to come to an end, and then he would go to the Pacific to kill Japanese. Everyone present seemed to enjoy Patton's unique brand of humor.

There are at least two versions of what happened next. One account has it that a reporter actually *was* present, and that he released the contents of the speech. Another story is that a representative of the British government was on hand, and he gave the details to the press. Whatever happened, the wire services picked up the story; it appeared in British newspapers the next day. Some accounts left out Patton's mention of Russia as one of the postwar rulers of the world. When the American press got hold of this edited version, all hell broke loose. It looked as though General Patton was advocating an Anglo-American alliance at the expense of the Russians.

Some newsmen and politicians were still angry with Patton over the slapping of two soldiers suffering from combat fatigue, which happened on Sicily during the previous August. Now they had another complaint, and complain they did, at the top of their voices. After the slapping incident, Patton was made out to be brutish, barbaric, and not much better than the Nazis he was fighting. Now, he was criticized for being loudmouthed, undiplomatic, and insulting, not worthy to hold the rank of lieutenant general. The press had a field day. A small local incident was blown into a major international crisis.

Patton found himself in serious trouble again because of misconduct, for the second time in less than a year. General Eisenhower sent him a strongly worded letter of rebuke, just as he had done following the slapping incident, and thought seriously about relieving him and sending him back to America in disgrace. It looked as though Patton's career was over.

How the contents of Patton's speech ever got beyond Knutsford, let alone out of the British Isles, has been questioned ever since the time of the incident. Britain was under strict wartime censorship; no story could be released without official clearance. No censor would have passed any story involving anyone as important as Patton. There was not much of a possibility that the story was released by mistake, as has been suggested. A report regarding someone of Patton's rank and reputation never would have gotten past any censor—unless it was intentional.

The only plausible explanation is that the Allied intelligence planners, either the British (London Controlling Section), the Americans (Joint Security Control), or both, decided to use the Knutsford incident to give Patton a very high profile. If Patton was in Britain, the thinking went, the German High Command would assume that Armeegruppe Patton would spearhead the landings at Calais. The fact that their tactics very nearly destroyed Patton's army career was beside the point, at least in the cold logic of British and American intelligence.

The Knutsford incident—or, rather, the distorting and magnifying of the incident—seriously injured Patton's reputation and jeopardized his Third Army command. Eisenhower said that he had deep reservations concerning Patton's "all-round judgment, so essential in high military position." General George Marshall, the chief of staff, was actually considering taking Third Army away from Patton. Of course, none of this mattered to the minds of either OSS or MI-5, who would have done more than ruin Patton's career to assure the success of Quicksilver. If it had suited their purposes, they would have had him assassinated.

But the episode did not end disastrously for Patton. His superiors decided that he was too valuable to be thrown onto the scrap heap, in spite of his well-publicized faults. Eisenhower chastised Patton but relented when it came to dismissing him. General Marshall agreed, calling Patton "the only available Army Commander . . . who had actual experience fighting Rommel."[5] Patton stayed in England, both as commander of Third Army and as the best decoy Quicksilver could ever wish for.

For all of its sound and fury, the Knutsford incident probably did not have very much of an effect on German intelligence or in convincing FHW or OKW that Overlord would come ashore in Calais. It served to reinforce the idea in the minds of those who were already convinced, including von Rundstedt, and did nothing to convince those who favored Normandy as the site. Patton was nearly thrown to the wolves for nothing.

Walter Schellenberg and his subordinates at SD had been receiving mixed signals about the Allied build-up, and about Allied plans regarding the Invasion. The double agents under the control of the Double-Cross Committee, Abwehr agents who had been captured and turned by counterintelligence and who were sending information supplied by the Allies, reported that the main invasion would come near Calais. These reports mentioned a massive build-up in Kent and Sussex, all part of a unit called the First U.S. Army Group. But there were also reports about troops in the south of England, in the Hampshire and Dorset area, building up for a landing in Normandy. The SD needed to know which of these reports was correct, or if they were both correct and the Allies planned a two-pronged assault in both Calais and Normandy.

The SD's man in England, Gwyn Evans, code-named Druid, could be relied upon for accurate information. Evans had always proved to be reliable in the past, and always managed to get whatever he was asked. Now Schellenberg needed Evans to put his cleverness and determination to use once again. This time, he wanted Evans to find out everything he possibly could about Overlord, especially its date and destination.

One of the main items that made Evans so valuable to the SD, apart from his hatred of all things English, was his ability to visit areas within the restricted zone along the south coast. A 10-mile deep strip along the Channel coast, extending from the Thames Estuary to Land's End, was closed to all outsiders. Barricades were set up at entrances to the zone; only those who had passes were allowed through. Anyone who arrived without a permit was put on a train by police, or was placed under arrest.

Evans could get in and out of the coastal zone without arousing anyone's suspicions. He had to show a pass before the military police would let him in, but this posed no problem at all; he had a genuine pass, not just a clever forgery, issued by ENSA. (ENSA was the Entertainments

National Service Organization, the British equivalent of the American forces' USO.) He was still touring military bases with his string quartet, performing pop renditions of Gilbert and Sullivan and light classics, and was actually welcomed in areas that were banned to British civilians. Once inside the restricted area, Evans was able to wander at will.

Evans took note of everything he thought might be of interest to the SD. On the pretext of arranging concerts for the string quartet, he took bus trips to Portsmouth and Southampton, where he was able to observe the loading of ships as well as the steady stream of traffic on the roads. He actually was able to count the number of military vehicles in one particular convoy. Evans noted the traffic heading toward the Channel ports in a long, encoded message to his contact in Germany, along with everything else he had seen. Walter Schellenberg's faith in the Druid had not been misplaced.

But Schellenberg and FHW also wanted as much data as they could get on the troops in the southeast of England, the First U.S. Army Group. Intelligence was forecasting that the Invasion might come at any time. More information on the forces in Kent and Sussex, FUSAG, would help FHW to predict where it would come, which would at least be half of the puzzle.

One item that FHW was using to predict where the Invasion would come was the concentration of Allied air strikes. American and British air attacks were hitting twice as many targets in the Calais area as in Normandy, which was another indication of Overlord's destination. The U.S. Eighth and Ninth Air Forces and the Royal Air Force (RAF) were turning the road and rail systems of northern France into a ruin. Bridges, roads, railway lines, and canals were cut by the repeated bombing, which would drastically curtail the movement of reinforcements into the area for a counterattack.

Railway bridges in and around Rouen, the main rail center linking Calais and Normandy, also had been a frequent target since the beginning of the year. But Rouen had been a target of Allied bombing for the past several years, and would affect the movement of troops into both the Normandy and Calais areas. The Luftwaffe's reconnaissance flights were showing an increase in traffic in the Channel ports opposite Normandy and Calais, which reinforced Gwyn Evan's reports. But this was not a clear indication of anything, either.

Beginning in April, the SD received quite a lot of information that ranged between inconclusive and totally useless. Agent Ricardo in Lisbon sent a "confidential" report that the Invasion would be launched in late April or early May—a span of four weeks. Word from contacts in Geneva, also based upon impeccable diplomatic sources, said that the landings would take place sometime in May or, if not in May, then by mid-June. A contact in Ankara predicted the landings for sometime in late May. Not one of these sources made any mention of where the Invasion would take place. Vague messages of this sort were to be expected when gathering intelligence on an operation as highly secret as Overlord; Walter Schellenberg realized this. British intelligence received the same kind of noninformative reports when monitoring Operation Sea Lion, the threatened invasion of England, which was to have taken place in the summer of 1940.

But there were also solid indications that the enemy across the Channel was beginning to stir. On 1 April, the Navy's radio intelligence unit discovered that the Allies had changed their code from a three-letter system to another, more complex, cypher. A week later, all radio traffic in Britain dropped off sharply, giving listeners on the Continent something to think about. And on 17 April, the government in London took perhaps one of the most drastic security measures ever; Britain virtually suspended diplomatic immunity for all foreign embassies and consulates, except for the Russians and Americans. It did not take Schellenberg very long to find out about this, or to figure out exactly what it meant.

According to this unprecedented order, all foreign diplomats were forbidden from leaving the British Isles. In addition, all diplomatic pouches would be searched before they could be sent out of Britain. All communiqués between foreign embassies and their home countries would have to be sent in clear language; diplomatic codes would not be permitted. These restrictions would remain in force, the ambassadors and their staffs were informed, until further notice—meaning until after the Invasion. Although the foreign diplomats objected and protested, it was to no avail. This was another lesson from 1940. During the Blitz, the nightly bombing of London, neutral reporters and diplomats sent word back home about bomb damage that had been inflicted the night before. These reports, which usually included mention of specific areas and even individual buildings, were of great help to Luftwaffe intelligence. The Allies were not about to have the same thing happen at this critical time, objections or not.

At the end of April, OKW decided that the Allies had reached their state of readiness and were prepared to launch their invasion. Clearly, something was going to happen soon. The Allies had changed their codes, and had turned Britain into a sealed camp. The High Command and FHW still did not know when the Invasion would be taking place, or what its destination would be. But the Luftwaffe, the radio reconnaissance units, and agents in Britain and the United States were doing their best to find out.

Colonel Alexis von Roenne, the chief of FHW, was another source who should have been helping OKW to learn about the enemy's intentions.

But he did not. The reason for his behavior is another of Overlord's surprises, as well as one if its mysteries.

Colonel Alexis Baron von Roenne had a distinguished military career, and came from a family that had a long and noteworthy history of service to Germany, a history that went back at least 200 years. His ancestors were solid old Prussian aristocrats, dedicated to the army, who had fought in battles as far back as the War of the Austrian Succession in 1741. The family received its baronetcy from Frederick the Great for their role in that war, and went on to other honors and achievements in other campaigns.

During the First World War, von Roenne was an officer in the Potsdam Regiment, which the Kaiser considered one of the best in the German army. His family lost their estates in eastern Germany after the war, but he went into the banking business, which was considered a suitable occupation for someone of his standing. When Hitler came to power, von Roenne rejoined his old regiment and was sent to the prestigious War Academy. The academy was also for officers of outstanding background and ability, most of whom were future candidates for the General Staff. In 1939, during the time of preparations for another move by the Wehrmacht, von Roenne was attached to Fremde Heere West's French division. His job with this department was to determine the intentions of the French government and its celebrated army, which was the most admired and respected in Europe.

Almost immediately, his powers of deduction were put to the test. Hitler was planning an offensive against Poland. But before he gave any orders to mobilize, it was vital for him to know what the British and French would do. Would they come to Poland's aid by staging their own offensive against Germany? Or would they sit by and do nothing, as they had done when he had gone into Czechoslovakia the year before? He did not have the men and resources to defend the German border from a combined British and French attack in the west and invade Poland at the same time. Hitler gave the problem to von Roenne.

FHW had volumes of information on both the French and the British, the cabinet members in both governments, and what they had done during the past few years, especially in the area of war preparations. Making use of all the resources at his disposal, von Roenne made a detailed study of the Western Allies and their actions so far. As the result of his study, von Roenne concluded that the British and French were afraid of starting another war. Both countries remembered the horrendous casualties of the First World War, when thousands of men were lost in a single day's fighting at the Somme and at Ypres, and would not risk another slaughter to come to the aid of Poland. They did nothing to defend the Rhineland or Sudeten Czechoslovakia. There was not much probability that they would do anything to protect Poland, either. Von Roenne said as much in a special report to Hitler: The Western Allies would protest a German attack, but would take no military action.

This was exactly what Hitler wanted to hear. He ordered an attack on Poland on 1 September 1939. Both Britain and France declared war but did not attack Germany in defense of Poland. Hitler was greatly impressed by von Roenne's intuition, as well as by the accuracy of his evaluation.

A few months later, von Roenne did a similar job. He began a deliberate study of the French army during the Phony War period, between the autumn of 1939 and the spring of 1940, and came to the conclusion that it was greatly overrated. Although it may have looked impressive on paper and in the newsreels, the French army was hopelessly outmoded when compared with the Wehrmacht, and the morale of the French private soldier was also well below that of his German counterpart. In short, the battalions garrisoned within the Maginot Line were living on their reputation. One strong show of force, von Roenne decided, would put the French on the run.

Von Roenne reported his conclusions to both Hitler and OKW, and also advised that the Maginot Line was nothing more than an elaborate static defense waiting to be outflanked. If a concentrated attack with infantry and armor were made across the River Meuse near Sedan, von Roenne said, the French army would give up. Hitler listened to von Roenne, and acted upon his advice. Germans troops and tanks attacked in force near Sedan on 14 May. French forces were routed. Within a month, German troops entered Paris, and France asked for an armistice on 22 June. A grateful Hitler awarded von Roenne the *Deutsches Kreuz* for his incisive study of the enemy and for his shrewd judgment.

When the Wehrmacht invaded Russia in June 1941, von Roenne volunteered for combat. He and his regiment saw their share of fighting, and von Roenne was wounded in the course of his service on the Eastern Front. After recovering from his wounds, he returned to FHW; by Hitler's personal recommendation, von Roenne was appointed its director. Hitler had implicit faith in von Roenne and in his reasoning ability, and seems to have liked him personally, as well.

As head of FHW, von Roenne once again held a position befitting his station. It was a highly prestigious job, but also a vitally important one. Every bit of intelligence involving the Allies and their war effort was received and evaluated by FHW. Its headquarters at Zossen, outside Berlin, could be called the lynchpin of German intelligence against the Western Allies. (Fremde Heere Ost [FHO] performed the same function of evaluating intelligence on the Eastern Front.) As its officer in charge, von Roenne evaluated every one of the many fragments of information that came in, and wrote the situation reports for both Hitler and the senior officers of OKW. He has been referred to as "the key figure" of pre-

Invasion German intelligence. "It was his mission to produce for the High Command the definitive intelligence they needed to make their dispositions," one historian said about von Roenne. "All the bustling secret services, the code-crackers, and the intelligence analysts worked for him. It was at his desk where the buck-passing ended."[6]

Colonel von Roenne would seem to have been the perfect German officer: loyal, patriotic, and clever, with an excellent war record, unquestioned authority, and a decoration presented by Hitler himself for service to the Fatherland. But there was also a side to von Roenne that very few people knew anything about: He was appalled by Hitler and the Nazi Party, and had contacts in the Schwarze Kapelle. The head of FHW, the single most important person in German intelligence, was an anti-Nazi conspirator.

Von Roenne's opposition to Hitler and his regime began before the war, although he did not do anything about it until much later. He did not have much of an opinion of the Nazis or their brutality, and was horrified by Hitler's encouragement of the SS reign of terror in Poland, the Low Countries, France, and the other countries occupied by the Germans. It has been suggested that this was simply a matter of class snobbery—the pedigreed Prussian aristocrat turning up his nose at the lowly National Socialists—the same way that Admiral Canaris was accused of being an upper-class snob. But von Roenne's dislike of Hitler went far beyond snobbishness.

In fact, von Roenne knew Admiral Canaris and had a great deal of respect for the admiral and his convictions. He was not a close personal friend of Canaris, even though he did admire him, but he did have a very close relationship with Major General Hans Oster, Canaris' associate as well as his confidant in the Schwarze Kapelle. It was not only a close relationship, but also a highly influential one.

Admiral Canaris' affect on von Roenne may have been largely indirect, since it came mainly through their mutual friend, Hans von Oster, but it was also strong and unmistakable. Oster worked very closely with Canaris in their intrigues against Hitler. He often acted on Canaris' behalf in sending intelligence out of Germany, as he did in 1939, when he warned Poland of the impending German attack. Oster was not only Canaris' friend, but was also his collaborator in the Schwarze Kapelle. Oster was also von Roenne's close friend; they saw each other nearly every day. During their many horseback rides together—they were both experienced riders—Oster exchanged his views with von Roenne on the subject of Nazism and the Schwarze Kapelle. Gradually, he strengthened von Roenne's anti-Nazi feelings, and turned them into a dedicated resistance.

Von Roenne was not a member of the Schwarze Kapelle. But his friendship with Hans Oster and other members of the group—including Count Claus von Stauffenberg, one of the leaders of the 20 July 1944 assassination attempt on Hitler—became a major influence on his actions as head of FHW. Through Oster, Admiral Canaris changed von Roenne's point of view. And so, Canaris was not as safely out of the way as Hitler and Walter Schellenberg thought. Even though the admiral was no longer head of the Abwehr, his impact upon German intelligence was as strong as ever.

But in spite of the anti-Nazi influence of Oster and Admiral Canaris, there is still a mystery about von Roenne. He gave Hitler the information he needed to go ahead with his planned invasion of Poland—in effect, he sanctioned the beginning of the war in Europe—but was appalled by the Nazi atrocities in Nazi-occupied countries. A few months later, he told Hitler exactly what the Wehrmacht should do to smash the French army, which led to one of the most astonishing feats of arms by any army of any era, but then he decided to work secretly against the Wehrmacht. If he was anti-Hitler and thought his Nazi regime not only repugnant but also immoral, why did he do such a brilliant job for him in the beginning?

There are a number of reasons. Although von Roenne was not a Nazi, he was still a dedicated German officer and still held strong patriotic feelings toward the land of his ancestors. In other words, he may not have wanted Hitler to win the war, but he did not want Germany to lose it, either. It took Oster and von Stauffenberg quite a while to convert von Roenne to their point of view, which was that Hitler was a criminal and that, if he won, the only thing that Germany would win would be a long, hard rule under a criminal despot.

Also, scheming and plotting went against von Roenne's nature, as well as everything he had learned as a German officer. As an officer of the old school, and a Prussian aristocrat as well, he probably knew this dictum of von Clausewitz by heart: "Rather than try to outwit the enemy with complicated schemes . . . on the contrary, try to outdo him in simplicity." The matter of his oath to Hitler was something else that troubled von Roenne; he had taken a blood oath, the *Fahneneid*, with his hand on the Bible.

Oster and his colleagues had to work very hard to turn von Roenne from a passive non-Nazi into an active anti-Nazi. They also needed time for their argument to sink in—that Hitler was an enemy to Germany, much more than either the British or the Americans. Von Roenne was not only a patriot but also a man of conscience. It required some persuasive discussion to convince him that working against Hitler was not treason—or if it was, it was justifiable treason.

Hans Oster pointed out to von Roenne that he was an indispensable part—if not *the* indispensable part—in the scheme to remove Hitler, because Hitler listened to him. He could be a great help to Hitler and the Nazis, as he had been in 1939 and 1940, or he could work against him and his atrocities. It was up to him.

Von Roenne listened to this line of reasoning for months, probably from the time of his appointment as head of FHW. He had a great deal of respect for Oster, as well as for Admiral Canaris. Although he agreed with Oster's anti-Nazi views, and became an ally of the Schwarze Kapelle, he took no active role in their conspiracy against Hitler.

At the beginning of 1944, something happened that changed von Roenne's life. It was a completely unexpected turn of events, an opportunity that fell out of nowhere and landed right in his lap. At the time, it seemed a very small and insignificant occurrence, but it would help to alter the course of the war.

A new staff officer joined FHW at the end of 1943, a Lieutenant Colonel Roger Michel. Colonel Michel was the new director of the English Sector. He had a unique background for the position: His mother was British, and he had played rugby in England as a member of the German national team. He would be responsible for reporting and evaluating all intelligence that came out of Britain—including information pertaining to Overlord.

After he had been on the job for a few weeks, Colonel Michel noticed that the SD had an annoying habit of changing his estimates of Allied troops in England. He was under orders to submit all information to the SD, so that they could check his numbers for accuracy. But when the staff officers at SD received his reports, they always altered his figures dramatically, usually, they reduced Michel's estimates of Allied troop strength by half. It happened every time: Michel would send his numbers to the SD; the SD would cut them in half. Only then would they send his report along to Hitler and OKW.

Colonel Michel complained to von Roenne about the SD's maddening behavior. Von Roenne sympathized, but explained that there was nothing he could do about it. The SD was a party organization, and could do pretty much what it wanted. Walter Schellenberg wanted all information that was gathered by any outside agency—meaning outside the Nazi Party—to be examined by his own intelligence staff first. After the SD absorbed the Abwehr, Schellenberg's organization became more powerful, and arrogant, than ever.

After having his figures changed several times in a row, for no apparent reason, Michel decided that there *was* something that could be done about it. If the SD took his numbers and cut them in half, then he would double his figures before sending them along to the SD. When Schellenberg's crew divided *this* number by two, they would then have a fairly accurate estimate of Allied troops in Britain. The SD would deliver an accurate report in spite of themselves—with the help of a little subterfuge by FHW.

When von Roenne first heard this suggestion, he immediately rejected it—again, it went against his nature and all of his training. But he began thinking about it, and the more he thought about Michel's idea, the more he liked it. The reason that Michel's proposal appealed to him had nothing to do with increased efficiency, or with providing Hitler and his generals with more accurate enemy troop estimates, however. In fact, it was for precisely the opposite reason.

Von Roenne realized that Hitler had a great deal of confidence in him. While it troubled his stiff Prussian conscience to use Hitler's trust against him—von Roenne shared Canaris' repugnance toward Hitler but had none of the admiral's duplicity—he also saw that it gave him a distinct advantage. If he submitted a set of inflated numbers himself, the SD might just send them along to Hitler without changing them. And if that happened, no one—not Hitler, not OKW, not even the SD—would have a true picture of the Allied build-up in England.

He took his scheme to one of his operations officers, a Colonel Lothar Metz, and asked for some help with putting it into action. Colonel Metz wanted no part of tampering with intelligence figures, and warned von Roenne to forget the whole thing. But von Roenne was determined to go ahead with the plan. Shortly after their conversation, Colonel Metz was transferred from FHW—a move that was far too convenient to be coincidental—leaving von Roenne to carry out his deception without any interference.

According to the most recent estimates compiled by FHW, which were based upon Luftwaffe reconnaissance, reports from agents in the field, radio intelligence, and other sources, the Allies had a total of thirty-five divisions in the British Isles. This estimate included British, American, Canadian, free French, and others, including three airborne divisions. Von Roenne took this number and more than doubled it.

In a report from 1 June, FHW listed twenty-two American divisions in the British Isles; actually, twenty divisions were stationed in Britain. This was only a slight exaggeration, however, in comparison with the numbers given in the rest of the document. The FHW report also included the number of other Allied divisions in Britain—British, Canadian, free French, and Polish—as fifty-seven. The actual numbers were: twenty-three British and Canadian divisions, along with one free French and one Polish division. Also mentioned were armored and paratroop units, which comprised another ten divisions. The true Allied strength in Britain stood at forty-five divisions. By the time von Roenne finished altering these figures, this number had become eighty-nine divisions.[7]

This represented a huge increase, almost a fantastic increase, over the last numbers that had been submitted. Colonel Michel's figures in his last report stood at about thirty divisions; the SD had reduced this to fifteen divisions. Von Roenne realized that he would have to justify his new total, especially to the naturally suspicious SD. Colonel Michel had an answer for this problem, as well: to include the troops that were stationed across the Straits of Dover from Calais, the First U.S. Army Group. Michel was not sure exactly how many troops actually made up FUSAG, or if the unit was only an elaborate deception. Luftwaffe photos had not been conclusive, and reports from Britain were still being awaited. But since the SD staff officers probably would disallow the figures, anyway, Michel reasoned, it did not really make very much difference.

Von Roenne took Michel's suggestion. In his report on Allied strength in Britain—or *feindbild* (literally picture of the enemy), as he liked to call it—he outlined the enemy's full order of battle. His picture included the fictitious First U.S. Army Group, with its make-believe American, Canadian, and armored divisions. The inclusion of FUSAG allowed von Roenne to justify the increase in the number of troops since the last report.

The figure that von Roenne had given the SD doubled the number of troops in Britain. It was such an unbelievable number that he probably had misgivings about submitting it. Even if the British and Americans did have that many men, there probably were not enough landing craft in the world to ferry them across the Channel. But he sent his incredible estimate, anyway, and waited to see what the SD would do with it.

To his astonishment, the SD accepted his report at face value. The fact that it had been sent by von Roenne himself, instead of by some minor staff officer, probably had a lot to do with it. It was widely known that Hitler held his judgment in high esteem, which was worth a great deal in a party organization like the SD. But whatever the reason, von Roenne's numbers were not cut in half, as had been the SD's usual practice. His estimation was sent along to Hitler and OKW intact, made-up Canadian divisions and all. Hitler believed von Roenne's report. He informed the Japanese ambassador that the Allies had about eighty divisions in the Britain Isles.

In an absurdist Catch-22, the SD did not alter the inflated numbers because of von Roenne's standing with Hitler, Hitler accepted von Roenne's numbers because they had been cleared by the SD. No one thought of questioning any of it, even though the report's figures were so much higher than they had been only a short time before; no one was suspicious, since von Roenne's estimate had the party's sanction. Because Hitler and OKW accepted the estimate, it became fact. Wehrmacht units throughout France had no choice but to believe what they had been told by their senior commanders.

Admiral Canaris' conversion of von Roenne to the Schwarze Kapelle, or at least to their way of thinking and reacting against Hitler, had a profound effect upon Overlord and, as a result, on the war against Germany. Von Roenne's decision to alter data compiled by FHW—and to risk his life by doing it—made Hitler and his generals believe that FU-SAG really existed. And if FUSAG existed, their reasoning went, then Calais *must* be the destination of Overlord. All those troops under General Patton were not in Kent just to enjoy the English countryside.

Once Hitler made up his mind, and after he ordered reports of his conclusions sent to Wehrmacht units in the field, all information became final—whether it was accurate or not. Von Roenne's number changing made FUSAG final, at least in the minds of Hitler and his senior commanders, and also was instrumental in the success of Quicksilver. Thanks to von Roenne, Quicksilver became one of the most successful deception schemes of the war.

Some questions have been raised concerning how much Colonel von Roenne actually knew about Quicksilver, and whether or not he realized, or at least suspected, that FUSAG was a hoax. Von Roenne was not an agent in any of the Allied intelligence services, and would not have had any firm knowledge of Quicksilver or any of its objectives. But he had been monitoring Allied movements since the beginning of the war, and was accustomed to making judgments based upon his own evaluation on enemy activities. And, as he had proved by his deductions regarding the French army in the spring of 1940, he was a master of his craft. If anyone in German intelligence had the ability to see through Quicksilver and recognize FUSAG as a fake, von Roenne was the man.

Quicksilver's bogus intelligence was meant to deceive the Germans and, according to a British author, "[von] Roenne knew very well that it might be a deception."[8] He also knew very well that once his recommendations were accepted by Hitler, and the fictitious Allied units were added to FUSAG's order of bottle, his altered figures would become permanent and unremovable. As head of FHW, von Roenne was not an officer who would have made such changes lightly.

Von Roenne certainly suspected that FUSAG was not what the Double-Cross agents and Quicksilver planners said it was. When he first began hearing reports from Allied-controlled agents in 1943, he dismissed them as nonsense—the "disparaged them as 'utterly fantastic' as recently as October 2, 1943," in the words of one writer. But in the spring of 1944, "he began to use them as a basis for his 'Allied order of battle in the UK.' "[9] In other words, von Roenne was convinced that the Quicksilver reports were a fraud until Colonel Michel gave him the idea of doubling his figures. After that, when he saw a way of using these made-up reports to suit his own ends, he kept his doubts to himself, and sent Quicksilver's fictitious reports along as fact.

Von Roenne's successor as head of FHW, a Lieutenant Colonel Buerklin, very quickly developed his own doubts about some of the SD's sources of information. The particular object of his misgivings was the

Stockholm-based agent Karl-Heinz Kraemer, who operated under the code name "Josephine" and had been sending intelligence to Berlin since the autumn of 1942. Kraemer had access to highly secret reports from the Swedish Military Attaché in London, and had acquired this access by means of a totally unorthodox arrangement. He had been given these secret files by the pretty secretaries of the Swedish Defence Staff in Stockholm. Kraemer would take the young ladies out for dining and dancing; they would reward him with copies of the attaché's official documents, along with the more conventional methods of repayment. These documents formed the basis for the regular communiques that Kraemer sent to his contact in Germany.

Kraemer's reports on what was taking place in Britain were of the very highest grade—including data on the build-up of American forces in Britain—until British agents managed to learn the identity of Josephine and, even more important, how Josephine received all the top-quality information that he had been passing along to German intelligence. Following this discovery, the reports of the Swedish attaché were deliberately adulterated with false data, which was supplied by British intelligence. The source of Kraemer's information had been seriously compromised, and the quality of Josephine's intelligence began to decline rapidly. This sudden falling off placed Kraemer in a suspicious light with a number of officers in German intelligence, including Colonel Buerklin.

Buerklin succeeded von Roenne at FHW in mid-August 1944. In the autumn of 1944, Karl-Heinz Kraemer was recalled to Berlin to answer charges that he was not a spy, but was a fraud and a swindler, and had been accepting money under false pretenses. He was subjected to a harrowing interrogation by Heinrich Mueller, the head of the Gestapo, which went on for an entire day. At the end of the interrogation, Mueller was satisfied that Kraemer's sudden unreliability was the result of Allied subterfuge and not his own double-dealing. But Kraemer also lost all credibility as a spy. "The evaluation of this operation by the Abwehr," the official assessment of Kraemer pointed out, "is no longer valid. The quality of the Josephine material, especially those concerning army matters, is generally inferior."[10]

As the director of FHW, the evaluation section of German intelligence, Buerklin was more than instrumental in the discovery of Kraemer's unreliability and the poor quality of his intelligence. Von Roenne was probably aware of the unreliability of Josephine's data, as well—British intelligence began planting their phony data in the Swedish attaché's records during his tenure—but there is no record that he ever reported any suspicions of Kraemer to his superiors. If he had any doubts, he never said anything about them, just as he never said anything about the Quicksilver reports. Von Roenne made no mention of ever suspecting anything regarding any irregularities in data from any source. This would indicate that he was either totally stupid or else was up to something. His past record strongly points to the latter view. And by the time Colonel Buerklin took over, it was much too late.

Colonel von Roenne clearly emerges from this episode as one of the Schwarze Kapelle's most able co-conspirators, as well as a prominent unsung hero of the Allies. The role of Lieutenant Colonel Michel is less clear. Michel may or may not have been working for either British or American intelligence when he made his timely and highly eventful suggestion to von Roenne. After the war, he almost certainly went to work for U.S. Army intelligence; he wore an American uniform and announced that he was a member of counterintelligence. But shortly afterward, he crossed to East Germany and defected to the Russians. If von Roenne is one of the heroes of this particular incident, at least to the Allies, Colonel Michel is its mystery man.

One senior officer who was not influenced—and would not allow himself to be influenced—by Colonel von Roenne's altered statistics was Feldmarschall von Rundstedt, the commander of Army Group West. Von Rundstedt had always been absolutely certain that Calais would be the site of the Invasion, and did not need any additional information to assure him of what he already knew. But even though von Rundstedt had already been convinced of Calais, many indications still pointed toward Normandy. There was no indication that SD leader Walter Schellenberg had made up his mind one way or the other. The Allies were still assembling troops in England, and all the evidence was not yet in.

Crotchety old von Rundstedt was not about to let any of the Intelligence Services change his mind. As far as he was concerned, all of German intelligence was stupid, incompetent, and unreliable, at best. Von Rundstedt distrusted intelligence to the extent that he would not allow any of his commanders to have direct contact with any intelligence agency. "The commander in Chief West, by means of a standing order, had forbidden the Army Group to work directly with the German Intelligence Service (*Abwehr*)," wrote General Hans Speidel, chief of staff to Erwin Rommel, Army Group B's commander. It probably made no difference to von Rundstedt that the Abwehr had been under the control of the SD, and the Nazi Party, for some time now. He trusted the Nazi Party's officials even less than he trusted the Abwehr.

Having no contact with intelligence made it, as understated by General Speidel, "difficult to assess the enemy potential." Army Group B did receive the occasional bit of information about the Allies and their preparations, but it always came in a predigested form, according to Speidel. News regarding Overlord was first received by Hitler and departments within OKW, and then passed along to Rommel and his command. "The Army Group received its reports second-hand, and there was not a single trained intelligence officer at Army Group Headquarters," General Speidel said.

Being kept in the dark made life difficult for Rommel and his officers.

Rommel himself was not even kept informed of what was happening in Italy or Russia, which should have been routine information for an officer of his rank and standing; it was only through personal connections within the army that he kept in touch. He did not even have access to information on the French resistance or their role in the coming Invasion, and Army Group B was charged with defending against the Invasion.

All of this can be attributed to what might be called the Canaris Effect. Admiral Canaris and his campaign to mislead Hitler and OKW had succeeded beyond all of his expectations. Von Rundstedt and most other senior officers shared Hitler's total lack of faith in the Intelligence Services; they had been misinformed and misled too many times in the past. The opinionated old field marshal summed up the general feeling toward intelligence officers when he called them "inefficient, unfailingly duped by the enemy, and incapable of discovering his plans."[11]

Von Rundstedt rarely agreed with Hitler; he made it a perverse point never to see eye to eye with the person he referred to as "that Bohemian corporal." But he was forced to agree with Hitler on this point: Intelligence should never be relied upon under any circumstance.

From his involuntary seclusion in Franconia, Admiral Canaris could be well satisfied that his plan to mislead and misinform Hitler was having its desired effect.

NOTES

1. Longmate, *How We Lived Then*, p. 488.
2. Author interview.
3. D'Este, *Patton*, p. 593.
4. Information regarding the Knutsford incident came from several sources, including D'Este, Farrago's biography of Patton, and periodicals from the spring of 1944.
5. D'Este, *Patton*, p. 587.
6. In Farago's *Foxes*, p. 785.
7. Kahn, p. 496.
8. Brown, p. 559.
9. Delmer, p. 145.
10. Farago, *Foxes*, p. 704.
11. Von Roenne's is one of the more interesting stories of the German resistance movement because he was recruited into it. I first encountered it when doing background on *Germany's Spies and Saboteurs*. It is also mentioned in Farago's *Foxes*, in Brown, and in Gehlen.

FIVE

Mounting Evidence

"All of southern England was one vast military camp," General Dwight D. Eisenhower recalled in his memoirs, "crowded with soldiers awaiting the final word to go and piled high with supplies and equipment."[1]

"The south of England was sealed off," Charles Cawthon, a captain in the U.S. 29th Division, also remembered after the war. "Troops were everywhere and every leaf-roofed lane packed with supplies."[2]

"Packed" was the perfect word to describe southern England in the spring of 1944. Howitzers and tanks, jeeps and prefabricated building materials, bulldozers and artillery shells were crammed into every vacant corner. Harbors all along the Channel coast—Falmouth, Weymouth, Plymouth, Newhaven—were alive with troop transports, landing barges, and supply ships. And thousands of men—over 200,000 U.S. troops arrived in Britain just during the month of April—began moving south toward the coast and their ports of embarkation. The local wits wondered out loud why the island did not sink under all the added weight.

This enormous arsenal of men, machines, and equipment was certainly a source of comfort for the men who were "awaiting the final word to go"; it was reassuring to know that the weight of all that support would be on their side when they went ashore against the Germans. But it was also a cause for anxiety: So much equipment in such a small area amounted to an open declaration that they were planning to invade, and very soon. If the Germans knew the invasion was imminent, they would be ready and waiting.

"I don't see how it would be possible to keep all that a secret," Second Lieutenant John Murphy of the U.S. Fourth Division wondered. He and the rest of his regiment were stationed in Seaton, a small resort town on the coast of Devon. All along the south coast, other units were also getting ready for the invasion that came nearer with each passing day. Murphy had seen the signs of all the preparations for himself—the long convoys of vehicles that filled the roads, the men and supplies that seemed to be crammed into every space, the troops on training exercises in all kinds of weather—and speculated on how much the enemy had seen.

"We were always being warned about 'security' and were told to keep our mouths shut about what was going on," Murphy recalls. "But nobody could miss all that—the training exercises, and all that equipment and stuff right out in the open for anybody to see." And if he knew what was happening in southern England—"a lowly second lieutenant, and in the army there's nothing lower"—he was sure that the Germans knew, as well.

Any civilian who lived anywhere near the coast was aware of the preparations and the massive build-up for the Invasion. There were signs everywhere—literally:

DANGER—TANKS ON ROAD—DRIVE WITH CARE

MILITARY NOTICE: THE PUBLIC ARE FORBIDDEN TO PASS BEYOND THIS
    POINT

And always:

CLOSED AREA

OUT OF BOUNDS

The tension grew with every day that went by, especially for the troops. "We knew that they knew," Murphy recalls. "We tried not to think about it too much, but we hoped that losses on the beach would not be too bad."[3]

Senior officers dropped in for a pep talk every now and then, mainly to keep up morale—a sure sign that something would be happening very shortly. Captain Cawthon of the 29th Division remembers a visit from Field Marshal Montgomery, "a small figure gesticulating from the hood of a jeep," as well as from General Omar Bradley.[4]

"We were told by the generals that casualties would not be too heavy, but we didn't know how much of this to believe," Murphy said. "All we knew was that we would be crossing over to France before long and that the Germans knew we were here. We were all pretty scared, although we tried not to let it show too much."

Lieutenant Murphy was right—the Germans *did* know. Thanks to radio reconnaissance, OKW knew that the 4th Division was in England and had known ever since they disembarked in Liverpool in January.

Communications Reconnaissance Battalion 13, the unit that monitored radio traffic in the British Isles, had been able to detect the presence of the 4th Division along with many other Allied units. German intelligence had built a very accurate estimate of the Allied order of battle. And they had been able to accomplish this in spite of the deliberate cutback in radio communications by British and American commanders.

Although radio talk had been drastically reduced, there was still enough activity to keep Battalion 13 occupied. Even seemingly innocent chatting by military policemen on their walkie-talkies produced useful bits of information. The mention of a particular officer or non-com, or possibly a company commander, could be linked to a specific unit within a division. Names and units were listed and kept on charts, and new information was always being added to keep records up to date. Exact locations of individual units were also determined by Battalion 13—including that of Lieutenant Murphy's regiment in Seaton—and were also kept current.

The radio listeners probably gave the most accurate picture of the Allied build-up in England; they worked seven days a week, listening to virtually every radio transmission in Britain. (Their colleagues in Battalion 12 performed the same job with radio broadcasts, including regular news programs, in the United States.) But the Luftwaffe also continued with its reconnaissance flights over the south coast of England, when the weather and Allied fighters permitted. At the end of April, pilots brought back photos that justified the risks they had taken.

During the last week of April, photos of Portsmouth, Southampton, and Weymouth showed that there had been a dramatic increase of traffic in those harbors. Only a short while before, pictures of the same ports showed only normal traffic. Now, suddenly, the enlarged prints revealed hundreds of landing craft, troop transports, and auxiliary vessels.

Both OKW and German naval intelligence sat up and took notice when they saw *those* pictures. The prints not only indicated that the date of the Invasion could not be very far off if the enemy was massing in the Channel ports, but they also gave a fairly strong hint that the attack would come either in Brittany or Normandy. Forces for an attack on Calais would not be assembling in Portsmouth.

The Luftwaffe's reconnaissance pilots had given German intelligence a vital piece of evidence. The photos could not stand by themselves, though. They would need confirmation from other sources, including the radio battalions and agents in Britain and on the Continent. But the pictures were proof that the Allies were on the move, at long last. It was now up to intelligence—the SD and FHW—to do something with the information.

Agents in the field kept sending in their data. Not all of it was of very high quality, however. In fact, some of it was absolutely worthless. A contact in Switzerland, who had access to the British military attaché in Bern, sent word that the Invasion had been called off, at least for 1944; the reason he gave was that there was so much bad feeling between the British and Americans that Overlord had to be scrapped. Nobody believed this one, anyway, so it did no damage.

There was also the ongoing litany of where the real invasion would take place. Among the places offered as the landing site for Overlord were Norway, the Balkans, the Mediterranean, and Denmark. One agent warned of a double landing, simultaneous invasions of southern France from the Bay of Biscay and from the Mediterranean.

Intelligence officers realized that most of these far-fetched reports were either from well-meaning but totally incompetent amateurs or—usually— double agents working for the Allies. These reports were filed away and forgotten. But any word on the two likely Invasion points, Normandy and the Pas de Calais, was treated with more respect. Reports on these sites were examined for any new evidence that might conclusively point to one place or another, or that might rule out one of the two sites.

But by the beginning of May, neither Hitler nor any of his senior officers were any closer to knowing the destination of Overlord than they had been several weeks before. There were the usual estimates and educated guesses, which were based upon the limited information that managed to get past Colonel von Roenne. This was becoming extremely limited, in spite of the activities of radio reconnaissance, photo reconnaissance, and all the other intelligence sources. Even as senior an officer as Erwin Rommel, a *feldmarschall* in command of an entire army group, was not very well informed. "I know *nothing* for certain about the enemy," he complained with conviction.[5]

Because they had no regular source of reliable intelligence, German commanders had to make decisions based on other means. Hitler was beginning to lean toward the Pas de Calais as the Invasion site; Colonel von Roenne's doctored numbers had a lot to do with this change of heart. Hitler reasoned that the First U.S. Army Group was in the perfect position for an attack on Calais; with George S. Patton in command, FUSAG also had the perfect general for the job. Also, he rightly concluded, Calais—not Normandy—was the most logical place for a cross-Channel invasion. The Allies might stage a secondary landing in Normandy, or possibly a diversionary attack, but Hitler was convinced that the main Allied attack would come ashore at Calais.

Stubborn old von Rundstedt stuck with his opinion that Calais would be the Invasion area, partly because he did not trust any of the intelligence services and partly because he was too rigid to change his mind. But Rommel was becoming less and less convinced about Calais. He had mentioned to General Hans Speidel, his chief of staff as well as his friend and confidant, that "the enemy would not ram his head against the hardest place in the defense just for the sake of a short sea voyage and short supply lines."[6]

Hitler might have been inclined to listen to Rommel at one time, but not any longer. Rommel had criticized Hitler too often and was too much of a pessimist—at least in Hitler's opinion. The Desert Fox might have been a legend among his troops and admired by an adoring public, but he was no longer a favorite of Hitler's.

In Hitler's eyes, Rommel was guilty of many sins. Prominent among them was his presiding over the loss of North Africa; even though this was more Hitler's doing than Rommel's, this made little difference to Hitler. Also, Rommel suffered from *Afrikanische Krankheit*, or African sickness, which was the name given to his pessimism toward Hitler and the High Command after returning from the desert. In short, Rommel came back from North Africa a changed man. He no longer had the same enthusiasm for Hitler or for National Socialism, and he was no longer a member of Hitler's charmed circle.

In the cast of senior officers who turned against Hitler, Erwin Rommel was probably the oddest character. Or, at least, he was the most reluctant. Although he has been portrayed as an anti-Nazi hero and martyr in any number of books, as well as in at least one Hollywood film, a British writer had a legitimate point when he said, "the C-in-C of Army Group B remained passionately devoted to Hitler until he became convinced that the war was militarily unwinnable."[7]

Until November 1942, when Hitler refused to allow him to make a strategic withdrawal, Rommel thought that Hitler was a true military genius. After that, he blamed Hitler for the defeat and destruction of the Afrika Korps, and became openly critical of Hitler. At the very least, he thought that Hitler should relinquish at least some of his military authority to his generals.

As the war continued and German fortunes steadily crumbled, Rommel began to entertain thoughts that an armistice should be negotiated with the Allied powers. He could see that there was no possibility that Germany would win the war unless some overwhelming miracle came to the rescue. He could also see that no political settlement could be reached with either Britain or the United States as long as Adolf Hitler remained in power.

Early in 1944, very soon after being given command of Army Group B, Rommel decided to visit a couple of old friends who just happened to be very powerful, as well as active, anti-Nazi conspirators. The two old acquaintances were General Karl-Heinrich von Stuelpnagel, the military governor of France, and General Alexander Baron von Falkenhausen, the military governor of Belgium. In the course of their conversation, Rommel mentioned his misgivings about Hitler and his conduct of the war as well as his feelings about an armistice. Von Falkenhausen and von Stuelpnagel recognized that they had a new recruit.

Rommel was just the man they needed. Members of the Schwarze Kapelle had been looking for someone of Rommel's stature, "a popular figure, a modern Hindenburg, to put at the head of it when the time came."[8] Von Falkenhausen and von Stuelpnagel decided to ask Rommel for his support.

Rather than approach him themselves, they decided to go through Dr. Karl Stroelin, who was mayor of Stuttgart and a long-time friend of Rommel. In 1918, Captain Stroelin had been in the same infantry unit as Rommel and had also served with him as a staff officer in the 64th Corps. After the war, Stroelin decided to go into politics; in 1933, he was elected Stuttgart's *Oberburgermeister*, and remained in office all throughout the war. His successful career as a politician is nothing less than astonishing, considering the fact that he had been an active anti-Nazi since March 1939, the result of the Nazi occupation of Czechoslovakia.

Actually, Dr. Stroelin's views had already begun to have their effect on Rommel. In 1943, he had signed a letter that demanded that the Nazi regime stop their persecution of the Jews and the Church, that civil rights be restored throughout the country, and that the court system be removed from party control. For his efforts, Stroelin was warned to stop his protests at once; otherwise, he would be put on trial for "crimes against the Fatherland" by the very court system he was protesting against. This notice served as a sharp announcement from the Hitler regime "that nothing could be done by legal methods."

He gave a copy of the letter to Lucie Rommel. When her husband came home on leave toward the end of the year, she showed it to him. "It made a profound impression on him,"[9] according to one biographer. Rommel had been thinking along these same lines for some time; this was the first time he had seen these ideas actually committed to paper.

By the time Dr. Stroelin finally had the chance to present his views in person—he had to make his visit in secret, since the Gestapo was watching him and had tapped his telephone line—Rommel was more than ready to meet him halfway. They talked about "the political and military situation of Germany" for several hours. Stroelin asked Rommel if he saw any chance of Germany winning the war. Rommel said that "he personally saw no chance" and doubted that Hitler knew how bad things were because "he lives on illusions."[10]

After questioning Rommel at length, Stroelin finally came to the point. He told Rommel that he was the only man who could prevent civil war in Germany if Hitler was removed from power. (The Schwarze Kapelle had an idea of asking Rommel to be president.) Hitler was incompetent at best, Stroelin said, and it was time for direct action. Rommel could not have agreed more. After thinking about what had been said, he announced, "I believe it is my duty to come to the rescue of Germany."[11]

Stroelin had his man. Rommel agreed to bring his name, his reputation, and his considerable energies to the anti-Hitler movement. His motives did not really matter, at least not for the moment. The important thing was that Rommel had aligned himself with the Schwarze Kapelle; the Desert Fox was now on their side.

Throughout the spring of 1944, while the Allied armies gathered strength in England, Stroelin kept in touch with Rommel on an almost daily basis. At the same time, General Hans Speidel worked with von Falkenhausen and von Stuelpnagel on armistice terms, which they hoped to present to either General Eisenhower or Field Marshal Montgomery. Speidel also kept Rommel informed on the progress of these meetings.

Rommel now found himself in an extremely awkward position. He wanted to fight against Hitler, but did not want to do anything that might cost Germany the war. He had sworn a personal oath of allegiance to Adolf Hitler, the *Fahneneid*—which Rommel did not take lightly—but had also become active in a conspiracy to overthrow Hitler and the Nazi Party. He "kept faith, professionally, with the Führer," while plotting against him. While planning secret negotiations with the Allied powers to end the war, he was also using every effort to make the defenses along the Channel beaches as formidable as possible against these same Allied forces. In the words of one of his many biographers, Rommel rode "two horses together." All the while, he hoped that neither horse would throw him and break his neck. [12]

Rommel's thoughts concerning a peace agreement with the British and Americans, as well as concerning exactly what terms should go into such an agreement, tended to be unrealistic and totally impractical. He wanted to reach an accord with the Allies, but he only wanted it on his own terms. One plan he had in mind was for the Allied air forces to stop bombing German cities. "Every day costs us one of our towns—to what purpose?" he said to his naval aide, Admiral Ruge. In return, the Schwarze Kapelle would put Hitler under arrest. As such, "The enemy would be spared the enormous human costs of invasion, and the political impossibility of negotiating with Hitler." [13] Apparently, he did not know that the British and Americans had agreed not to reach terms separate from the Russians. Either that, or he did not want to acknowledge it.

His decision to become involved in the anti-Hitler movement had a great deal in common with Colonel Alexis von Roenne's entry into the conspiracy. Like Rommel, von Roenne also needed a lot of prodding and persuading before he finally made up his mind. Plots and stratagems went against the grain of both men. Also, both were dedicated German officers, and considered themselves patriots. And both men had also served Hitler well, if not absolutely brilliantly, earlier in the war, and both had impressive records during the First World War.

Von Roenne's reluctance continued even after he became an ally of the Schwarze Kapelle. He did not actually do anything against the Nazi regime for quite some time after throwing in his lot with Admiral Canaris' colleagues—not until the very end of 1943, when Colonel Roger Michel talked him into changing the numbers on the Allied troop estimates. But once von Roenne had found his own unique way of opposing Hitler and become comfortable with it, he carried on with his work in support of the Schwarze Kapelle.

In February 1944, Rommel finally made his decision to throw in *his* lot with Dr. Stroelin and the Schwarze Kapelle. Like Colonel von Roenne, Rommel also had a great deal of power and influence—although a completely different sort of power than von Roenne's. How would he use his influence to oppose Hitler, he must have wondered. He probably had nothing specific in mind, other than a determination to arrest Hitler, take all power, political and military, away from him, and come to terms with the Allies. There were no time restrictions on any of this. Like von Roenne, Rommel would wait for an opportunity to drop in his lap; he had no idea how this opportunity would take shape, or when it would come.

Throughout the spring of 1944, Rommel traveled up and down the Channel coast, making inspection tours of coastal defenses in his big black Mercedes, issuing orders, giving pep talks to the troops, overseeing the placement of mines and beach obstacles. While he was doing all these things, Rommel kept his discussion with Dr. Stroelin at the back of his mind, and he waited for his chance.

While the Luftwaffe and radio reconnaissance kept a close watch on the gathering Allied strength in England, Allied intelligence was keeping an eye on what the Germans were doing in Normandy. British and American commanders needed to know what the enemy had done on the invasion beaches, and exactly what to expect on D-Day.

British and American reconnaissance pilots flew hundreds of low-level flights over the French beaches—at considerably less risk from enemy fighters than their German counterparts—taking countless photos of the shore and every obstacle on it. These photos were pieced together, like a gigantic jigsaw puzzle, to make a huge, minutely detailed picture of the Normandy coast and its defenses. The resulting picture was, in the words of one British historian, "so accurate and detailed that warships could lay their guns according to the grids superimposed on it."[14] Scale models of the beaches were also made from this aerial picture, complete not only with obstacles but also with landmarks and prominent buildings. These detailed models were used by landing crews to familiarize themselves with their objectives.

Although the air photos certainly served their purpose, senior officers needed a closer view of the enemy defenses. They had heard about the land mines, about "Rommel's asparagus" (wooden stakes topped by land mines), as well as other devices to destroy landing craft. A closer view of the beaches, and their obstacles and booby traps, was needed, a view that even the clearest of aerial pictures could not provide.

In order to obtain this particular point of view, specially trained commandos were put ashore on the Normandy beaches at night. These men landed by submarine to scout the shore, especially at low tide, and to see what the Germans had put there—on all five of the Allied landing beaches. They explored the area, making notes and taking infrared pictures, and did their best to avoid German patrols that guarded this particularly vital stretch of seaside.

Many of these commandos were foreign nationals and had to be especially careful of the patrols—if caught, it meant instant death. "If one was captured, and they discover that you're Hungarian, they hang you on the spot," said one commando who had made a reconnaissance of Omaha Beach. "So that's why I always pretended to be a Welshman." After taking their pictures and "getting a closer view of what the defenses are looking like," the same commando said, "we then had to ease our way out, looking as much like seals as possible."[15]

The most consistent and reliable source of first-hand intelligence was the French resistance, which was actually an irregular army of soldiers, spies, and saboteurs. Many groups within the resistance were trained and equipped by Special Operations Executive (SOE), a British unit that trained and equipped guerilla groups in enemy occupied territory. The *maquis* were probably most famous—or infamous, from the German point of view—for blowing up trains and assassinating high-ranking German officers. But as far as Overlord and its planners were concerned, the resistance members were most useful for watching the enemy and reporting on his activities.

The resistance had a network of spies and observers in place all across Normandy. These were ordinary civilians, who went about their daily business without arousing any suspicion from the occupation troops. There were some who had the authority to travel within the coastal prohibited zone because of their jobs. (The Germans, like the British, closed a strip of Channel coast to any French civilians who did not live in that area.) Nonresidents of these districts needed a pass from the Germans before being allowed to enter the coastal zone, including farmers who brought their produce to market, or salesmen who made periodic trips to towns and villages along the Norman coast. Once inside the coastal area, a resistance member could make his surveillance of whatever section of the Atlantic Wall he had been sent to observe. Afterward, he would write down everything he could remember, or sometimes make a sketch of a particularly noteworthy fortification. The report and the drawing would be given to a contact, who would send it off to London.

The most valuable, and usually the most reliable, resistance contacts were those who lived within the prohibited zone; they could make daily observations of the Germans and their movements without leaving home. Marie-Louise Osmont lived in the Chateau Periers, just outside the village of Periers, which is about midway between the city of Caen and the section of Channel coast that would become known as Sword Beach. Madame Osmont made hundreds of comments about her guests—both the soldiers who occupied her house and the troops who moved in and out of her part of Normandy. She was not a member of the *maquis*, but the things she had to say about the local German soldiers, which she kept in a diary, were exactly the kind of information needed by both British and American intelligence.

At the end of April, she had some observations concerning the troops occupying her village. These soldiers were not of very high quality; they consisted of Germans, Russian laborers and French truck drivers, most of whom did as little as possible all day and did not seem very keen on fighting. These were replaced by much more professional troops—"three times a day, muster inspection, rifle drill, heels clicking, etc." On 10 May, an artillery battery at Merville was hit by bombs from an Allied air raid. At the end of May, a motorized unit arrived in Periers: "Once again, there are more soldiers than inhabitants in the village." The low morale of the enlisted men was another topic of comment: "They are afraid, they are controlled like sheep or tools, they are often childish, sometimes stupid. Actually, like me, they are *unhappy* (for reasons far different from mine)."[16]

This was precisely the sort of intelligence that the resistance were interested in compiling: morale of enemy soldiers, the position (and condition) of German artillery batteries, troop movements, damage done by bombing. Because this activity took place in a zone that was so vital to Overlord, the resistance undoubtedly made note of these same items and sent them along to London. In England, the information would have been used to update information on enemy operations in the Caen area. One person who would have been very glad to receive this intelligence was Major General Thomas Rennie, commander of the British 3rd Division. General Rennie's appointed landing area was Sword Beach; he certainly was interested in knowing that a German motorized unit had moved to within three miles of his assigned objective.

All across Normandy, as well as the rest of occupied France, thousands of people like Madame Osmont made similar observations about the Germans and their movements. Their reports gave Allied intelligence a steady flow of accurate and up-to-date information on enemy fortifications and troop strength in the area of each of the five landing beaches—Gold and Sword for the British, Omaha and Utah for the Americans, and Juno for the Canadians. This data would prove invaluable.

The resistance were also involved in a more direct rebellion against German military rule, by means of sabotage and assassination. Throughout the war, they had been doing as much damage to the Germans as they could manage—derailing trains, setting fires in factories, blowing up power generators, disrupting communications. In England, the organizers of Overlord, along with the SOE, were encouraged by the chaos being inflicted upon the enemy by this determined, and highly organized, group of guerillas. Not only were the resistance inflicting real damage upon the enemy, but they also were keeping the Germans in a high state of anxiety over the impending Invasion. But the SOE were afraid that the resistance might provoke a murderous retaliation, which would result in their destruction just when they were needed most.

In order to exercise some sort of control over these enthusiastic amateurs, London worked out a way of communicating with the various resistance groups. It was a fairly simple plan, and could be carried out right under the noses of the Germans. Every night, the British Broadcasting Corporation (BBC) in London would send a series of cryptic messages from Bush House, in The Strand—the personal messages, *messages personnels*. Everyone in France who owned a radio or had access to one listened to these nightly broadcasts, even though getting caught meant imprisonment, or worse.

The method by which the underground groups received these messages has been reenacted many times in films about the Second World War. The broadcast would begin with the first four notes of Beethoven's Symphony No. 5—the three dots and a dash of the Morse Code *V*, for victory. ("V for Victory" was the symbol of the resistance and was chalked on walls all over occupied France.) Immediately after this dramatic opening, the broadcaster would announce, *"Ici Londres. . . . Voici quelques messages personnels* (This is London. . . . Here are some personal messages)."

The announcements that followed usually consisted of short, simple sentences: "Josephine loves Napoleon"; "The cow jumped over the moon"; "Rain is forecast for Tuesday." Each message was always repeated, spoken much more slowly the second time. None of them would have made any sense to anyone outside of the group for whom it was intended, since they were prearranged signals to carry out a specific task. "Napoleon loves Josephine" might be an alert to blow up a particular stretch of railway line in Normandy. "The cow jumped over the moon" could be an order for the sabotaging of a telephone transformer in the Pas de Calais. [17]

By issuing these orders over the BBC, SOE was able to coordinate and control, at least to some degree, the activities of an entire network of resistance groups. London feared a premature uprising throughout northern France unless some sort of control was exerted, and that this up-rising would have disastrous results for the resistance and for Overlord.

With the approach of D-Day, SOE had a specific campaign in mind. Just prior to the Invasion, the resistance would begin a series of coor-dinated sabotage operations near the Channel coast. Plan Blue was the code for a prearranged attack on power lines; Plan Violet was a similar attack on telephone and telegraph lines; Plan Green was a sabotage cam-paign against the rail system; and Plan Tortoise was an organized cam-paign to block roadways. These would be triggered by the BBC's messages, so that some overly enthusiastic resistance group would not start things prematurely—which might tip off the Germans regarding the immediacy of the Invasion, and might also get them killed for their efforts.

The primary signal, the call that would put every *maquisard* in northern France on alert, was a passage from Paul Verlaine's poem "*Chanson d'Automne*":

> Les sanglots longs
> Des violins
>   D l'automne
> Blessent mon coeur
> D'une langeur
>   Monotone.

("The constant sobbing of autumn's violins / Pains my heart with their monotonous lethargy.") The passage was to be broken into two seg-ments, which were to be sent several days apart. Part one, "*Les sanglots longs Des violins D l'automne*," was to be sent on the first or the fifteenth day of the month of the Invasion, and would serve as a general alert. When the second part was heard, "*Blessent mon coeur D'une langeur Mon-otone*," this meant that the Allied landings would take place within forty-eight hours, beginning at midnight on the day following the broadcast.

Every resistance group in northern France knew what the Verlaine poem meant, and every listening post waited for the broadcast. What the resistance did not realize—and neither did Allied intelligence—was that the Germans also knew what it meant, and were also waiting for it.

German counterintelligence had penetrated a number of resistance groups, and had learned a great deal about the way they operated and communicated. The agency behind this was Abwehr Section III, which operated from the Hotel Lutetia in Paris under the direction of Major Oscar Reile. (Although Admiral Canaris was a dedicated anti-Nazi, his subordinates did not always share his thoughts regarding the Hitler re-gime.) Major Reile made it his special project to infiltrate the resistance and find out as much about them and their organization as possible.

Under Major Reile's direction, Abwehr III did to the resistance what British counterintelligence did to any German spies they caught in England—turned them, gave them the option of working for them or being tortured to death by the Gestapo. This method of persuasion was as effective for the Germans as it had been with MI-5. Captured members of the resistance, only too aware of what awaited them at the hands of the Gestapo, reluctantly agreed to work for the Germans as the less excruciating of two very painful alternatives.

With the help of these turned resistance members, German counterintelligence was able to penetrate any number of French underground groups. They had at least ten German-controlled radio operators in touch with London, sending messages that contained either misleading or totally false information, and were able to destroy and disperse several sabotage organizations in the north of France. The *Carte* group, which specialized in sabotage and guerilla activities, was led by a man named Michel; Michel was under German control, and was actually being paid by the Gestapo. The *Mithridate* group had three radiomen sending false reports to SOE in London; none of the other members had any idea that these radio operators were under German control. "Unable to wipe out the Resistance movement," a French writer reflected, "the German counter-espionage services had at least succeeded in contaminating it."[18]

Another group under German control was Butler, which consisted of three men: Francois Garel, the leader; his radioman, Marcel Rousset; and a courier named Marcel Fox. The three of them parachuted into France on the night of 23 March 1943. Because all of their equipment went astray in the drop, they had to be resupplied by SOE and did not begin operations for nearly two months.

It did not take Major Reile and his agents very long to find Butler and their whereabouts. Counterintelligence tracked the group throughout the summer of 1943, while they were busy drawing up a listing of communications and transportation to be sabotaged. At the beginning of October, they were arrested in a Paris café. A turned British agent identified Rousset as a member of the resistance, and Butler became pawns of the Germans.

Earlier in the war, the three unfortunates would have been turned over to the Gestapo, and, following a brutal interrogation, they would have been transferred to a concentration camp and shot in the back of the head. But with the impending Invasion in mind, Reile had a more useful role for them. Instead of handing them to the Gestapo, Reile gave them over to the custody of the SD.

The SD's leading radio expert, Josef Goetz, used Rousset's set, and his identity, to send false—but convincing—messages to London. Under Rousset's name, Goetz sent requests for money, materiel, and several agents—all of which was sent by SOE and all of which was immediately picked up by waiting German troops. But the most important result of

Butler's capture was the cracking of the Verlaine code, which was a genuine intelligence windfall.

Shortly after being captured, one of the group told Reile's interrogating agents about the passage from Verlaine's poem as well as what it meant. This was very probably Francois Garel himself, since the report of the incident, dated 14 October 1943, described the informer as "the leader of a sabotage organization directed from England." The methods used by the interrogators were anything but gentle; the outcome was predictable. Reile wrote poetry himself, and recognized the passage.[19]

As the result of good, persistent detective work by Reile and his men, OKW now had a priceless clue, and an intelligence key that could tell them one of Overlord's two most closely guarded secrets—*when* the Invasion would take place. In the 14 October report, this bit of information was called "the password to announce the impending Anglo-American invasion of France."[20] An American writer, being a bit more effusive, said that it gave "the High Command the definitive clue to anticipate the invasion."[21]

Admiral Canaris, who was still head of the Abwehr, probably wished that there was something he could do to destroy Reile's report, or at least keep it from reaching OKW. But the SD was also involved in the Butler interrogation, which meant that Walter Schellenberg knew about it. Because of this, Canaris knew that there was nothing he could do to stop the information from being passed along.

Allied intelligence had no idea that their code had been broken, or that any resistance groups were being controlled by the Germans. As far as both the British and American intelligence services were concerned, their *messages personnels* were still as safe as ever. And SOE still thought they had a foolproof way of harassing German communications and transportation.

The German High Command now had the means of determining when Overlord would take place. But they still had no real idea as to where the operation would come ashore.

In order to give OKW some solid clue, Walter Schellenberg and his organization would first need to answer several very basic questions, the same questions they had been trying to answer for the past few months. The SD needed to know exactly where, in what part of England, was the main Allied build-up taking place. Were most of the troops gathering in the southwest, opposite Normandy, or in Kent and Sussex, across the Straits of Dover from Calais? Was FUSAG the prime Invasion force, or were the units west of Portsmouth the main body? Solving these ongoing questions would also provide the answer to Overlord's second riddle: What was the objective for all this manpower and equipment? Was it Normandy or Calais?

Both the radio reconnaissance units and the Luftwaffe were still at work trying to come up with an answer. So was Gwyn Evans, agent Druid, who was still touring the British Isles with his string quartet while keeping his eyes open for clues. Evans was the SD's best bet. Anyone who could get close to the empty camps and dummy supply depots in Kent and Sussex would realize that there was no First U.S. Army Group. General Patton's Third Army was there, but was assigned to reinforce the troops in Normandy. And if FUSAG did not exist, then there could be no landings in the Pas de Calais.

If Evans could find out the truth about FUSAG, and get his story across to his contacts, OKW would have the second half of the D-Day secret. Hitler and his generals would know when the Invasion was coming, and also would know where. It then would be just a matter of building up their defenses in Normandy—taking troops from Calais, where they were no longer needed, and sending them to reinforce units that were already stationed in Normandy. After that, they would only have to wait for the BBC to broadcast the lines from the Verlaine poem.

NOTES

1. Eisenhower, p. 249.
2. Cawthon article, pp. 50–51.
3. Author interview.
4. In Cawthon.
5. Fraser, p. 461, from a German biography of Rommel by Lutz Koch.
6. In Speidel, p. 24.
7. Hastings, photo caption facing p. 69.
8. Young, p. 219.
9. Quotes about Stroelin and Rommel in Young, p. 221.
10. Ibid., p. 222.
11. Ibid., p. 223.
12. The biographer is Desmond Young.
13. Fraser, p. 461.
14. Botting, p. 57.
15. Comments from the commando in *D-Day* (video).
16. Remarks by Madame Osmont in Osmont diary.
17. The method by which the resistance received its *messages personnels* has certainly been reenacted in many films. My favorite is *The Longest Day*, for its mood and background more than for factual content.
18. Perrault, p. 140.
19. The date of Reile's report on Verlaine's *"Chanson d' Automne,"* which was 14 October 1943, in Farago's *Foxes*. Farago criticizes Cornelius Ryan for giving the date as January 1944 in *The Longest Day*. Ryan also cites Admiral Canaris for passing the report along to OKW, which is just as inaccurate.
20. Farago, *Foxes*, p. 798.
21. Ibid.

SIX

Elaborate Fakery

While the SD was employing every trick they knew to discover the second part of the Overlord secret—namely, *where* the Invasion would be put ashore—Allied counterintelligence had a few tricks of their own.

In the early days of May, the Quicksilver deception began a new, more energetic phase. While the Invasion force commanded by General Bernard L. Montgomery, the *real* Invasion force, was building its strength and resources in the west and southwest of England, Quicksilver frantically worked to give the impression that General Patton's First U.S. Army Group was making its preparations in the Dover area. The British and Americans used every device short of black magic to convince the Germans that Calais was the site of Overlord, and that FUSAG was the principal attack force. And if either the OSS or LCS had known of a reliable expert in witchcraft or voodoo, they would have employed him, as well, and pressed him into service as a special advisor.

A certain kind of magic *was* employed by the planners of Quicksilver—the magic produced by the film makers at Shepperton Studios, near London. To the Shepperton set designers, creating a make-believe world of wood and canvas was all in a day's work. But now, instead of inventing an illusion to entertain an audience of filmgoers, they had been enlisted to produce a different sort of illusion, for an entirely different purpose.

Because of wartime restrictions, prop makers throughout the British film industry did not have very much to work with in the way of material—the bows and arrows of the English archers in Laurence Olivier's film of Shakespeare's *Henry V*, for instance, were made of cardboard. But the builders at Shepperton managed to create about 400 landing craft out of canvas and wood, and floated them on pontoons made from oil drums. These 400 ships were transported to ports along the Kentish and Sussex coast, including Dover and Folkestone, as well as to harbors in eastern England, such as Lowestoft. Chemical generators made smoke for their funnels, and men were sent from ship to shore via motorboat to add to the illusion. And so, a landing fleet was assembled across from Calais without the benefit of either ships or sailors.

The same sort of deception was used to create fleets of vehicles on land—convoys of trucks, troop transports, and armored cars. Some of these dummy vehicles were made of inflatable rubber. Others were built from wood frames that were covered with canvas. Still others were nothing more than headlights—rows of shaded headlights, giving the impression at dusk of columns of trucks parked along a road, waiting for the order to move out.

Dummy tanks also came in two varieties: inflatable and wood-and-canvas. The men in charge of blowing up the inflatable type had to be careful of puncturing the vehicles, which sometimes occurred. Anyone who happened to witness one of these mishaps was treated to a rare sight—a full-sized Sherman tank collapsing into a blubbery heap, like an oversized inner tube. Tanks had to make tank tracks, of course, so the next step was to make twin sets of tracks in the vicinity of each dummy tank unit. This was done by a special machine, which was towed by a truck.

Entire divisions of supply vehicles were also created, in the same way. These would either be left out in the open or camouflaged very poorly, so that they would be visible from the air. At night, floodlights—also improperly camouflaged—gave the impression of intense, round-the-clock activity, as though the men attached to these units were working against time to prepare for the impending Invasion.

Kent and eastern England had enough dummy vehicles, inflatable tanks, wooden guns, canvas ammunition dumps, fake camps, phony fuel dumps, and empty headquarters buildings to make a hundred war films. Nothing was overlooked. A 3-square-mile fuel oil dock was built at Dover, which was never intended to hold oil. It was made of scraps of construction material and pipes, and was put together by film and stage scenery designers. After it was completed, the king came to inspect the facility, so did generals Eisenhower and Montgomery. The big, long-range German guns across the Straits of Dover fired shells at the dock, and hit it on several occasions. When that happened, large, smoky "oil fires" were set, to give the impression that the installation's tanks had been set on fire.

The entire point of making all of this elaborate stage scenery was so that the Germans could admire it. And so, whenever the Luftwaffe sent one of its photoreconnaissance Messerschmitts to take pictures of FUSAG and its preparations, the pilot was allowed to take all the snaps he wanted—as long as he stayed above 30,000 feet. From that altitude, his cameras would not be able to pick out any telltale flaws in the wood and canvas facilities below. If the photos were too good, or at least too clear, the SD would be alerted that all the impressive camps and installations across from Calais were actually fake.

A lone reconnaissance aircraft would have been picked up by British radar while it was still over France. By the time it arrived over the coast of southern England, the defenses would have been ready for it. If the pilot remained above the required 30,000 feet, he would have been allowed to do his snooping without risking his life. Fighters would have been sent to intercept the intruder, and might even have fired their guns at him, but they would not have shot him down. Antiaircraft fire would have been just as ineffective—near enough to seem threatening, but not close enough to do any damage.

When the pilot returned to base, and the film was removed from his cameras and processed, the resulting photos would have shown exactly what Quicksilver intended. The enlarged prints would have shown rows of poorly hidden supply trucks, brigades of tanks, tons of supplies and equipment of all description—in short, everything that the builders from Shepperton Studios had put there for them to see. The tank tracks were evidence that these armored units had only just arrived, and that the build-up in eastern and southeastern England was still increasing. But the photos would not have shown any evidence of fakery, even under high magnification, because the pilot was at too great height. The official explanation for this was that he had to fly above the intense antiaircraft defences.

Over Portsmouth, where the 21st Army Group, under the command of General Montgomery, was assembling for the landings in Normandy, such a reconnaissance flight would have been worth a pilot's life. But over Dover, or anywhere else where General Patton's First U.S. Army Group was grouping its largely nonexistent forces, a pilot was assured of a successful run—as long as he did not venture below 30,000 feet.

Radio deception relating to FUSAG was also intensified at the beginning of May. The number of messages sent by operators in make-believe units increased with every day that passed, creating the effect of more troops moving into the area, as well as the effect that these units were entering into the final phases of their training. In the course of these messages, operators would sometimes commit casual breaches of security, just to give German intelligence a bit more false information. A radioman might let slip a unit name within the First Canadian Army, which existed only on paper, or make a fleeting reference to a totally made-up American airborne unit. A place name in Kent or East Anglia would accidentally drop from a communiqué—a vehicle had broken down on the road from Ashford (Kent) and had to be retrieved.

Engineers even diverted telephone messages from General Montgomery's headquarters near Portsmouth to Dover Castle, more than 100 miles away, so that radio activity relating to the 21st Army Group could be broadcast from southern Kent. This served two purposes: It helped to keep the real Invasion force under protective silence, while adding still more radio traffic to the already noisy east and southeast. From the sheer volume of broadcasts, the listeners of Radio Reconnaissance Battalion 13, eavesdropping from Vitre in Brittany, must have thought that Kent and East Anglia were about to sink under the weight of all the men and equipment of FUSAG.

General Montgomery had a role in the Quicksilver deception himself, although it was done by proxy. In March 1944, a lieutenant colonel in Ops B, one of the many Allied deception units, saw a photo of a junior British officer in the London *News Chronicle*. The photo was of Lieutenant Clifton James, attached to the Royal Army Pay Corps. Before the war, James had been an actor in British provincial touring companies. The Ops B colonel was struck by Lieutenant James' close resemblance to General Montgomery, and decided to turn him into "Monty's Double." This particular deception plan would be known as Operation Copperhead. By impersonating the popular British general, it was hoped that Lieutenant James might help to mislead German intelligence as to Montgomery's whereabouts and, just possibly, mislead them as to the time and destination of Overlord.

But before he could even hope to give a convincing impersonation, James had to make a thorough study of the general. He spoke with Montgomery at length, so that he could observe his nasal speech, clipped accent, and brusque gestures. He also noted Montgomery's walk and his general manner—self-confident to the point of arrogance. After nearly two months of this intensive study, which must have been the longest and most uncomfortable dress rehearsal in James' acting career, he was ready to play his part in front of a live audience.

After Lieutenant James arrived at the point where he looked and acted like Montgomery, he also had to learn to dress like him. He was outfitted in an exact copy of the general's uniform, complete with all decorations and insignia—including the famous black beret with the two regimental badges. At Montgomery's insistence, James was also issued a general's pay as long as he wore a general's uniform.

Following weeks of study, training, and outfitting, and with a little help from a hairdresser and make-up artist, James' resemblance to Montgomery was almost supernatural. There were just two items, two differences between James and Montgomery, that threatened to give the game away. James was missing a part of the middle finger of his right hand, a result of his service in the First World War, which would immediately attract attention every time he gave a palm-out army salute. The famous Monty salute was as much a part of his public persona as his eclectic headgear. This rather obvious fault was remedied fairly easily by fitting James with an artificial finger. While he was wearing this, no one could tell that James had any sort of handicap, and he would be able to salute his crowds of onlookers as often as he liked.

The second item could not be fixed so easily. General Montgomery had an almost self-righteous aversion to both tobacco and alcohol, a trait that was widely known both in Britain and to German intelligence. On the other hand, Clifton James both smoked and drank—especially drank, often to excess. He was sometimes so fond of the bottle that it got the better of his judgment, particularly when he was under stress. It quickly became apparent that keeping James away from the bottle would be a major chore during this operation.

James made his debut in the role of General Montgomery on 25 May 1944. During the late afternoon, he was driven to Northolt airfield, to the west of London, by staff car. From Northolt, he was to proceed by an American-built Liberator to Gibraltar, so that German agents across the water in Algeciras would see him and conclude that Montgomery was not in England. He later admitted that he was overtaken by the worst case of stage fright he ever had, and that he felt like a "hypnotized rabbit"—playing Shakespeare in the provinces was never like this!

The trip to the airport was a small success. As the staff car made its way through London, James was seen by small groups of people, whenever the car slowed for traffic, onlookers would shout, "Hooray for Monty!" and other bits of encouragement. In return, James would smile and give his famous salute. The word quickly spread that Good Old Monty had passed through on his way to Northolt.

The Liberator took off on time and traveled toward Gibraltar through the night. James' attendants gave him a sleeping pill, to make sure that their charge would stay calm, and also to ensure that he would arrive well rested. But, unknown to them, James had brought along a tranquilizer of his own—a pint flask of gin. While everyone else was asleep, James made his way to the toilet at the rear of the aircraft. When his aides went to check on him a short while later, they found him very much the worse for about half of the gin he had smuggled aboard.

Their little plan had backfired. Not only had the sleeping pill not calmed James down and given him a good night's sleep, it had mixed with the gin and turned him into a staggering drunk. At that point, the Liberator was only about two hours from Gibraltar. James had to be sobered up, and in a hurry.

Drastic situations call for drastic measures, and James' escorts acted quickly and drastically. The first thing they did was take his clothes off.

There was no cold shower on board, but the subfreezing temperatures at the Liberator's cruising altitude had the same effect. Next, to purge most of the gin and sleeping pill from his system, they forced him to throw up. To keep him from going to sleep, they kept him on his feet while slapping him on the face. After a series of extremely brisk rub-downs, James was shaved and dressed. When the Liberator touched down at Gibraltar, and a fit-looking "Monty" stepped out of it, no one was any the wiser about the ordeal that had taken place during the past couple of hours.

As soon as he set foot on the tarmac, James began his performance as General Montgomery. He was driven to Government House in an open car, onlookers along the way, including some German agents, got a good look at him. The governor of Gibraltar, General Sir Ralph Eastwood, had attended Sandhurst with Montgomery, and had been told all about Lieu-tenant James and his masquerade. The two greeted each other like old friends. Sir Ralph invited James to a party that night, which was to be held at Government House in honor of the general's visit.

During the party, James made several references to Plan 303 in a voice just loud enough to be overheard. He also mentioned that he was on his way to Algiers. Among the other guests were several Spaniards who were known to have pro-German sympathies, including two bankers who were SD informants. Before morning, the SD in Algeciras (formerly an Abwehr post) would be well informed of Montgomery's trip to North Africa, as well as of a Plan 303.

In the morning, James was driven back to the airport in a reprise of the previous day's performance—open car, Monty salute from James, and "Good Old Monty!" from the onlookers. While the Liberator was being inspected for some nonexistent minor problems, which allowed James to be seen by more people, he once again told Sir Ralph about Plan 303, just in case anyone missed it the night before. Finally, after doing all he could do on Gibraltar, James was finally permitted to take off for Algiers.

Clifton James had certainly done his job, and Operation Copperhead was off to an extremely encouraging start. James had given an astonish-ingly convincing impersonation of General Montgomery, managed to drop several intriguing bits of misleading intelligence in enemy ears, and even managed to entertain crowds of onlookers at the same time. Now that he had got the hang of it, all he had to do was repeat his perform-ance in Algiers.

When he got off the plane at Algiers' Maison Blanche airfield, James made another glittering impression. He reviewed the guard of honor, was introduced to the British commanding officer, Sir Henry Wilson, and shook hands with several British, French, and American staff officers.

Following this ceremony, James was driven to his hotel, the St. George, in a staff car decorated with the general's flag. Everyone knew that General Montgomery had arrived—including German intelligence. James was carrying off the second phase of Operation Copperhead with as much panache as he had done with his initial success in Gibraltar.

But James' stage nerves apparently never went away, in spite of his successes. In Algiers, they evidently flared up. At SHAEF headquarters, outside London, a fantastic report was received by General Eisenhower and his staff. General Montgomery has been seen stumbling about the streets of Algiers, obviously drunk and smoking a cigar. James' escorts received what must have been a frantic message to get him out of there as quickly as possible. The order was carried out; James disappeared from Algiers and was rushed back to England at once, and in strictest secrecy.

When he returned and was safely back in his lieutenant's uniform, James received a very harsh reintroduction to reality. He was told, in no uncertain terms, that if he mentioned anything about Operation Copperhead to anyone, he would be court-martialed. He was then reassigned to the Pay Corps, which must have come as a great relief following the strain of the past few weeks.

But his excitement had not yet ended. Operation Copperhead was so hush-hush that nobody told James' commanding officer about it or the fact that Lieutenant James would be required for other duties. He was threatened with a court-martial for being absent without leave; his fellows in the Pay Office assumed that he had been off on an extended drunk and began spreading gossip about an alcoholic binge. To make matters even worse, the War Office accused James of using his position in the Pay Corps to embezzle army funds—how else could he explain drawing the pay of a general?

The entire Copperhead affair was finally straightened out. But the goal of the operation—which was to convince the Germans that Montgomery's presence in North Africa meant that there would be no cross-Channel invasion in the immediate future—was never realized.

The SD did not believe that this particular episode had anything to do with Overlord. James had done an excellent job of passing himself off as General Montgomery, at least until his stage fright overwhelmed him, but the Germans simply did not think that Montgomery's presence in Gibraltar and Algiers would have any impact on the coming Invasion. The main Allied attack would be in northern France; Walter Schellenberg realized this, and knew that any operation in the Mediterranean would be secondary, at best. In spite of what Clive James said in his imaginative postwar memoirs, which he called *I Was Monty's Double*, Operation Copperhead was not the success everyone hoped it would be.

Colonel Alexis von Roenne, head of FHW, was giving a degree of credibility to Quicksilver that even the most elaborate Allied fakery could not hope to accomplish. All the double agents, false radio messages, and extravagant film sets may have told convincing lies about FUSAG, but von Roenne swore to them.

Of course, having a supply of good, true-sounding lies to work with was a great help. One source of these lies was Captain Roman Garby-Czerniawski, a Polish officer who had the code name Brutus. As Brutus, Garby-Czerniawski supplied the SD with misleading reports that fit right in with von Roenne's own deception scheme.

Until Poland was overrun by the Wehrmacht in the autumn of 1939, Garby-Czerniawski had been attached to the general staff of the Polish army. After Poland surrendered, he elected to go to France instead of becoming a prisoner of the Germans. In Paris, he became an agent for the Polish underground and collected data on the German army. When France was overrun in the spring of 1940, he joined the resistance. He could not escape from occupied France, so he decided that this was the next best thing.

As a member of the resistance, Garby-Czerniawski was given the code name Paul. He became a member of an underground cell that had about 100 members, and also became involved romantically with one of the group's encoding clerks, a girl named Mathilde Carre. Paul may have been an excellent staff officer and a first-rate intelligence man, but he did not know very much about women. He soon began to look elsewhere for feminine companionship, and apparently did not try to hide his wandering eye. When Mathilde found out, which did not take long, she became extremely jealous. Rather than give him up to another woman, she turned Paul over to the Gestapo.

Under usual circumstances, Garby-Czerniawski would have been shot, either summarily or following a brutal interrogation at Gestapo headquarters. But because of his background, German counterintelligence became interested in him as a possible double agent. A colonel named Joachim Rohleder visited him in his cell at Fresnes Prison and made an offer: If Garby-Czerniawski would go to work for German intelligence, the hundred or so members of his resistance cell would be treated as prisoners of war instead of as spies and saboteurs. But Garby-Czerniawski had no intention of going to work for the Germans. He presented Rohleder with an unreasonable demand regarding Polish independence, which he knew Rohleder would not be able to accept.

For the next seven months, Garby-Czerniawski remained in prison. Colonel Rohleder must have thought that his prisoner would eventually change his mind; at any rate, Garby-Czerniawski was not executed. And, eventually, he did change his mind, but not for reasons that Rohleder expected.

While he was sitting in his prison cell throughout the winter and spring months, Garby-Czerniawski must have given a lot of thought to Rohleder's proposal. There was nothing he could do, though—if he changed his mind at that point, it would have seemed too suspicious. But when the Germans invaded the Soviet Union on 22 June 1941, he realized that he now had another opportunity. He told Colonel Rohleder that he now would go to work for Germany against Russia; the Russians were Poland's ancient enemy, and he would do everything possible to fight them.

Colonel Rohleder accepted Garby-Czerniawski's change of heart, as well as his story. It seemed logical; the Poles and the Russians had been at each other's throats for centuries, so there was nothing suspicious about a Polish officer wanting to fight his country's natural enemy. The first step in putting Garby-Czerniawski to work for German intelligence was to get him out of prison, which would not be difficult for someone of Colonel Rohleder's imagination and resources.

Rohleder knew that he could not simply ask for a release—Garby-Czerniawski was a member of the hated *maquis*—so he had to arrange for a trumped-up escape. According to his plan, Garby-Czerniawski would be transferred from Fresnes Prison by car; during a prearranged stop to avoid a stalled army vehicle, he would be allowed to break out of the car and get away. With the help of German counterintelligence, he would cross the border into Spain. From Spain, he would travel to neutral Portugal and then to England, where he would begin sending information on any subjected requested by German intelligence: airfields, shipping, or anything else that might be of timely importance.

After he agreed to become a German agent, Garby-Czerniawski was given the code name Armand. Armand succeeded in making his prearranged—and very convincing—escape on 14 July 1942, running from his car after the driver actually crashed into the stalled army vehicle, which was the only aspect of the operation that was not planned. As had also been arranged, he headed south toward the Spanish border after making his getaway, and linked up with an Abwehr contact in Madrid. He was given a crash course on espionage techniques: how to obtain sensitive information, and how to send it back to his contact. When he completed his training, Armand was driven to Lisbon, where he left for England on a commercial British Overseas Airways Corporation (BOAC) flight.

Garby-Czerniawski never had any intention of spying for the Germans. As soon as he made his phony escape, he notified a contact in the resistance; when he reached Spain, he told his story to a British agent code-named Monday. It was Monday who drove Garby-Czerniawski to Lisbon for his flight to England. He managed to talk his way out of prison to work against the Germans; now he was in a position to outwit them in a different way.

The Double-Cross Committee—which actually had been formed to control captured German agents—was glad to have him. They gave Garby-Czerniawski yet another code name; this time, it was Brutus. The first thing they did was to send him to the Royal Patriotic School at Battersea, so that he could be questioned in depth and generally watched over. After it was determined safely that Brutus was what he claimed to be, Double-Cross decided to put him to work.

But Brutus was not an ordinary agent, or even an ordinary double agent, and activating him presented several problems. The first difficulty was that he was a serving Polish officer, and owed his first allegiance to Poland. The second problem was political: Neither the British nor the Americans wanted to offend the Soviet government by using a Polish officer as an agent for the Western Allies. But the most pressing difficulty was a practical one: Could anyone be certain that the Germans would trust him or the information he would be sending? There was fear that the Germans might, in the words of John C. Masterman, one of the directors of Double-Cross, "expect him . . . to revert to his former ideas and attach himself to the Allied cause once more." But Masterman and his colleagues finally decided to ignore their fears and give Brutus a try, "for a time at any rate."[1]

If Brutus was to operate as an agent, the first thing he needed would be a contingent of subagents—contacts who would obtain information and report back to him. And so Double-Cross Committee invented a string of subagents, and also supplied the information that Brutus would be sending. Everything possible was done to convince the SD that Brutus was not only trustworthy, but was also a first-rate spy. In fact, some historians have insisted that Double-Cross Committee may have gone overboard in their efforts to make Brutus and other double agents seem genuine in the eyes of German intelligence.

Several allegations have been made (especially by James Campbell in *The Bombing of Nuremberg* and Martin Middlebrook in *The Nuremberg Raid*) that Double-Cross gave the Luftwaffe advance warning of the air raid on Nuremberg on the night of 30 March 1944—accurate information, supposedly sent by German agents—to make the Double-Cross agents more credible and reputable. The result was a major triumph for the Luftwaffe's night fighters, and one of the war's great disasters for RAF Bomber Command. Of the 898 bombers that took off to bomb Nuremberg that night, 94 were shot down, 10 more had to be scrapped, and another 70 sustained enough battle damage to keep them on the ground while they underwent repairs. Also, 745 crewmen were killed or wounded, and another 159 were taken prisoner.

Confidence in Brutus was certainly established fairly quickly; the SD came to rely upon him and the reports he sent. John C. Masterman called Brutus "the best placed of all our agents for sending over military information . . . as confidence grew both in him and in the Germans' belief in him, he was used more and more, and took a large part in the deception for Overlord."[2]

Brutus certainly played a role in averting a possible crisis in late April. On the night of 27 April, a flotilla of nine German E-boats, or *schnellbooten*, left their base at Cherbourg to look for a convoy in the Channel. Radio reconnaissance, always listening for any unusual activity, had picked up heavier than normal radio traffic off the Devon coast; it sounded like the ships of a large convoy talking to each other. Just before 2 A.M. on 28 April, Oberleutnant Gunter Rabe, the captain of one of the E-boats, saw "indistinct shadows of a long line of ships." He could not tell exactly what kind of ships they were. At first, he thought "they were tankers, or possibly destroyers."[3] Each of the E-boat captains lined up their targets and launched two torpedoes.

Oberleutnant Rabe had not located a convoy; he and the other E-boat captains had run into Exercise Tiger, which was a rehearsal for Overlord. Eight Landing Ship Tanks (LSTs) were making their way through Lyme Bay, taking a long, looping route to simulate the length of a Channel crossing. Their destination was Slapton Sands, in Devon, which was chosen because its shoreline resembled Utah Beach. The LSTs were carrying the men, vehicles, and equipment of the U.S. 4th Division and 1st Amphibian Engineer Brigade, who were scheduled to land on Utah Beach on D-Day.

The first salvos of torpedoes missed. Rabe launched two more, aiming at the last ship in the column. Another E-boat captain did the same. "At 0207," Rabe reported, "we saw that we had hit the target. Fire was spreading from bow to stern rapidly, and a dense cloud of smoke rose from the ship."[4] Rabe's target was LST 507. Fuel tanks of the Jeeps, tanks, and other vehicles caught fire; burning gasoline set fire to the ship's leaking fuel oil.

About ten minutes later, another attack was made. A torpedo struck LST 531; minutes later, LST 289 was also hit by a torpedo. Both LST 507 and LST 531 sank; LST 289 was badly damaged, but was towed back to port. Following this attack, the E-boats broke off and went back to base.

In the two torpedo attacks, a total of 749 men had been killed. Exercise Tiger was immediately canceled, and the surviving LSTs returned to Plymouth. Lieutenant James Murphy, who had been on one of the LSTs, was shaken by the experience. "If this is what happened in a practice drill," he said, "we all wondered what the hell the real thing was going to be like."[5]

The sinking of the two LSTs and the loss of life were not the main concern of SHAEF, however; nor was the damage to the morale of the troops. Supreme Headquarters was wild to know if any of the E-boats had picked up survivors from the LSTs. Ten officers who had Bigot status—Bigot was the code name for anyone with extensive knowledge of Overlord—had taken part in Exercise Tiger and might know both the time and place of the Invasion. If any had been taken prisoner by the Germans, and had been made to talk, either by trickery or more physical means of persuasion, the future of Overlord would have been in serious jeopardy. In a near panic, the assistant chief of intelligence at SHAEF, General Thomas J. Betts, and the head of Security, Colonel Gordon Sheen, were sent to Devon to make absolutely certain that all Bigoted officers had been accounted for.

The E-boats had not stopped to pick up prisoners. Oberleutnant Hans Schirren, another E-boat captain who took part in the attack, later said that there was never any intention of stopping. "Our system to keep alive and avoid destroyers and escorts was to hit and run always at high speed," he recounted. "It did not occur to us to stop."[6]

But General Betts and Colonel Sheen were not aware of this. Betts checked a listing of the dead, as well as of the survivors, against his own, and managed to account for every one of the Bigoted officers. Even this did not put SHAEF's mind at ease. There were others in Exercise Tiger who also had sensitive information relating to Overlord—if not the exact time and location of the Invasion, then perhaps details about planned Allied strategy once the landings were ashore, or possibly information concerning tactics to be employed against Panzer units. To make absolutely certain that no one had been taken prisoner by the Germans, it was decided to account for everyone who had taken part in the exercise.

It was a relatively simple matter to make sure that all the survivors were safe in England, but the dead and missing had to be located, as well—all 749 of them. Divers were sent to investigate the two sunken LSTs on the bottom of Lyme Bay. They cut their way into compartments and removed dogtags from bodies. The tags were checked against unit rosters. By this method, most of the dead were accounted for, although it was decided that some of the corpses must have been carried away by the tide. Based on this painstaking investigation, SHAEF concluded that no one with secret information had been captured.

But even if no prisoners had fallen into German hands, one nagging fear still remained: Did the discovery of Exercise Tiger give away one of the prime Overlord secrets, namely that Normandy was its objective? The landing exercise had been held off the coast of southwestern England, nowhere close to the Pas de Calais, and other realistic drills were scheduled to be held there, as well. SHAEF was afraid that the location might give German intelligence the clue it needed to reach the conclusion that Normandy, not Calais, would be the site of the Invasion.

It would not have been feasible to stage decoy landing exercises in the Straits of Dover, opposite Calais. Any such exercises would have been well within range of the German coastal guns on the Channel cliffs, which could inflict losses far in excess of what the E-boats did to Exercise Tiger. Instead of risking men, ships, and equipment to fool the enemy, SHAEF and Ops B decided to have Brutus, along with other agents, launch another kind of deception campaign.

Brutus was given instructions to play down the importance of the landing rehearsal in his reports. He informed his SD contact that Exercise Tiger was only a preliminary drill, and not a very important one, at that. Many other such exercises were planned for the spring and summer, he reported, and the dress rehearsal for the Invasion would take place in July. He went on to say that the actual Invasion was scheduled for the end of July.

Allied intelligence took full advantage of the SD's confidence in Brutus. False landing exercises were invented for May, June, and July, to be added to the long list of so many things that had been invented to keep the Germans from learning the truth about Overlord. It was just one more hoax in the already full Allied box of tricks.

But Brutus' main job was to pass along false information about the most elaborate hoax of all: Quicksilver. He sent daily reports on the make-up and activities of FUSAG to his contact, all of which were concocted by the Double-Cross Committee. In May, Double-Cross Committee invented a liaison post for Brutus. He informed the SD that he had been attached to General Patton's staff at FUSAG headquarters, where he would serve as a liaison officer between FUSAG and the Polish forces in Britain. This meant that he would have more access to information regarding the impending invasion in the Pas de Calais, and of FUSAG's readiness. His detailed reports mentioned completely made-up Polish units, as well as fictitious Free French and American paratroop units. The SD was in possession of FUSAG's complete order of battle, every one of its make-believe divisions and regiments; Brutus amended and updated it daily.

All of these reports looked entirely believable to the SD; after all, Walter Schellenberg and his intelligence experts had been kept informed of General Patton's activities for months, along with every development dreamed up by Allied counterintelligence. And after Brutus sent his information, and his contact forwarded the report along to his superior, all the data was then turned over to Fremde Heere West for evaluation. It was up to FHW to determine the reliability and accuracy of the information.

Fortunately for SHAEF, Colonel Alexis von Roenne, the head of FHW, was involved in basically the same activity as Brutus and the other Double-Cross agents—falsifying information and inflating estimates regarding FUSAG. Brutus' fictitious reports on the mainly nonexistent Allied forces in Kent and eastern England complemented his own. Colonel von Roenne endorsed all of the data that Brutus forwarded. In fact, von Roenne may have taken Brutus' figures and inflated them still further, to make FUSAG seem even more threatening to the Pas de Calais.

While Brutus and his colleagues sent fabricated reports about a massive Allied army in southeast England and East Anglia, complete with unit identification and other specific details, FHW passed them along as genuine. At this critical time, during the last few weeks before the Invasion, Colonel von Roenne gave Quicksilver—and SHAEF—an enormous advantage. With an intelligence officer of von Roenne's background and reputation saying that Double-Cross Committee reports concerning FUSAG were accurate, what else could the SD have done but believe them? Information from radio reconnaissance units and aerial photographs added their share of feasibility to the Quicksilver ruse, but von Roenne's sanction gave all the misleading information the final stamp of approval.

Brutus was not the only double agent who sent long and imaginative messages regarding FUSAG. Another agent reporting on the made-up army was a highly imaginative fellow code-named Garbo. John C. Masterman called Garbo "something of a genius,"[7] not only for the amount of misleading and totally false information he fed German intelligence, but also for the manner in which he did it.

Garbo was born in Spain, and apparently developed his extreme dislike of Fascists during the Spanish Civil War of 1936–1939, when he was forced to go into hiding for two years. (He hated Communists with just as much zeal.) In January 1941, he tried to enlist as a British agent, requesting either Italy or Germany as his base of operations, but the British turned him down. Undaunted, he went across town to the German embassy in Lisbon and enlisted in the Abwehr, with the view of becoming a double agent. The Germans took him up on his offer, and made arrangements to send Garbo to England. In July 1941, Garbo acquired a forged Spanish diplomatic document to get himself out of Spain, said good-bye to his German employers, and set out for England.

But Garbo did not go to England; he went to Lisbon. He pretended to be in England, however, for the benefit of his German contacts, and sent "long and colorful letters to his German friends"[8] about his espionage activities in the British Isles. His main sources of information about Britain—he had never even visited the country, and knew almost nothing about it—consisted of a travel guide, a map of the country, an old railway timetable, and an occasional article in the Lisbon press. With these scanty references, along with three subagents that he invented, Garbo fabricated any number of reports about troop movements, rail traffic, and pillbox defenses. Even though these reports were based upon nothing but his own imagination, they sounded genuine. And German intelligence swallowed them whole.

In February 1942, MI-6 learned that the Kriegsmarine were deploying a large number of U-boats to intercept a convoy that was to depart Liverpool en route to Malta. This was cause for alarm until several inquiries disclosed that there was no Malta-bound convoy due to leave Liverpool. The convoy had been another one of Garbo's inventions, but German naval intelligence believed it. On the strength of Garbo's report, U-boat headquarters diverted several submarines from their Atlantic patrols, where they might have done real damage to Allied shipping, and sent them on a wild goose chase.

At that point, Garbo was still a freelance double agent; he was working against the Germans, and having a lot of fun doing it, but was not working with anyone in particular. The Malta convoy deception convinced MI-6 that he belonged on their side, or, as John C. Masterman put it, "Garbo was more fitted to be a worthy collaborator than an unconscious competitor."[9]

In April 1942, Garbo was brought to England. He was given four more subagents—also fictitious—to add to his original three. Just to be creative, Garbo killed off his Liverpool contact—the one who informed him of the Malta convoy—after a long illness. He reported the death to the *Liverpool Daily Post* which ran an obituary of the nonexistent dead man. He then sent a copy of the death notice to his contact in Germany, and was asked to extend a grateful Fatherland's condolences to the grieving widow.

As a member of the Double-Cross Committee's organization, Garbo kept up the quality of his work. Now that he had the resources of MI-6 behind him, instead of just a map, a railway timetable, and a travel guide, he was even better and more deceptive than before. His activities went "from strength to strength" during the next year, as "the one-man band of Lisbon became an orchestra"[10] after arriving in Britain. By the spring of 1944, Garbo had become the main agent to fourteen subagents, all of whom were fictional—or, as Double-Cross Committee liked to refer to them, "notional." And German intelligence trusted each and every one of them implicitly.

Garbo sent about 400 letters and 2,000 cables to his German contact. These were clever, imaginative, and totally believable stories. One of his made-up tales involved an underground depot for storing arms and ammunition in the chalk caves near Chislehurst. These caves, Garbo went on, also served as a communications center. This fit perfectly with the Quicksilver deception—a hidden ammunition dump just across from Calais would be just what FUSAG would need.

Along with Brutus, Garbo also sent messages to confirm that Exercise Tiger was not an Overlord dress rehearsal, but just one landing exercise among many. But his most important job was to keep his contacts supplied with news pertaining to FUSAG and, in short, to make Quicksilver a success.

A third double agent who took part in the Quicksilver subterfuge was a Yugoslav named Dusko Popov, who would be known by the code name Tricycle. Popov came from a family that was well-off financially, and had the luxury of attending French schools and of studying at Freiburg University. At Freiburg, he met another student named Johann Jebsen, who came from a wealthy shipping family from Hamburg. The two of them would remain friends after leaving Freiburg, and would play their own part in Overlord.

Early in 1940, while he was negotiating the sale of two ships to Germany, Popov was required to go to the German consulate in Belgrade to fill out some forms. While he was there, one of the secretaries suggested that Popov might be in the position to do some "useful work" for Germany because of his background and family connections. But Popov had no intention of going to work for the Germans. Instead, he reported the conversation to the British representative in Belgrade.

The MI-6 contact in Belgrade surprised Popov by asking him to take the Germans up on their request. Popov complied. The Abwehr then asked him to go to England to collect some secret papers. Again, Popov complied, and the German staff arranged Popov's departure for England. Unknown to them, MI-6 made certain that all their arrangements went ahead without interference—they had their own reasons for wanting Popov in England. Before he left Belgrade, Popov met his old friend Johann Jebsen. Jebsen said that he had been an employee of the Abwehr for some time and happily told Popov that they now worked for the same organization.

In London, Popov made "a most favorable impression" with MI-6. He had excellent family connections, he had a business cover for any trips to the Continent that might be necessary, and, in Johann Jebsen, he even had a friend who was an Abwehr official. Popov was given the code name Tricycle; Double-Cross Committee furnished all the information he would be sending to his contact in Lisbon.

Although most of Popov's journeys were to Lisbon, where his contact had his base, he was sent to the United States in June 1941 by his Abwehr employers. His assignment in America was to supply detailed information, including sketches, of Pearl Harbor and the installations in and near the naval base—ammunition depots, floating drydocks, and airfields, including "Wicham Field" (Hickam Field). British intelligence kept track of Tricycle's activities but did not inform American authorities of the German curiosity concerning their naval base in Hawaii; there was a fear of being snubbed by the Americans, and also of putting their nose where it was not welcome. After the war, John C. Masterman regretted not having at least mentioned Tricycle's American assignment to the FBI, and admitted that "we ought to have stressed its importance more than we did."[11]

Popov did not give the Germans any information connected with Pearl Harbor or its defenses. He did not send much information at all from the United States; he blamed the Abwehr for not sending enough money. By the end of 1942, he was back in Lisbon, and then back in London to pass along Double-Cross Committee reports.

During one of his frequent trips to Lisbon, this time in July 1943, he visited his friend Johann Jebsen to see if he might have any news worth reporting about the Abwehr. Jebsen had some news for Popov, but it was not about the Abwehr. Popov was surprised to hear Jebsen say that he was having his doubts about Hitler and the Nazi regime; after all, Jebsen was still in the Abwehr, and had risen in rank several times since the early days of the war. Now, he said, he had joined the growing ranks of those who had turned against Hitler and his government.

As it turned out, Jebsen's new anti-Nazi point of view was not entirely his own. Part of Jebsen's transformation was based upon personal motives, to be sure, but the change also bore the stamp of Admiral Wilhelm Canaris. Canaris had arranged for Jebsen's trip to Lisbon, a visit which may have had something to do with an errand for the Schwarze Kapelle. Somewhere during one of their conversations, Jebsen dropped a hint that his faith in Hitler was fading; Canaris took things from there. It is fairly safe to assume that his change in opinion was in no small measure caused by the Canaris Effect, just as Colonel Alexis von Roenne's views has been shaped by Canaris and his co-conspirators in the Schwarz Kapelle.

As soon as he returned to London, Popov reported Jebsen's change of heart to his contacts in the Double-Cross Committee. Through Popov, Jebsen was recruited into Double-Cross league of deception and duplicity, and was given the code name Artist. Once again, the two university pals were working for the same espionage organization.

As agent Artist, Jebsen was able to provide Popov with some valuable information regarding the German Vengeance weapons—the V-1 flying bomb and the V-2 rocket. Both the British and the Americans had known about the V-weapons for some months and were impressed by the content of Artist's reports. But Popov, as agent Tricycle, had also been doing some impressive work of his own. In the early months of 1944, he was sent to Lisbon to pass along further misinformation regarding FUSAG—Double-Cross Committee had decided to put his talent for deception to work as part of Quicksilver.

In February 1944, Popov hand-delivered a detailed listing of First U.S. Army Group units and personnel to his German contact in Lisbon, an order of battle that had been carefully constructed by Double-Cross Committee. The man's reaction took Popov completely by surprise: He said that he did not think very much of Popov's work in general and that this phony information was not worth the money he was being paid for it. Although he was completely unprepared for this, Popov was a veteran in the business of duplicity by this time and quickly recovered. He protested that his information was not at all phony; in fact, it was far from it. The data that he was passing along was the result of keeping his eyes and ears open, and every fact had been double-checked. The report he was now being given regarding Allied forces in Britain was both up to date and accurate, and should be sent to Berlin immediately— the SD were well informed of the situation, and would appreciate the importance and the timeliness of his data.

Popov's German contact probably did not believe a word of this, but sent the information on to Berlin anyway, probably with misgivings. The next time Popov saw the man, which was two days later, his entire attitude had changed. He apologized to Popov for doubting him and his information, and went on to say that Berlin was absolutely delighted with the reports he had submitted. Popov was hugely relieved—he had not been sure what to expect.

What had happened between the first and second meetings was that Colonel Alexis von Roenne had, once again, come to the rescue. Popov's information had been sent to Fremde Heere West for evaluation and promptly came to the attention of Colonel von Roenne. Von Roenne immediately saw the significance of the new report, and wrote a memo that was read by both Hitler and OKW defending Popov's information. He described the V-mann (*Vertrauensmann*, or confidential agent) dispatch as containing "particularly valuable information" and went on to say that the "authenticity of the report was checked and proved" and that data regarding the "3rd Army, 3rd Army Corps, and twenty-three large formations . . . confirms our own operational picture."[12]

Von Roenne's endorsement not only made Popov's information—actually Double-Cross Committee's information—acceptable; it also defused any suspicions regarding Popov himself. In Popov, Double-Cross Committee now had another agent to plant bogus information regarding FUSAG. As the day of the Invasion approached, Quicksilver would be needing all the help it could get if it was to succeed.

For the next few weeks, Popov, as agent Tricycle, continued to send his reports that named nonexistent units or gave inaccurate locations for existing units: The 42nd British Armoured Division, presumed to be in Devon, was being sent to the Mediterranean; the 34th British Armoured Brigade was in southern England. But in May, an incident involving his friend Jebsen, code-named Artist, put Popov's career as Tricycle, as well as the future of Quicksilver, in jeopardy.

In early May, Jebsen was arrested by the SD. The exact reason for his arrest has never been clarified. John C. Masterman of Double-Cross Committee suggested that Jebsen "had become suspect only because of his financial dealings."[13] But there may have been another, more ominous reason, as well. Jensen had become the good friend of the mother of a former Abwehr agent named Erich Vermehren and often visited her at her home in Lisbon. Erich Vermehren had defected to the Allied side in February 1944. Jebsen's frequent visits to her house may have aroused suspicions among the SD.

For whatever reason, Johann Jebsen had been taken prisoner. Not only had he been arrested, but he also had been drugged and sent to Germany inside a steamer trunk. When Double-Cross Committee was informed that their agent Artist had been arrested and was being interrogated at SD headquarters, the reaction was predictable. "Under interrogation," Masterman later said, "it was to be presumed that much, if not all, of the history of his activities would come to light."[14] Jebsen's arrest also meant that agent Tricycle, who had been so useful up to that point and seemed to have so much potential as part of Quicksilver, would have to be discontinued.

The most frightening aspect of Artist's arrest was that nobody in Double-Cross Committee, or anywhere else, knew what it might mean to Quicksilver. Nobody was even certain of the motive for the arrest. Was it because of some illegal financial dealings, as John C. Masterman thought, because of his association with Erich Vermehren's mother, or for some other reason that no one knew anything about? Jebsen certainly knew enough about Tricycle/Popov to put a stop to his role in Quicksilver—the Double-Cross Committee feared that if Popov returned to Lisbon, he would be picked up by the SD, as well. Popov also had acquired enough information about Quicksilver to compromise that operation, and to expose FUSAG as a fake.

No one at SHAEF panicked because of the situation. Realistically, there was not very much that could be done. Quicksilver could not be scrapped, not at this point; there was too much riding on it, and the Invasion was now only a matter of a few weeks away. The most prudent thing to do, it was decided, was to wait and see what happened.

It did not take very long for something to occur, and what happened was exactly what SHAEF feared most: Hitler ordered reinforcements moved into Normandy, although forces in the Pas de Calais remained in position. The diary of Rommel's Army Group B noted on 6 May: "The Führer is of the opinion that . . . attacks will occur primarily at Normandy and to a lesser degree at Brittany. The most recent information once more points in that direction."[15]

Two days later Feldmarschall von Rundstedt's chief of staff, General Blumentritt, sent this message: "The Führer attached extreme importance to Normandy and the defense of Normandy. In the coming enemy offensive, very strong landings by air and heavy bombing raids, as well as the main attacks from the sea, are to be expected."[16]

Again, SHAEF and the various Allied intelligence services were perplexed; nobody seemed to know what to make of this shift to Normandy. Was the strengthening of Normandy purely a coincidence, the result of one of Hitler's intuitions? Was it only a temporary measure? Or had German intelligence been tipped off regarding Overlord and its objective?

Neither General Eisenhower nor anyone else at SHAEF had been very encouraged by the events of the past few weeks. First, Exercise Tiger had been discovered off the coast of Devon by German E-boats; then Artist was arrested. Immediately afterward, German forces in Normandy were ordered to be reinforced. The only ray of hope was that the Calais defenses were left in place. If Fifteenth Army's Panzer Divisions had been transferred from Calais to reinforce Normandy, the reaction at SHAEF headquarters would have been something close to panic.

Another note of encouragement was that Brutus and Garbo were still active, and were still feeding their SD contacts authentic-sounding data about FUSAG. But Overlord's real—and totally unknown and uncelebrated—source of strength in this crisis was Colonel Alexis von Roenne. Von Roenne would continue to approve all Double-Cross Committee reports pertaining to FUSAG and would pass them along as genuine. Dispatches from the Allied V-Men placed genuine U.S. Army units, including the 6th Armored Division and 28th Infantry Division, in the East and Southeast of England as part of FUSAG's build-up for the Calais invasion. Von Roenne duly relayed this information in FHW's situation reports. He even added his opinion that these reports provided mounting evidence that the main Invasion force was assembling in Kent and East Anglia. And, because he was head of FHW, his word was not questioned. Without von Roenne and his activities, all of the Allies' elaborate fakery very well might have been exposed, and Overlord might have turned out very differently from the way that it did.

NOTES

1. Masterman, p. 205.
2. Ibid., p. 206.
3. Greene and Allen, p. 27.
4. Ibid., p. 28.
5. Author interview.
6. Greene and Allen, p. 34.
7. Masterman, p. 206.
8. Ibid., p. 173.
9. Ibid., p. 174.
10. Ibid., p. 206.
11. Ibid., p. 124.
12. Delmer, p. 156.

13. Masterman, p. 221.
14. Ibid.
15. Ruge, p. 153.
16. Brown, p. 552.

Feldmarschall Erwin Rommel was a welcome recruit into the Schwarze Kapelle; he brought his reputation and prestige to the anti-Hitler movement. But Rommel found himself in an awkward position—he wanted to overthrow Hitler, but did not want to do anything that might cost Germany the war. (Author's Collection)

Adolf Hitler and his commanders, including General Jodl (pointing) and Field Marshals Göring and Keitel, examine a map of the Normandy coast on 6 June. As supreme military commander of the Third Reich and head of all German forces, Adolf Hitler was the target of Admiral Canaris' and Colonel von Roenne's misinformation and deception campaign. His first instinct was that the Allies would land at Normandy. (National Archives, Captured Foreign Records)

General Dwight D. Eisenhower aboard the cruiser U.S.S. *Quincy*. As Supreme Allied Commander, General Eisenhower's most pressing worry was how to keep the massive preparations for Operation Overlord a secret from German intelligence. (National Archives)

Feldmarschall Gerd von Rundstedt, commander of all German forces in the West. His disdain for Hitler was matched only by his distrust of the German Intelligence Services. (National Archives)

Three Canadian soldiers examine a German coastal artillery emplacement at Boulogne, on the Calais coast, in September 1944. Hitler and his senior commanders were not fully convinced that the Allies did not intend to invade Calais until British and Canadian troops had actually advanced into that area. (National Archives)

Huge concrete caissons, sunk in place, form the outline of one of the Mulberry artificial harbors. The Mulberries allowed the Allies to bring their own port across the Channel. German intelligence knew about the caissons, but did not know what they were for. (National Archives)

American infantry at the base of the Cherbourg Peninsula, prior to their breakout at St. Lo. If Colonel von Roenne's campaign of misinformation had not succeeded, the fighting all along the Normandy front would have been much heavier. The Allied forces would have had the German Fifteenth Army to contend with as well as the Seventh Army. (National Archives)

General George S. Patton, in a photo taken in Sicily in 1943. Patton nearly had his career destroyed to assure the success of Quicksilver. (National Archives)

Captain Wilhelm Canaris (left), head of the Abwehr, with SS Lieutenant General Reinhard Heydrich, chief of the SD, in 1936. Heydrich suspected Canaris of plotting against Hitler. Heydrich's assassination in May 1942 cut short his investigation, and allowed Canaris to continue with his Schwarze Kapelle activities. (U.S. Army)

While troops of the U.S. 2nd Division moved inland on 7 June, Hitler waited for word about the "real" invasion on the Calais coast. (U.S. Army)

A Messerschmitt Bf 109, and crew members installing a camera into one of the fighters. German reconnaissance aircraft were allowed to photograph the dummy tanks and empty camps of FUSAG—just as long as they did not fly too low. (Above: U.S. Air Force; below: National Archives)

A local farmer walks his horse-drawn cart past a field of U.S. Army vehicles. Anyone in England would have been able to witness similar evidence of Invasion preparations. Allied planners realized that keeping the massive build-up of men and equipment a secret would be impossible. (U.S. Army)

An American reconnaissance photo of beach obstacles on the Normandy coast. Allied intelligence sent commandos ashore at night to get a close look at the defenses on all five landing beaches. (U.S. Air Force)

Colonel Alexis von Roenne, the head of Fremde Heere West (FHW) and the key figure of German intelligence in the West. It was his job to evaluate the countless fragments of information gathered by German intelligence on the pending Invasion. His decision to alter the data compiled by FHW was a main factor in convincing Hitler and his generals that FUSAG really existed.

Lieutenant General Sir Frederick E. Morgan, one of the original planners of
Overlord. His successor was General Eisenhower, when COSSAC (Chief of
Staff, Supreme Allied Command) became SHAEF (Supreme Headquarters,
Allied Expeditionary Force). He was well aware of the risks involved in
landing an army on the French coast. (U.S. Army)

Lieutenant Wilhelm Canaris (center) poses with the officers and crew members of the submarine *UB-128* in the summer of 1918. Canaris had a distinguished career as a naval officer before he became head of German Military Intelligence, the Abwehr, in 1934. (National Archives)

A famous D-Day photograph: men of the U.S. 1st Division landing on Omaha Beach on the morning of 6 June 1944. The success of the landing depended upon many factors, including the activities of Colonel von Roenne. (National Archives)

Field Marshal Bernard Law Montgomery conferring with some of his commanders. General Omar Bradley (wearing helmet) and General Sir Alan Brooke (to extreme right). Shortly before D-Day, a British actor, Clifton James, impersonated Montgomery at Gibraltar to give German intelligence the impression that Allied activity might be pending in the Mediterranean. (U.S. Army)

A communiqué written by General Eisenhower, which he had planned to release if Overlord had not succeeded: "Our landings in the Cherbourg-Havre area have failed to gain a satisfactory foothold and I have withdrawn the troops. My decision to attack at this time and place was based upon the best information available. The troops, the air and the Navy did all that bravery and devotion to duty could do. If there is any blame or fault attached to the attempt, it is mine alone." (It is misdated July 5 instead of June 5, an indication of the tension that he was feeling.) If Quicksilver had not succeeded so spectacularly, Eisenhower might have been forced to send it. (Eisenhower Library)

Rommel, his aide Captain Hellmuth Lang, and his Chief of Staff Major General Dr. Hans Speidel in the Libyan desert (left to right). Speidel was also an established member of the Schwarze Kapelle and often acted as a liaison between Rommel and other Schwarze Kapelle associates. (National Archives)

Hitler (left) and Generalissimo Francisco Franco (right) at their meeting in October 1940. Franco had been warned by Admiral Canaris about Hitler's intention to invade Gibraltar via Spain and refused to submit to Hitler's demands or to join the Axis. (U.S. Army)

Map 1

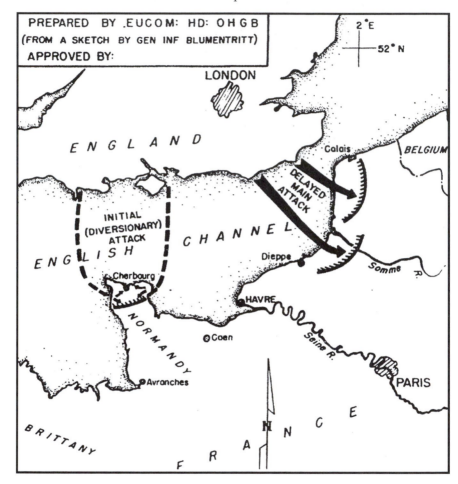

PREPARED BY .EUCOM: HD: OHGB
(FROM A SKETCH BY GEN INF BLUMENTRITT)
APPROVED BY:

Two maps that were based upon sketches drawn by Major General Gunther Blumentritt, Feldmarschall von Rundstedt's Chief of Staff. The maps illustrate what Hitler and his generals expected the Allies to do: (see Map 1) land a diversionary force in Normandy and follow up with a main attack in the Pas de Calais. From Calais (see Map 2), Allied forces would be in position to move through Belgium and into Germany. Colonel von Roenne's misinformation persuaded Hitler to keep the Fifteenth Army in Calais for weeks after the Invasion. (National Archives)

Map 2

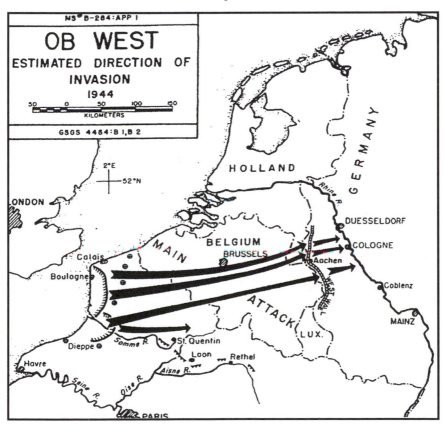

SEVEN

Invasion Nerves—"When Will They Come?"

In May 1944, the Invasion was the leading topic of conversation on both sides of the Atlantic. New York bookmakers took bets on the exact time of D-Day. British factory workers had pools, similar to football pools, on the day of the Invasion. Newspaper columnists and magazine writers in both countries put together countless stories on Invasion preparations, Invasion forces, Invasion commanders, and any other aspect of D-Day that they thought might satisfy their readers' curiosity. Everyone knew that the big day was coming, but they could only guess at when.

People in England, especially southern England, felt the tension caused by the uncertainty of the coming Invasion. Everyone could see that D-Day was not far off. Roads were still crammed with military vehicles of all types; some road convoys stretched for miles, heading south toward the embarkation ports. The pubs were filled with uniforms of Free French, Poles, Australians, New Zealanders, Indians, Americans, and British soldiers. All of this could only mean that the landings were imminent. The weather, which had been sunny and clear and looked to continue that way, was another source of tension; the Invasion was sure to be launched very soon, everyone said, before the weather turned.

The tension was just as wearing in Germany and in German-occupied France, although for completely different reasons. Dr. Goebbels' Propaganda Ministry showed all the symptoms of Invasion jitters. The propaganda machine insisted that the Invasion would actually be welcome, since the defenses of the Atlantic Wall were fully prepared for it. Photos of German soldiers standing guard on the French beaches appeared in newspapers and magazines throughout Germany and France. Newsreel footage of coastal artillery batteries firing out to sea were shown in cinemas. The German and French public were assured that the invading Allied troops would be stopped by the defenses of the Atlantic Wall, just as they had been at Dieppe. The official German line on the impending Invasion radiated supreme confidence: Let them come, the Propaganda Ministry said; we're ready for them.

But senior Wehrmacht officers, especially officers commanding units along the French coast, knew better. The defenses were anything but ready. The port city of Cherbourg was well fortified; so was the Pas de Calais. Defenses in between were spotty, at best. Some artillery units did not have their guns in place; other batteries had their guns mounted, but did not have ammunition for them. Concrete pillboxes were another problem: The fortifications that already existed seemed adequate, but there were not enough of them. But the biggest problem was air and naval support. The British and Americans had complete air and naval superiority, while the Germans had practically no air or sea defenses that were capable of stopping the Overlord offensive.

Invasion nerves at OKW were evident in a communiqué that was issued on 10 May, which concerned Allied intentions. "OKW expects the enemy attacks to begin in the middle of May," the report began. "Especially 18 May seems a potentially favorable day. Irrefutable documentary proof is, of course, not available. Point of concentration first and foremost: Normandy; secondly, Brittany."

The message went on to warn that the enemy would try to destroy ground troops with heavy attacks, possibly simultaneous attacks by sea and air, and that "the use of new weapons is not impossible." In the final part of the communiqué, the warnings continued: "deploy the troops in a cleverly camouflaged and dispersed manner," "dig in everything not protected by concrete," and "special attention should be given to airborne landing troops."[1] OKW's evaluation was an excellent one, except for the date, and might have meant possible disaster for Overlord had it been heeded.

OKW was clearly in a full state of nervous tension. They must have felt as though they were staring into the muzzle of the proverbially loaded gun—the enemy had been building his strength for months, and was about to unleash all this stored-up power and might against them. The best course of action, most senior officers agreed, was to dig in and stay alert, which is why everyone's nerves were stretched to the breaking point. "Every thought in the weeks before the invasion centered upon means of saving the Reich,"[2] wrote General Hans Speidel, Rommel's chief of staff.

The continual stress gave rise to wild stories about the landings. In mid-May, rumors circulated that the Invasion had already begun, at Calais, and that (1) Allied soldiers were being slaughtered en masse, or (2) the resistance had taken to arms and were slaughtering German troops.

No one's composure was helped by a Berlin radio announcement that "sensational news" would be released within the next few days. This breathless news turned out to be that a violin piece was going to be performed "by a very talented Berlin artist . . . on a violin that was made in 1626."[3]

When the predicted 18 May landings did not take place, tension increased still further. Both army and naval commanders were well aware that the Allied forces in Britain had finished their training, and were ready to move at any time. Exactly when they would be moving depended upon factors that were beyond the control of either the Germans or the Allies. Specifically, these factors were the tides, the brightness of the moon, and the weather.

From the Allied point of view, the tides were a main consideration when planning the exact day of the Invasion. Ideally, the tide already would have reached its lowest point, and would have begun coming in, when the first wave landed. This would allow the landing craft to touch the shore without coming in contact with any of the potentially fatal beach obstacles—although it also meant that the landing troops would have to cross a longer stretch of beach, probably under enemy fire. Since the tide would already be coming in, this would also prevent any of the boats from being stranded on the sand.

Moonlight was important mainly for the airborne landings, which would take place on the night before D-Day. The paratroops would need the light of a late-rising moon to help them locate landmarks in the night and the moonlight would also assist the various units, as well as individual soldiers, in finding each other. But this also had a negative side: The bright moon would also make the aircraft carrying the paratroops easier for antiaircraft gunners to spot.

Weather was probably the most critical element in planning the Invasion. It was certainly the most unpredictable. Attempting to land Overlord in a storm would bring about a disaster, everyone on General Eisenhower's staff agreed. They also realized that the bright, sunny weather of recent weeks would not hold forever, and could only hope that the god of storms would favor them when, at long last, the time came to launch Overlord.

General Dwight D. Eisenhower designated Y-Day, the day on which Overlord would be declared ready, to be 1 June, and assigned it the code name Halcyon. Based upon a consideration of the moon and the tides, as well as readiness reports from senior commanders, it was decided that D-Day would be either the 5th, 6th, or 7th of June. Monday, 5 June, the earliest day, was selected as the actual day for launching the Invasion, but the following two days would also be suitable.

"Looks as if Y plus 4 is D-Day," wrote Commander Harry C. Butcher, Eisenhower's naval aide, in his diary entry for Thursday, 18 May. ("Y plus 4" translates as four days after Y-Day, or 5 June.) "Y plus 5 and Y plus 6 are also acceptable in case unsuitable weather makes it necessary to postpone the assault."[4] The next favorable tidal period would be between 19 June and 22 June or, as Commander Butcher phrased it, "about Y plus 18."[5]

The planners at SHAEF were not the only ones who had been keeping a close watch on the moon and tides of northern France. Hitler and OKW had been looking at similar records, and had come to the same conclusions: Because of the tides and the moon, the most likely time for the Invasion would be 5 June, 6 June, or 7 June. And if the enemy was not able to make his attack on any of these three days, the next time that conditions would be favorable for a landing would be toward the end of the month. The Admiralty and naval intelligence had been keeping their own charts for over a year, and had kept OKW and all the various commands—including 15th Army (Calais) and 7th Army (Normandy)— informed of their findings.

It was common knowledge that the enemy always landed at dawn. This had been their practice at North Africa, in Sicily, and in Italy. They always came at dawn, and only when the weather was perfect. Weather was another vital factor; everything depended upon the weather.

Hitler and his OKW were as preoccupied with the weather as with the moon and tides, and were as concerned about it as the planners at SHAEF headquarters. The navy could keep charts on the currents and the tides, and the Intelligence Services monitored the activities of enemy forces in England, but nobody could say what the weather would be like in June. The Allies had to come by sea, and could not land his forces in a storm. The question, "When will they come?" was always coupled with, "What is the weather forecast?"

The commander of Army Group B, Feldmarschall Erwin Rommel, also was concerned with the winds, the tides, the weather, and how they all tied in with the enemy's intentions. Because of the lethal variety of obstacles that had been positioned on the landing beaches, some of which had been designed by himself, Rommel concluded that the invaders would land when the tide was out. A low tide that came just before dawn indicated that the Invasion could be expected during the first full week of June: Monday, 5 June; Tuesday, 6 June; or Wednesday, 7 June.

The feldmarschall was still riding two horses at the same time, and riding them just as fast as ever. On the one hand, he was waging a campaign with Hitler himself for the control of all the armored units in France, all seven of them. (Allied intelligence, through the Ultra deciphering of German codes, knew all about the exchanges between Rommel and Hitler.) His plan was to throw every tank unit in the Calais/ Normandy area at the invading Allied armies as soon as they came ashore, and to make the landings into such a bloodbath that the enemy would be forced to withdraw before they could establish a foothold on the beaches.

Rommel's campaign was only partly successful. Hitler turned three of the seven panzer divisions over to Rommel: the 2nd, the 21st, and the 116th. The other four remained under Hitler's direct control, although Rommel was assured that these units would be released for operations as soon as the enemy's intentions were determined. Allied intelligence also knew about this development.

But while he was arranging to make the Overlord landings a complete disaster for the Allied forces, he was also conspiring to bring about the downfall of Adolf Hitler and his regime. Rommel remained in constant touch with the Schwarze Kapelle plotters throughout the spring of 1944, including generals von Stuelpnagel and von Falkenhausen, and also confided in his chief of staff, General Hans Speidel, another leading anti-Hitler conspirator, on an everyday basis.

"Rommel struggled to determine at what point obedience must end for a general who feels responsible for the fate of his nation," Speidel said, "and at what point human conscience would demand insurrection."[6] Rommel would often quote passages from Hitler's *Mein Kampf*, and use them to point out the ironic contrast between Hitler's words and his actions: "When the Government of a nation is leading it to its doom," Hitler wrote, "rebellion is not only the right but the duty of every citizen. . . . Human laws supercede the laws of the state."[7]

On 15 May, Rommel met with General Karl Heinrich von Stuelpnagel, General Alexander von Faulkenhausen, General Heinrich von Luettwitz, the commander of the 2nd Panzer Division, and General Gerhardt von Schwerin, commander of the 116th Panzer Division. General Speidel was also present. The meeting was called to address the "necessary measures," according to Speidel, for ending the war in the West, and for overthrowing Hitler. It was held in a country house in Mareil-Marley, near St. Germain, which was surrounded by the men and tanks of the 21st (Afrika) Panzer Division. The 21st Division had been a unit in Rommel's Afrika Korps; at that moment, units of the 21st were serving as Rommel's personal bodyguard. The feldmarschall was taking no chances, either with inquisitive outsiders or with the Gestapo.

Although Rommel wanted Hitler removed from power, he was rigidly opposed to having him assassinated. He did not want to turn Hitler into a latter-day John Brown, a martyr that might inspire Nazi fanatics to start a civil war. The most prudent course of action, Rommel insisted, would be to use reliable Panzer detachments to take Hitler prisoner, and then to bring him to trial for crimes against Germany and against humanity. "He should be tried by the people who elected him," were Rommel's sentiments concerning Hitler's punishment.[8]

This may have been a noble approach, but it was not a very practical one. For one thing, killing Hitler would have been the only sure way of ending the Nazi regime and of shortening the war. Fanatical Nazis were more inspired by a living Führer than by his dead body. When Hitler finally committed suicide in April 1945, the Nazi Party collapsed; he *was* the Nazi regime. Also, the Western Allies had no intention of negotiating an armistice separate from Soviet Russia and, in spite of the Schwarze Kapelle's promises of a full-scale German evacuation of all occupied territories, would have rejected any suggestion of a separate peace.

The Hitler problem—whether to arrest him or assassinate him—was the only point of disagreement at the meeting. Apart from the stipulation that fighting would continue along the Russian front, the major decisions reached by the conspirators were that Rommel would be de facto leader of the movement, and also that the unseating of Hitler must take place before the Allied Invasion. If the Allies landed, and the landings were successful, the Schwarze Kapelle would lose a great deal of negotiating leverage; they would be bargaining from a position of weakness, they feared, instead of strength. As such, it was absolutely imperative to make contact with the Allies as soon as it could be arranged safely, and to begin taking steps toward the elimination of Hitler.

While Rommel and his colleagues were making their arrangements, Luftwaffe intelligence discovered that the Allies had a scheme of their own for shortening the war. A captured American Air Force officer, identified by General Speidel as Colonel Smart, spoke at length about an attempt to make contact with Rommel about negotiating an armistice. Colonel Smart had been shot down over Vienna on 10 May 1944. Under interrogation, he admitted that a plan existed to contact the feldmarschall to arrange for an ending of the war, and that he was a part of that plan. Smart's testimony was written down in the officers' Prisoner of War Stockade at Oberursel; copies were sent to Reichsmarschall Hermann Göring, Propaganda Minister Josef Goebbles, and the Air Ministry. Rommel was not told anything about Colonel Smart or his testimony, and never heard about the secret Allied plan to contact him.[9]

Feldmarschall Rommel certainly loomed large in Allied thoughts during the spring of 1944. While an American colonel admitted to being part of an attempt to contact Rommel for the purpose of ending the war, a British plot had been concocted to kill or kidnap him. Rommel was regarded as the very best general that the Germans had, and his position as commander of Army Group B was fairly common knowledge. With Rommel out of the way, the logic went, the German forces in northern France would be leaderless at a very critical time. No one was sure exactly what would happen if Rommel was assassinated, but the results could not be good for German forces in France, and could only be an advantage for the Allied invaders. But the plan did not work out. Both

Army Group B and the Schwarze Kapelle retained the services of one of their most valuable members.

Although this might seem a contradiction of huge proportions—planning to talk to Rommel about arranging an armistice while, at the same time, plotting to kill him—Rommel's life at this point was a riddle of contradictions. On the morning of 15 May, a few hours before he met with his fellow conspirators at Mareil-Marley to discuss removing Hitler from power, Rommel and his naval aide discussed the necessity of having concrete emplacements for artillery batteries along the Channel coast. Only guns protected by concrete pillboxes would survive the pre-Invasion naval shelling, it was agreed, and would be able to fire back at the attackers. While the discussion was in progress, Hitler telephoned and "talked with Rommel about the multiple rocket launchers."[10]

Within the next few days, Rommel would make several stops along the French coast to inspect offshore obstacles and airborne landing barriers, to give pep talks to his troops, and to talk with his officers about preparations for killing as many Allied soldiers as possible on D-Day. At the same time, he would remain in communication with generals von Stuelpnagel and von Falkenhausen and their Schwarze Kapelle associates, either directly or through General Speidel. Although he was an anti-Hitler accomplice, Rommel was also a career soldier. He wanted to see Hitler removed, but could not let his role in the Schwarze Kapelle interfere with his duties as a German officer and the commander of Army Group B.

While Feldmarschall Rommel was under constant tension from his double life, Admiral Wilhelm Canaris was feeling a different kind of pressure. Even though he had been dismissed as head of the Abwehr and banished to the hinterlands, Canaris had not been stopped from carrying out his own campaign to subvert Hitler. He kept in touch with the Allied intelligence services throughout his exile, and managed to send some extremely useful information on German forces in Normandy as well as on defenses along the Channel coast.

Apparently, Canaris had begun contacting the Allies as early as February 1944—in other words, as soon as he had been relieved of his job as chief of intelligence. No one is exactly sure how he managed to stay in touch, although it was probably through his contacts in Spain. However he did it, Canaris sent many reports and much information, and kept sending right up to D-Day. This is apparently why Canaris left his post at the Abwehr so quietly. He had not given up his fight against Hitler; he had just moved it to Lauenstein Castle in Franconia. And nobody in the SD, from Walter Schellenberg down, ever caught on.

An unnamed former British intelligence officer told one of Canaris' biographers, "As you know, we had Admiral Canaris."[11] Another British official, also unnamed, probably came a lot closer to the mark when he said that Canaris "helped us all he could, didn't he?"[12] Canaris was not actually employed by MI-6, but he went out of his way to be as helpful as possible to British intelligence and to the Allied cause in general.

In the late winter of 1944, an American colonel in SHAEF intelligence found out just how valuable Admiral Canaris had become to Allied intelligence. The colonel was James O. Curtis, senior American intelligence evaluator at SHAEF. His job required him to analyze reports sent by agents in the field, and to judge their accuracy and reliability. Not only was Colonel Curtis the senior American in his department; he was the *only* American. The other evaluators—Colonel Eric Birley, Major John Austin, and Colonel Foord, the director—were British.

Even though he was on good terms with his three British colleagues, Curtis had the feeling that they did not trust him completely. This distrust was not based entirely upon historical prejudices stemming from the Declaration of Independence and the Battle of Bunker Hill, although Curtis realized that they probably had something to do with it. The major bone of contention was Curtis' skepticism concerning the source of some of the information he was supposed to be analyzing. Some of the data he had been reading seemed to be too detailed and too accurate as far as he was concerned—too good to be true. He told Colonel Foord that he could not pass such information along to the American planners at SHAEF as genuine unless he knew something about its origins.

Colonel Foord finally decided to let Curtis in on the secret. He took Curtis aside to explain the situation in private: Although much of the top-quality information he had been reading had come from Ultra decrypts of German radio traffic, including intercepts from OKW, some of it originated from Admiral Wilhelm Canaris. Curtis recognized the name, and was absolutely astonished by Foord's disclosure.

Curtis found out that some of the items that Canaris sent personally to SHAEF included the German order of battle. Foord said, "The only reason that I am telling you this is that we want you to regard this information as being priceless and copper-bottomed."[13] Foord also explained that only a select few high-ranking individuals—including Churchill, Roosevelt, Eisenhower, and Montgomery—knew anything at all about SHAEF's connection with Canaris.

Intelligence reports received at SHAEF were assigned a classification based upon their authenticity and reliability. The highest quality reports were classified A-1; the lowest were F-6. All of the information sent by Canaris had been classified A-1 by Curtis long before he was told where it was coming from, and he certainly recognized it as top quality— "priceless and copper-bottomed." What made Curtis suspicious was that so many of the reports he was receiving were A-1, a larger percentage than he thought feasible. Now that he knew their source, his suspicions were put to rest.

Canaris worked unconditionally for the Allied cause and against Hitler, and used all of his considerable resources to undermine Hitler. Unlike Feldmarschall Rommel, Canaris did not feel any loyalty at all toward the current German government. Even though he still held a government position, he did not think that this job, or even his past service in the German navy, created any sort of conflict with his role in the Schwarze Kapelle.

In fact, Canaris had occasion to speak with Rommel concerning this very subject. He met Rommel during the early part of 1941, when Rommel—who was still a general and not yet a field marshal—was commander of the Afrika Korps. Canaris had compiled a listing of SS atrocities that had been committed against "undesirables" throughout occupied Europe, and gave a copy of it to Rommel. He meant it as an indictment against Hitler and the Nazis, but Rommel just shrugged it off. The general was "hardly sympathetic," a Canaris biographer said, "and so keen on his desert war that he had no time to be shocked by mass murder and racial extermination."[14]

Canaris was irritated by Rommel's lack of concern, and warned him that he "will one day be held responsible for what is happening behind the lines." But Rommel was not impressed. His attitude was: "That's not behind my front—not my concern at all. . . . I'm just a fighting man."[15] Eventually, Rommel would change his mind but not until Hitler's conduct affected him personally.

Canaris' activities during his exile remain shadowy, at best. He had been given a government job in the Economic Warfare Department, a bureaucratic dead end designed to keep him busy with minor duties. But this did not prevent him from contacting his fellow conspirators in the Schwarze Kapelle and may have provided him with information of value to the Allies. At any rate, he remained as active as ever in his campaign to oust Hitler, and kept SHAEF supplied with invaluable reports on German defenses in Normandy. Canaris was not the only source of intelligence on German movements and intentions in northern France, but he was one of the most reliable. Also, the data he provided served to supplement the other sources. Reporting the movement of the Panzer Lehr Division, for instance, might confirm the same information that had been intercepted by Ultra.

Delivering the German order of battle was one of Canaris' major achievements. He had the connections to obtain this highly secret information, as well as the means of sending it to Britain. Supplying the Wehrmacht's listing of men and divisions was a very great help to Allied intelligence, and made their own work much easier. Both MI-6 and SHAEF intelligence probably could have pieced it together themselves, but it would have taken a good deal of time and effort—energy that was put to use on other projects.

And from the point of view of SHAEF and the Allies, the demotion of Canaris from head of the Abwehr was the best thing that could have happened. Now that he was no longer chief of intelligence, Walter Schellenberg left Canaris alone. Schellenberg thought he had won; he was now chief of the combined Abwehr/SD, while Canaris had been sent off to some insignificant office job out in the sticks, a million miles from nowhere. Schellenberg paid no attention to Canaris, and suspected nothing about him.

Since Canaris was now much too small a fry to rate surveillance by the SD, he was free to carry on his intelligence war against Hitler without fear of being observed. His new home in Castle Lauenstein may not have been in Berlin, but his position as head of a department, no matter how insignificant, allowed Canaris to travel—to Berlin or anywhere else. In short, Canaris was now able to do everything he had been doing while he was head of the Abwehr, including remaining in contact with the Allies as well as with his colleagues in the Schwarze Kapelle, except that he now could carry on his activities without worrying about the SD constantly checking his movements and looking over his shoulder.

The fact that his dismissal as Abwehr chief had been on the grounds of incompetence also helped him carry out his new deception. The prevailing thought among senior German officers was that Canaris was a dim-witted little man who never should have directed the Abwehr in the first place. Hitler would have agreed with this point of view, and would have added that Canaris did not do very much, and that everything he attempted turned out wrong. Suspecting Canaris of conspiring with the Allies simply would not have come to mind. Hitler believed that anyone with Canaris' record of failures and shortcomings—including misinforming OKW about Allied intentions just prior to the invasion of North Africa as well as about the landings at Anzio—would not have either the intelligence or the ability to contact SHAEF, even if the thought happened to occur to him.

The myth of the addle-brained little admiral, which Canaris himself went out of his way to establish, lasted for many years after the war had ended. In the late 1950s, Admiral Karl Doenitz, commander of the German U-boat fleet, wrote that "the German Intelligence Service under Admiral Canaris failed completely, just as it failed throughout the war, to give U-boat command one single piece of information about the enemy which was of the slightest use to us."[16]

This particular accusation was absolutely not true. German intelligence gave considerable help to U-boat Command by advising Doenitz of the sailing times of convoys, especially convoys sailing from the east coast of the United States. But Doenitz had already made up his mind, and told anyone who would listen—including Hitler—his opinion of Canaris and how he ran his intelligence service.

Admiral Doenitz and everyone else who ridiculed and criticized Canaris, including Walter Schellenberg, was actually helping Canaris with his plan to unseat Hitler. This kind of criticism undermined the credibility of the German espionage network as a whole—the phrase German Intelligence Service also referred to the SD. The lack of confidence in Canaris and his organization was transferred to the combined Abwehr/SD of Walter Schellenberg. This side effect of Canaris' studied "incompetence" would be of enormous service to SHAEF and to Overlord.

During this critical time, both for Overlord and for von Rundstedt, Admiral Canaris was left to himself in Castle Lauenstein to play with his pet dachshunds and to run his meaningless little Economic Warfare Department. Walter Schellenberg thought that was all the absent-minded little admiral was capable of doing. All the while, Canaris continued to send his invaluable information to SHAEF, and carried on with his secret campaign against the very people who had written him off as incompetent and had dismissed him.

Second Lieutenant John Murphy of the U.S. 4th Division had heard that the chances of surviving the Invasion were being put at fifty-fifty. These were not official figures, just a grisly estimate based upon nothing more substantial than rumors—"latrine rumors," Murphy called them. The talk was that the Germans had guessed that they were coming and would be waiting for them. Survival would depend upon luck, and the odds of being killed during the landings were given at even money.

Lieutenant Murphy would not have been encouraged if he had known that General Eisenhower's chief of staff, Lieutenant General Walter Bedell Smith, reached the same basic conclusion. General Smith said that he had "no misgivings about our troops getting ashore," but he predicted that "our chances of holding the beachhead, particularly after the Germans get their build-up, is only fifty-fifty."[17]

Both Lieutenant Murphy and General Smith would have been greatly encouraged to know that the Germans were not as well informed of Allied plans as they feared. Although the timing of Overlord was tied to the moon and the tides, which placed the landings either during the first week of June or sometime near the middle of the month, nobody had been able to determine exactly *where* the Invasion would come.

Feldmarschall von Rundstedt was convinced that the Allies would come ashore near a major port. The two largest Channel ports were Boulogne and Cherbourg. While Cherbourg remained a possibility, he had always believed that Boulogne and the Pas de Calais would be the goal of the Allied landings. He had not heard anything that might have convinced him otherwise, although he probably would not have listened to anything that intelligence had to say, anyway. By nature, von Rundstedt was not inclined to let anyone change his point of view, and his opinion of the German Intelligence Services were just about as low as Admiral Doenitz's.

Unlike his stubborn old field marshal, Hitler had allowed his mind to be changed; he was now convinced that the main Allied attack would come at Calais. In this instance, at least, Hitler would have been better off if he had been inflexible like von Rundstedt, and a bit less inclined to listen to intelligence. His first instinct had been that Normandy would be the Invasion site. But the elaborate FUSAG trickery had changed his mind, and the manipulations of Colonel von Roenne of FHW had sealed it. By mid-May, Hitler believed that the objective of all those troops in southeast England would be Calais, although there might be other landings in other places. All the reports on the activities in Kent and East Anglia could not be wrong.

But even though he now thought that Calais was the objective of Overlord, Normandy was still very much on Hitler's mind. He reached the conclusion that the beaches along the Calvados coast would be the most likely place for a diversionary landing. Those gently sloping beaches were simply too obvious, and seemed to be an open invitation for attacking enemy forces.

With this in mind, steps were taken to reinforce Normandy. In May, the 21st Panzer Division was ordered to move from Brittany to Caen, in a position just south of what would become the British and Canadian sector of the Normandy beachhead, and the Panzer Lehr Division moved to Normandy from Hungary, which must have come as a relief to the men of this unit. The peace and quiet of Normandy was a welcome respite from the rebellion in Hungary, which they had just put down. With these two moves, and with the increase of beach obstacles, the defenses in Normandy suddenly became formidable.

When word of this activity reached SHAEF headquarters, the reaction was alarm. The addition of two Panzer divisions to the defenses came as a very nasty surprise, especially in view of the fact that Overlord was scheduled to be launched in just a few weeks. General Eisenhower himself was taken aback by this unexpected development, and wondered if the Germans had somehow discovered the intended site of the Invasion.

The only encouraging news was that the defenses in the Pas de Calais had not been dismantled. Ultra kept track of everything that was happening, both in Normandy and in Calais, and kept General Eisenhower and SHAEF informed and up to date. "There continued to be no signs of a move by any of the infantry divisions of the Fifteenth Army from the Pas de Calais area,"[18] wrote the officer in charge of the Ultra operation.

On 20 May, Eisenhower's naval aide, Captain Harry C. Butcher, attended a briefing on Overlord and came away from it somewhat depressed and demoralized. The speaker, one of SHAEF's navy planners, certainly did not pull his punches when he described the German defenses and what would be in store for the attacking Allied forces. Among the topics he touched upon was the concentration of German troops—heaviest near Calais and only somewhat less near the actual Invasion beaches—and the likelihood of a fast and powerful counterattack in an effort to drive Overlord back into the sea. "I must say that since I have heard the briefing I am not as optimistic about the forthcoming Invasion as I was,"[19] Butcher wrote.

Captain Butcher's pessimism would certainly have been alleviated, or possibly would have lifted entirely, if he had known that the recent activity in Normandy was the result of one of Hitler's hunches and had nothing to do with German intelligence. In fact, Hitler and OKW still had no real idea where the Invasion would be coming ashore—a shortcoming that was entirely the doing of his intelligence services.

The secret intelligence campaign against Hitler and the Nazi regime was certainly achieving its intended purpose. Not only was it keeping Hitler and his generals in the dark regarding Allied intentions, but it also was helping to give the Allies a very good idea of what the Germans were up to in France. A British historian noted that "Eisenhower on the eve of D-Day was the best informed military commander in history"[20]— in large measure because of Admiral Canaris and his contacts with British intelligence. At the same time, Hitler and OKW were being completely misinformed and misled regarding the actual Allied strength in England.

Although Hitler had been put at a major disadvantage, this could change instantly if he determined that the real destination of Overlord was Normandy and not Calais. With the reinforcements that were now in position, the Invasion could still be turned into the bloodbath that Hitler hoped for. And he did have the means for making this diagnosis, including the radio reconnaissance units, which listened for the slightest clue regarding the time and the place of the landings, and Gwyn Evans, agent Druid, who was still at large in England, touring army camps with his string quartet.

The SD received another indication of the time of the Invasion, if not the place, on 15 May: The resistance, every underground group in northern France, were to go on full alert on 20 May. Major Oscar Reile, whose counterresistance units had infiltrated several *maquis* groups, already knew that the resistance in the Le Havre area had been put on full standby. But this latest development, which amounted to a general mobilization of the entire underground organization, served as a warning that a major operation was imminent. The only operation that could possibly justify an alert of this magnitude was the Invasion itself.

This small but significant piece of information all but confirmed that the Invasion would take place during the first favorable tidal period—5 June, 6 June, or 7 June—as opposed to the next time the moon and tides would be in a position favorable for the landings. If the Allies had not been planning to launch their Invasion until 19 June or 20 June, the *maquis* would not have been put on alert on 20 May.

Also, the number of communiqués between London and the resistance increased toward the end of May—another sign that the Invasion was not far off. These communiqués came in two forms: *messages personnels*, largely addressed to sabotage squads throughout northern France, and operational instructions, which were requests for information about the enemy. Some of these operational instructions included, "Note the markings on enemy vehicles and try to find out the regiment, formations, or group to which they belong." Other broadcasts asked resistance units to be as accurate as possible when supplying information: "How many roads come into the town or village? . . . Are there any roadblocks? If so, is there any way around them?"[21]

Germans were already tense and agitated concerning the *maquis* and their activities, an uneasiness that sometimes bordered on the hysterical. They knew all too well that the resistance was an invisible army, always watching their every move and waiting for the chance to murder them. These broadcasts made them even more nervous than usual. The Vichy Minister of Information warned of "terrible and bloody reprisals" by the Germans if the *maquis* made any attacks on German soldiers, and went on to say: "Consider carefully before you listen to General Eisenhower. The Allied invasion is a gamble, and its success is a very open question."[22] (Vichy was the German puppet government that controlled France following the French surrender in June 1940.)

These Allied communiqués with the *maquis* were two-way streets. They actually did serve to keep the many resistance groups informed about what they needed to know about the Invasion and the part they would be playing in it, and they also kept morale at a fighting pitch. But these broadcasts were also picked up by the Germans, and served to keep the Wehrmacht geared up and on the alert. Radio monitors logged the BBC's *messages personnels*, and kept records of exactly what kind of messages were being sent. Toward the end of May, these monitors were able to determine that a major percentage of all the communications sent by London were pre-Invasion alerts—sabotage alerts that would preface the Allied attack. And so, the BBC were giving German intelligence another indication that Overlord was not very far off.

Even though Hitler and OKW were confused as to the place of the impending Invasion, if not the time, there were any number of things that could allow the truth to slip out. Colonel von Roenne had consistently misled Hitler and his generals regarding Allied troop strength, and Admiral Canaris had done irreparable harm to the reputation of German intelligence with his campaign of misinformation, but the SD was still functioning. Walter Schellenberg and his organization kept their eyes and ears open for the slightest breach of security, from SHAEF headquarters or from any radio operator attached to any unit in the British Isles. One slip—the mention of a British port on the southwestern coast at the wrong time, or the slightest suggestion that FUSAG was only an elaborate deception—would be all that it would take to give the game away. Schellenberg and his group were waiting for the chance, and listening for the smallest of clues.

NOTES

1. Ruge, p. 157.
2. Speidel, p. 69.
3. *Newsweek*, 5 June 1944, p. 21.
4. Butcher, pp. 542–43.
5. Ibid., p. 543.
6. Speidel, p. 70.
7. Ibid.
8. Ibid., p. 66.
9. Ibid., p. 71.
10. Ruge, p. 161.
11. Colvin, p. 1.
12. Ibid., p. 2.
13. Brown, p. 665.
14. Colvin, p. 160.
15. Ibid.
16. Doenitz, p. 277.
17. Butcher, p. 538.
18. Winterbotham, pp. 186–87.
19. Butcher, p. 544.
20. Botting, p. 56.
21. *Newsweek*, 5 June 1944, pp. 22–23.
22. Ibid., p. 23.

EIGHT

"Les Sanglots Longs..."

"Living on this little island just now," noted London journalist Mollie Panter-Downes, "uncomfortably resembles living on a vast combination of an aircraft carrier, a floating dock jammed with men, and a warehouse stacked to the ceiling with material labelled 'Europe' "[1] But when she made this entry in her diary, the great, bulging floating dock/warehouse already had begun taking its first steps toward unloading its cargo on the Far Shore.

Throughout the month of May, the troops left their camps and headed toward their assembly areas. Convoys of vehicles, many of which stretched for miles, made their way southward toward the Channel. Signs along the way pointed the drivers in the right direction, arrow-shaped signs that all had the same message: "To The South."

Most of the convoys were bound for assembly areas close to the Channel ports—Plymouth, Dartmouth, Portsmouth, Newhaven, Poole, Portland—although some British units were moved to West Ham football stadium, as well as other destinations in East London. Once the men were safely inside their designated areas, barbed wire fences were set up and guards were posted around the perimeter. The troops were "sealed"—no one was allowed inside, and no one was allowed out. Once they had arrived in their sectors, everyone inside was cut off from the outside world.

After the troops had been sealed, the final operations order was distributed to officers—"which we pounced on like the Book of Revelation," according to Captain Charles Cawthon of the U.S. 29th Division. The order contained all the vital details they had guessed at and wondered about for the past several months "on smudged mimeographed sheets."

Captain Cawthon first learned that he and the rest of his unit would be landing on a stretch of Norman beach that had been code-named Omaha. As set down by the directive, the landing was to proceed on a "split-second schedule"—amphibious tanks would go in first, followed by rifle companies and combat engineers, then by heavy weapons, battalion headquarters, and artillery. Within the first thirty minutes, according to the plan, the entire battalion would be ashore. After the Invasion had actually taken place, Cawthon realized how absolutely unrealistic this order was.[2]

Now that the men were aware that they would be landing on the French beaches in a matter of only a few weeks at best, reactions to their impending ordeal were as varied as the men themselves. To Captain Cawthon, the realization that the heaviest fighting would fall to the infantry "engendered in us what was probably an obnoxious arrogance."[3] But Lieutenant James Murphy, who would land on Utah Beach with the U.S. 4th Division, did not feel anything approaching arrogance. He felt that he and his men had been well trained for their assignment and that they were fully prepared to carry it out, but his attitude came a lot closer to resignation than arrogance. "We hoped and prayed for the best but were prepared for the worst," Murphy said. "We knew that the Germans had a hell of a lot of stuff on hand to stop us. Our one big fear was that they had been tipped off and that they would be laying for us."[4]

While the Allies were getting ready for their assault, the Germans were making preparations of their own. "Each morning at five o'clock, the company assembled and disappeared into the fields or forests for combat training—assault, defense, counter assault," recalled a sergeant who was stationed near Caen.[5] A 30-year-old medical officer remembered, "We were living under tension, expecting the invasion, and there were constant air raid attacks. We knew it would come."[6]

For some of the defenders, preparations consisted of little more than digging in and waiting. "Today, they're digging foxholes to shelter themselves from future bombardments," Marie-Louise Osmont wrote about the Germans who were billeted in her chateau. "They're everywhere: in the paths, under the thornbush, behind the house, in the farmyard. . . . I spent the morning fighting with men who were taking the doors of the outerbuildings to cover their foxholes."[7]

Toward the end of May, reinforcements arrived in the district. "Arrival in Periers of a new unit, cavalry this time, coming from Plumetot and Cresserons."[8] Mme. Osmont noticed that a noncommissioned officer (NCO) with this unit had the death's head insignia of the SS on his collar. On 30 May, she saw a "motorized unit, tanks and others, led by a noncommissioned officer who spoke remarkable French" pass her estate. The following day was her birthday, prompting her to wonder, "What will the coming year be like?"[9] Everyone on both sides of the Channel, including Hitler and his generals, wondered the same thing.

Mme. Osmont was not the only one who kept her eyes open regarding the movements of German units in Normandy. Members of the resistance also made note of the comings and goings of the enemy, especially the arrival of new units. At the end of May, the 91st Air Landing Division moved to the southern end of the Cotentin Peninsula, in the vicinity of Carentan and St. Mere Eglise. By 29 May, SHAEF headquarters had been informed of the move as well as of the fact that the 6th Parachute Regiment had also moved into the same vicinity.

No one can be absolutely certain as to who sent the news about these troop movements. It could have been the resistance, or it could have been Admiral Canaris, or it even could have been both. Having two sources of information on enemy activities was certainly a great help, both to SHAEF and to the various branches of Allied intelligence; one source served to confirm the reports sent by the other and gave intelligence two separate sets of numbers to check against.

The news that the 91st Air Landing Division had taken up a position in Normandy was received with alarm by Allied planners. When Air Chief Marshal Sir Trafford Leigh-Mallory heard about it, he sent General Eisenhower a letter to warn that the proposed parachute landings in the St. Mere Eglise area would end in disaster if they were carried out. Leigh-Mallory, who commanded all the Allied air forces supporting Overlord (Allied Expeditionary Air Force), had never been enthusiastic about the airborne operation in the first place. Now, he feared that the result would be "colossal losses" for the paratroops.

In his letter to Eisenhower, Leigh-Mallory had gone on record about his misgivings concerning the planned U.S. airborne operations. According to plan, the U.S. 82nd and 101st Airborne Divisions were scheduled to jump into Normandy on the night before the main landings, and would be flown to their drop zones in about 915 C-47 troop transports. Because they would be flying across the Cotentin (Cherbourg) Peninsula in moonlight, and at low altitude, Leigh-Mallory feared that many of the aircraft would be shot down before they ever reached their appointed zones. And because the 91st Air Landing Division was now known to be in the very area where the American paratroops were to be dropped, Leigh-Mallory was also concerned that the men who actually made it as far as the drop zones would be slaughtered as soon as they landed.

Eisenhower realized that Leigh-Mallory's warnings were well-founded. But he also realized that the planned air drops were vital to the success of keeping the Germans from making a counterattack against the troops that would land on Utah Beach. "General Ike replied promptly that Leigh-Mallory was quite right in communicating his convictions to the hazards," Captain Butcher said, "but a strong airborne attack is essential to the whole operation and it must go on."[10]

General Eisenhower and SHAEF continued to be kept well informed of the Wehrmacht's actions, thanks to Ultra, the resistance, and Admiral Canaris. Eisenhower had been advised very quickly of the arrival of the 91st on the Cotentin Peninsula, and had made his decision regarding the air drops with that information at hand. When Hitler had called for the reinforcing of Normandy in early May, SHAEF headquarters and Allied intelligence knew about it at once. Later in the month, when the 21st Panzer and Panzer Lehr Divisions were transferred to Normandy, Eisenhower received word immediately, just as he had been informed of the 91st Air Landing Division's arrival near Carentan.

At the same time, Hitler and OKW continued to be kept totally confused and misinformed by their intelligence services, particularly by FHW. Colonel Alexis von Roenne was given regular estimates of Allied troop strength by his specialists—as head of FHW, he had several under his command—and proceeded to change every one of these estimates and updates to suit his own ends. With the help of his assistant, Colonel Lothar Metz, von Roenne inflated each of the reports he was given for evaluation. Only after he had doctored the figures on Allied forces in Britain did he pass them on to Hitler.

And von Roenne had become an expert on inflating and exaggerating numbers and estimates, as well as in making his inflated numbers believable. Since he had been changing the numbers of the Overload survey for the past several months, no one suspected that the reports he submitted contained anything out of the ordinary. His secret accumulation of fictitious divisions and regiments had gone on all throughout the early part of 1944, subtly and steadily.

One of the many deceptions performed by von Roenne took place in mid-May, when he received word about a U.S. Eighth Army Corps. He immediately mentioned the Eighth Army Corps in his situation report, and went on to say that the unit was probably in the Folkstone area— on the Kentish coast, just across the Straits of Dover from the Pas de Calais. He also made it seem as though it was almost ready to become operational, and likely would be one of the units in the initial Invasion. While the U.S. Eighth Army Corps actually did exist, it was not made operational until 15 June, over a week after D-Day, and most of its component units were not based anywhere near Folkstone. This was the type of deception that was being delivered to Hitler and OKW—making it seem as though Allied units were massing in southeast England for a massive assault on Calais by means of lies, half-truths, and distortions.

By 1 June, the fictional army that von Roenne had created was almost twice as large as all the Allied forces in the British Isles. A total of forty-seven divisions were stationed in the British Isles: twenty Americans, twenty-three British and Canadian, two Commonwealth, one French, and one Polish division. But von Roenne's figures stood at eighty-nine divisions: twenty-two American; fifty-seven Allied (British, Canadian, French, and Polish), and an additional ten armored and airborne divisions—forty-two more divisions than actually existed.[11] He had built an entire army out of guile, distortion, and exaggeration. And Hitler accepted all of von Roenne's divisions, all eighty-nine of them. And if Hitler believed that eighty-nine Allied divisions were based in England, poised to attack, what else could OKW do but follow suit?

These figures provided the evidence Hitler needed to reinforce his idea about the location of the coming Invasion—eighty-nine divisions were more than enough to stage two separate landings on the French coast. By the end of May, Hitler's views regarding the Allies and their plans were that Calais would be the site for the main Invasions, and that secondary, or diversionary, landings would come ashore either at Normandy or Brittany. This belief was almost entirely the work of von Roenne. Quicksilver and FUSAG may have been thought up by Allied deception committees, but von Roenne's misinformation made the deception real, at least in the mind of Adolf Hitler. Von Roenne filled the empty tent cities of FUSAG with troops from his own imagination.

General Eisenhower had an idea of his own to help keep the Germans in the dark. He asked Prime Minister Churchill to continue the ban on foreign diplomatic staff to communicate with their governments, even after the landings had taken place. Foreign embassy staff were already prohibited from sending any sort of information out of Britain via diplomatic pouch—a security measure to prevent any word pertaining to Overlord from leaking out. But Eisenhower was concerned "that the lifting of the ban would indicate to the enemy that our main effort has been launched."[12] In other words, lifting the ban would indicate that the Normandy landings were the primary Invasion, and that there would be no secondary or diversionary landings.

Churchill agreed with Eisenhower's assessment and kept the ban in force. But the governments that were affected by the ban, including the Belgians, Dutch, and Poles, were not happy about it, and protested that they felt that they had been reduced to secondary allies by the British and Americans. Churchill was informed of this protest, but decided that it was better to offend these governments than to risk the security of Overlord. Eisenhower and SHAEF agreed. "If the Germans learn that we have shot our wad," Captain Butcher pointed out, "they will be able to collect their reserves and concentrate them against our beachhead, and this is just what we don't want."[13]

The Allied air offensive was also employed to give a false impression. During the last weeks in May and the first days in June, more than twice as many bombing sorties were flown against targets in the Pas de Calais area than against Normandy—in excess of 10,000 sorties against Calais; just over 5,000 against Normandy. But the attacks in Calais were not solely for the purpose of misleading the Germans concerning the destination of Overlord. Calais was also the launching site for the V-1 flying bombs, and the nearness of Calais to England, such a prominent factor of Overlord, also made it the most convenient location for launching the pilotless Doodlebugs against London. Sorties against the V-1 launching ramps, which were known as "Noball missions," went on right through D-Day, and increased after the flying bomb campaign against London actually began in mid-June.

German agents in the field unwittingly played their own role in misleading German intelligence. These were not anti-Nazis in league with Colonel von Roenne or Admiral Canaris, but well-meaning operators— and sometimes well-meaning amateurs—who passed along genuine-sounding information that they had heard. Walter Schellenberg continued to be plagued by the same array of conflicting reports regarding where and, especially, when the Invasion would take place.

Some of the reports received by SD Headquarters included: "No invasion is to be expected in the near future." "There will be an attack in the Pas de Calais at the end of May." "The assault will come in July between Dunkerque and Dieppe." "Many parachutists will be dropped on northern France beginning May 20.""The invasion will come in July in the Pas de Calais." "The invasion will take place as soon as weather conditions permit."[14]

A few of these reports were rejected out of hand: "The Allies will land in Denmark before June 18"; "The Allies have decided to call off the invasion", "Technical difficulties have made the invasion impossible for the time being," "Belgium will be invaded between May 15 and May 22."[15]

There were reports from the field that did indicate Normandy, and were fairly accurate in their assessment of Allied plans. A few days before D-Day, an officer in British naval intelligence reported to a gathering of the Cabinet Committee in London that a Czech agent in Lisbon had learned the time and the place of the Invasion. This agent, an employee of the SD, advised his superiors that the landings would definitely take place between 4 June and 7 June because of the tides (the SD had already been told this), that airborne forces would be employed to secure the flanks of the Invasion, and would probably be dropped near the Orne River in the east and on the Cotentin Peninsula in the west (the British 6th Airborne Division would land in the Orne River/Caen Canal area, and the U.S. 82nd and 101st Airborne Divisions would parachute into the southern end of the Cotentin Peninsula during the night of 5/6 June) and that the Invasion itself would take place in Normandy, in the vicinity of Ouistreham (Ouistreham was situated on the eastern extremity of

Sword Beach). Everyone who heard the report was startled by its accuracy, and could only hope that no one in German intelligence would pay any attention to it.

The Cabinet Committee was granted its wish—no one in German intelligence took note of the revelation, for several reasons. The main cause for ignoring this perceptive piece of information was that there was no overwhelming evidence that pointed to Normandy, only this isolated report, along with a series of similar unrelated reports. Hitler had concluded that the beaches of the Calvados coast might be the site for an Allied invasion, but there was no clear-cut indication that this would be *the* attack, the *grossinvasion* that everyone had been fearing for nearly a year. Another consideration as to why the Normandy report was ignored is the Canaris Effect: Because of what Admiral Canaris had done to mislead Hitler and OKW during his tenure as chief of the Abwehr, Hitler was not inclined to believe any intelligence report at this stage.

Colonel von Roenne played a more immediate role in this deception. If von Roenne had not inflated the numbers that he had been given for evaluation, it would have been fairly easy to conclude that the Allies only had the manpower to attempt one landing along the French coast—either Calais or Normandy, but not both places. Without von Roenne's made-up divisions, Quicksilver almost certainly would not have succeeded as impressively as it did, and may not have succeeded at all. Forced to choose between Calais and Normandy, and without von Roenne's reinforcing Quicksilver's imaginary threat against the Pas de Calais, Hitler stood an excellent chance of determining that FUSAG was nothing more than an intricate fake, and that the troops in southern and southwestern England were bound for the beaches of Normandy.

One Allied design that succeeded without any help from either Admiral Canaris or Colonel von Roenne was the plan to keep the artificial Mulberry harbors a secret. Allied planners had known that they would need the use of a port, with all of its facilities, to keep the Invasion forces supplied once they had secured the beaches. From their experiences at Dieppe, they also realized that capturing a port would not be practical: First, it would take too long, and second, the enemy would destroy the very facilities—docks, cranes, and equipment—they needed to load and unload supply ships.

When Admiral Lord Louis Mountbatten first suggested the idea of taking a port over to France along with the invading forces, everyone thought he was trying to be funny. The idea of a portable harbor seemed so fantastic that no one believed that it might be practical—which is one item that helped to keep Mulberry safe from the SD.

Sections of the prefabricated Mulberry ports were built in various places throughout Britain. There were to be two separate ports: one for the British beaches and one for the American sector. Each would be the size of a major port—they are generally compared with the size of Dover harbor—and would be made up of huge concrete breakwaters as well as sunken ships (which were code-named Gooseberries). Twenty thousand men worked on hundreds of these concrete caissons, called Phoenixes, seven days per week in several locations, including the Barking marshes, east of London; the Channel waters off Selsey Bill, on the Sussex coast; and North Wales. Although none of the residents of these places were quite sure what to make of these strange concrete megaliths, they were so big—each of the caissons weighed 6,000 tons and stood as tall as a six-story building—that no one could miss them or resist talking about them. In Conway, North Wales, the residents speculated about what went on in "the jam factory," as they called the construction site for the Mulberry pier.

No one could stop local gossip; everyone at SHAEF hoped that none of it would be picked up by the wrong pair of ears. In the spring of 1944, it seemed that this was exactly what had happened. SHAEF received a very bad scare from William Joyce, "Lord Haw-Haw," the British fascist who had defected to Berlin and made radio broadcasts for Dr. Josef Goebbels' Propaganda Ministry.

On 21 April 1944, Joyce directed his remarks at the sailors and Seabees on the Selsey Bill Phoenixes: "We know exactly what you intend to do with those concrete units." His message became more ominous as he went on. "You think you are going to sink them off the coasts in the assault. Well, we're going to help you, boys. We'll save you the trouble. When you come to get under way, we're going to sink them for you." From what Joyce had said, it looked as though German intelligence had discovered the Mulberries, as well as their role in Overlord. "Every Seabee took that broadcast practically as his obituary notice," wrote an officer assigned to the project.[16] SHAEF intelligence decided to find out exactly how much the Germans really knew.

During the next few weeks, Ultra listened for any other radio messages that might allude to the artificial port. But even though virtually all German signal traffic was monitored, no mention of Mulberry or anything resembling it was ever detected. The probable source of information for Joyce's panic broadcast was the Swedish naval attaché in London, Count J. G. Oxenstjerna, who had heard talk that some very large floating concrete structures were built off the Sussex coast. The attaché mentioned this information, imprecise as it was, to a German agent in Stockholm, the veteran Karl-Heinz Kraemer. The Stockholm contact passed the word along to Berlin, and the Propaganda Ministry decided to use the story to stir up as much trouble as possible with SHAEF. Joyce's broadcast certainly did stir up trouble, at least temporarily, and the fright he gave was a bad one. But SHAEF reached the conclusion that the broadcast had only been a shot in the dark, and the fear soon died down.

But at some point in time, several of the Mulberry Phoenixes apparently had been sighted by Luftwaffe reconnaissance aircraft. Images of the huge caissons turned up on a photographic plate—they were as obvious to observers in the air as they were from the ground—and investigators tried to determine exactly what the things were. It was decided that they must be prefabricated parts for a dock, but this was as close as anyone came to puzzling out a solution. Analysts, possibly from naval intelligence, reached the conclusion that the mysterious objects would be used to repair facilities of a port that had been damaged in the upcoming Invasion. In other words, the Germans did discover Mulberry and, although they did guess that the Phoenixes had something to do with port facilities, they were not able to figure out their real purpose.

If Mulberry's true function had been discovered, it would have been another indication that Normandy was Overlord's intended objective. Had German intelligence known that the Allies were building artificial harbors to support the Invasion during its early phases, they also would have understood that the landings were not going to take place anywhere close to a port—which would have ruled out Calais, Boulogne, and Le Havre. Also, the coast of the Pas de Calais was not suitable for an artificial port. The only feasible place for the Mulberry harbors on the Channel coast was Normandy.

By not determining the secret of the Mulberries, the Germans lost an enormous opportunity, and the Allies were given a priceless piece of luck. But the Germans simply could not grasp the concept of Mulberry—a portable, prefabricated harbor that could be moved from England to the coast of France. It was such an unbelievable idea that it never occurred to anyone—not to Walter Schellenberg or the SD, or anyone in naval intelligence, and certainly not to Hitler or any of his generals. And Lord Haw Haw's broadcast made a bigger impact in England than in Berlin. It was too imprecise to be of any value. Besides, OKW was even less inclined to believe the Propaganda Ministry than its Intelligence Services.

Another factor that made SHAEF apprehensive concerning to the success of Overlord was the weather. All of SHAEF's plans depended upon good weather, and upon the accurate forecasting of it. And there was no way by which it could be kept secret from the Germans—no deception plan could be *that* clever.

As it happened, the weather served as an ally to the Germans and German intelligence, because it helped to pinpoint the exact day of Overlord. Both naval intelligence and the SD were aware that the Invasion would have to be postponed until the middle of June if storms made landing on 5 June, 6 June, or 7 June impossible; they realized that the Allies would not be able to come ashore on 9 June, for instance, because the tides would not be right.

General Eisenhower and SHAEF realized it, as well, and were not happy about being so dependent upon the elements. "There will be all sorts of chaos and disappointment if it [D-Day] had to be postponed two or three weeks," wrote General Eisenhower's naval aide.[17] But a postponement would cause more chaos than disappointment. By 1 June, all the assault troops had been sealed. Officers, as well as many of the noncommissioned officers, had been briefed about their objectives. If the Invasion had to be pushed back two weeks, it was inevitable that men who had information about Overlord and its objectives would be leaving their encampments—with or, most likely, without orders. The urge to talk about what they knew would be too great for some of them to resist. And the longer the postponement, the greater the risk to security.

The weather requirements for Overlord had already been defined. The wind at the landing beaches would have to be less than 15 miles per hour; visibility in the Channel would have to be at least 3 nautical miles; and the ceiling could not be lower than 3,000 feet. No one at SHAEF, not to mention any of the commanders who would be taking part in the Invasion, was certain if these requirements were realistic—the Channel had a mind of its own, they knew, and did not pay much attention to the best laid plans of generals or admirals.

Until the last weekend in May, it looked as though the god of storms had every intention of complying with these requirements. The winds along the Channel coast had been gentle, the Channel itself had been reasonably calm, and the sky had remained blue and cloudless. German officers, including Feldmarschall Erwin Rommel, wondered why the Allies had not launched their long-threatened Invasion in May—they certainly had the weather for it. But Rommel was not entirely convinced that the enemy would come when the weather was calm and clear, in other words, when they were expected.

On 17 May, during one of his inspection trips, Rommel told the men of a unit in the Cotentin Peninsula not necessarily to expect the enemy during the day, or in good weather. "They would have to be prepared for the enemy to come with clouds and storm, and after midnight."[18] The feldmarschall was still fence-sitting: He was opposed to Hitler and his government, but he was also a serving German officer and the commander of Army Group B.

But all of the many and infinitely complex components of Overlord had not been ready in May, good weather or not. Not until the very end of the month, on 29 May, did General Eisenhower send the message that confirmed the definite date of D-Day. Using the code name Halcyon for Y-Day—which was 1 June, the day on which Overlord was formally declared ready and fully prepared—Eisenhower sent the message, "Halcyon plus four," across to Army Chief of Staff George C. Marshall in Washington, D.C. It meant that Overlord was still planned for 5 June.

The signal seemed a good omen—halcyon being a synonym for calm and quiet, especially regarding the sea. In Greek mythology, the halcyon bird, or kingfisher, was able to calm the seas after the winter solstice. But at the same time that Eisenhower's message was being sent to the United States, a weather reconnaissance aircraft over Newfoundland was reporting bad news, for SHAEF and for Halcyon. The weather was beginning to make a change for the worse, the crew reported; a pronounced low pressure system over the Atlantic was deepening and moving east. An Atlantic storm was headed for the British Isles and northern France, and should arrive by the end of the week. By 5 June, rain and high winds were expected to be buffeting the Channel, providing extremely rough conditions just in time for D-Day.

A weather syndicate made up of meteorologists from the army and air force of both Britain and the United States, had been given the delicate job of trying to forecast Channel weather. This syndicate, headed by Group Captain J. Stagg, RAF, a Scot with an ironic sense of humor, christened the Atlantic depression L5. The group kept a very close watch on L5, not always agreeing on what they were seeing, and tried to come up with a prediction of the storm's progress.

Although the members of the weather syndicate could not agree on the storm's future course, Group Captain Stagg and his American counterpart, Army Air Force Colonel P. N. Yates, arrived at the conclusion that the Channel coast was due for a period of foul weather. By Thursday, 1 June, they were certain: The weather for 5 June and 6 June appeared to be, in Stagg's words, "potentially full of menace." [19]

It was Stagg's unpleasant duty to report this conclusion to General Eisenhower at Southwick House, SHAEF's headquarters north of Portsmouth. On the evening of 2 June, Stagg gave his forecast to Eisenhower and his commanders, Admiral Sir Bertram Ramsay, Air Chief Marshal Sir Trafford Leigh-Mallory, and General Sir Bernard Montgomery.

It was not encouraging news: Expect rain and gale force winds on June 5 through June 7. Stagg and Colonel Yates wondered if this dismal forecast might cause a postponement of D-Day. But General Harold R. Bull, SHAEF operations officer, left the conference to inform them that there would be no change in plan regarding Overlord for the next forty-eight hours.

On the other side of the Channel, German meteorologists were also following the track of the storm. The Luftwaffe's weather officers reached the same basic conclusion as Stagg and Yates: Stormy weather and heavy seas could be expected in the English Channel during the coming tidal period. This would almost certainly preclude an invasion during the first week of June, unless the enemy decided to reverse his usual practice of landing only during perfect weather. Or, unless the weather took a sudden and dramatic turn for the better.

Feldmarschall Rommel decided to use the weather to his advantage. He was still carrying on a running debate with Hitler over the control of all armored units in northern France; Rommel had three of the seven Panzer divisions under his direct control, but Hitler would not give up his hold on the remaining four. All of his arguing and protesting had been done via the radio—which Ultra followed with rapt interest—and had accomplished exactly nothing. Rommel had wanted to go to Berchtesgaden to present his case in person to Hitler. But he had not been able to leave France, not with the Invasion about to break.

If the weather was going to interfere with the Allies' plans, however, and delay the landings, that would change everything. Now, he would be able to travel to Germany and meet with Hitler, and would still be able to return to France in time for the next favorable tidal period. "Rommel above all wanted to go to the *Obersalzburg* and speak with Hilter personally," Admiral Ruge, Rommel's naval aide, noted in his diary, "and to ask for the transfer to Normandy of two additional Panzer divisions, one antiaircraft corps, and one mortar brigade."[20] He had often told his adjutant, Captain Hellmuth Lang, "The last man who sees Hitler wins the game." [21]

At the point in time, the Invasion was certainly foremost in his thoughts, along with what he would say when he met Hitler. His colleagues in the Schwarze Kapelle and their plans to overthrow Hitler, must also have been on his mind especially since he had such a prominent role in those plans. But during the first days of June, he was primarily concerned with his impending eight-hour drive to Germany—because of the hazard of Allied fighters, high-ranking officers had been forbidden to go anywhere by plane.

But before he went on to Berchtesgaden, Rommel intended to go home to Herrlingen, Ulm, for a very short leave. It would be his first furlough in months, and he sorely needed a rest from the pressures he had been under since the beginning of the year. But in addition to being a brief holiday, the journey would also be a sentimental one; he wanted to be at home for his wife's birthday, which was Tuesday 6 June.

While Feldmarschall Rommel was getting ready for his trip, SHAEF sent a message that would affect both Rommel and the outcome of his journey. On 30 May, Supreme Command headquarters directed that all *messages personnels* connected with the Invasion—325 of them—be broadcast beginning 1 June. This directive was issued with some misgivings, since it was feared that such a torrent of these messages might trigger a general uprising among resistance units—which would be fatal not only to the members of these units but to the security of Overlord, as well.

But the many and various resistance groups had to be put on alert, and there was no other practical way of doing it. Among the communiqués to be broadcast was the first part of the Paul Verlaine passage from "Chanson d'Automne": *"Les sanglots longs / Des violins / De l'automne."* This signal was a general alert and only signified that the Invasion was imminent.

As had been ordered, the BBC began sending the alerts on 1 June. And as soon as they were broadcast, the messages were intercepted by German listening posts on the Continent. None of the Allied intelligence branches realized, even at this time, that Major Oscar Reile's counter intelligence team had infiltrated several resistance groups, and that the SD was capable of deciphering the coded announcements.

One of the monitoring posts was at Fifteenth Army headquarters at Turcoing, close to the Belgian border, which listened in on the BBC's broadcasts every night. Not all of the announcements made sense to the operators; some seemed to be nonsense, such as "Marie has dark brown hair," or "The apples are ready to be picked." But they knew the Verlaine passage and what it meant, and had been instructed to listen very, very closely for it.

On the night of 1 June, Sgt. Walter Reichling was on duty in the radio hut at Turcoing. Just after 9 P.M. he began recording the BBC's messages—every one of them—so as not to miss the Verlaine passage. The very first message read by the announcer was the long-awaited signal: *"Les sanglots longs des violins de l'automne."* When he heard it, Sergeant Reichling held his breath and put his hands to his earphones. The announcer repeated the message, speaking more slowly the second time: *"Les sanglots des violins de l'automne."*

Reichling ran out of the building and across to the quarters of Lt. Colonel Hellmuth Meyer, Fifteenth Army's intelligence officer. Colonel Meyer returned to the radio hut with Reichling, and listened to the recording with him. It was a relief to hear it; after all this time, the first part of the Verlaine passage finally had been broadcast.

Colonel Meyer telephoned the news to Fifteenth Army's chief of staff, Major General Rudolf Hofmann. "The first message has come," Meyer said. "Now, something is going to happen."

"Are you absolutely sure?" Hofmann wanted to know.

"We recorded it," Meyer assured him.[22]

Major Oscar Reile also intercepted the BBC's *"Les sanglots longs"* alert. He apparently made the interception before anyone else, having heard the message several times between 1:30 P.M. and 2:30 P.M. on 1 June. [23] Reile's first instinct was to inform the Intelligence Services. By teletype, he relayed the news to von Rundstedt's intelligence officer, Colonel Wilhelm Meyer-Detring, as well as to the head of FHW, Colonel Alexis von Roenne. Notifying Colonel von Roenne, Reile must have thought, would be the equivalent of putting all forces in northern France on alert, including Rommel and Army Group B. Von Roenne had the most important military intelligence post in the West; Reile concluded that the head of FHW would know exactly what to do with such a vital piece of information.

The first part of the Verlaine passage was not the most important part, however. It only served to alert the Germans that the second line of the poem would be broadcast soon, possibly in a matter of days. That passage, *"Blessent mon coeur d'une langeur monotone,"* would indicate that the Invasion would take place within forty-eight hours. When it was broadcast, both Major Reile and Colonel Meyer would be waiting to intercept it.

On the other side of the Channel, no one at SHAEF knew anything at all about Meyer or Reile or their activities. No one, not General Eisenhower or any of the intelligence groups, had any idea that the enemy had been alerted, or that the Germans had the means of determining the exact day that Overlord would be coming ashore on the French beaches.

NOTES

1. Panter-Downes, p. 322.
2. Cawthon, p. 52.
3. Ibid.
4. Author interview.
5. Miller, *Nothing Less Than Victory*, p. 108.
6. Ibid., p. 124.
7. Osmont, pp. 34–35.
8. Ibid., p. 35.
9. Ibid., p. 39.
10. Butcher, p. 552.
11. National Archives Record Group 165, and Kahn, p. 496.
12. Butcher, p. 552.
13. Ibid.
14. Perrault, p. 208.
15. Ibid.
16. Ellsberg, p. 155.
17. Butcher, p. 553.
18. Ruge, p. 162.
19. Stagg, pp. 87–88.
20. Ruge, p. 162.
21. Ryan, p. 30.
22. Ibid., p. 33.
23. Farago, *Game of the Foxes*, p. 799. Although Farago dismisses Ryan's contention that Colonel Meyer intercepted the BBC broadcast, Ryan was given Meyer's story by Meyer himself in the late 1950s. The probability is that both Meyer and Major Reile intercepted the broadcast at different times on 1 June.

NINE

"...D'Une Langeur Monotone"

Captain Charles Cawthon and the rest of the U.S. 29th Infantry Division left their sealed marshalling area on Saturday, 3 June. Cawthon remembers that the ride to the docks was a short one. From the dock, he and the others in his unit were ferried out to the transport *Thomas Jefferson*, which would take them across the Channel to the coast of Normandy. "It was like loading for a training exercise, except for the mountains of equipment," Cawthon said.[1] And except for the knot in the pit of his stomach.

Actually, Cawthon was better off than any of the enlisted men in his unit—or worse off, depending upon a person's point of view—because he knew that this was going to be the real thing and not just another training exercise. Most of the men who were clambering aboard troopships throughout Britain had no idea where they were headed.

Operation Overlord and the thousands of men, the five thousand ships, and untold tons of equipment that were part of the almost unimaginably vast undertaking, were ready to depart for the enemy-held Continent. The landings were scheduled for dawn on Monday, 5 June. The only thing that could stop it at this stage was the weather.

To Group Captain Stagg, the head of SHAEF's meteorological syndicate, it looked as though the weather was going to do just that. He and his American colleague, Colonel Yates, had been watching the development of the depression labeled L5 and were not feeling very encouraged about its progress. By 3 June, while Captain Cawthon and thousands of other soldiers were boarding their transports for the cross-Channel journey, Stagg had reached the conclusion that the weather on 5 June, as well as for the following two days, would not be suitable for a landing on the French coast. The forecast he had decided upon was essentially the same prediction he had given before—rain, heavy overcast, and gale force winds.

Stagg had given his verbal weather report to General Eisenhower and his staff at 10:15 P.M. that Saturday. He was ordered to return to Southwick House at 4:15 A.M. on Sunday to give an update—hopefully an improvement. But on Sunday morning, Stagg could offer neither encouragement nor any improvement. He had forecast ten-tenths cloud, three thousand feet thick, along with limited visibility and Force 5 winds. Now, Stagg told his anxious audience that "since the last meeting no development had occurred which allowed any substantial change in the forecast."[2]

Admiral Ramsay said that he was prepared to go ahead with the operation, in spite of the weather, and General Montgomery was against any delay. But air chief marshals Leigh-Mallory and Tedder, speaking for the air force, agreed that they could not carry out their pre-Invasion bombing offensive in such weather. Bombing through 3,000 feet of solid cloud was impossible.

That consensus settled the postponement question for General Eisenhower. In spite of the fact that the navy and the army were willing to go ahead with the operation, there could be no Invasion without air cover. Without air support, Eisenhower realized that he had no choice but to postpone. He ordered his chief of staff, General Walter Bedell Smith, to issue the signal to delay Overlord. Aboard the Mulberries off Selsey Bill, the code word Bowsprit—meaning that the Invasion had been pushed back for twenty-four hours—came over from Portsmouth. Similar coded signals were sent to every unit in Britain.

"Here was the whole business completely suspended," Group Captain Stagg remarked.[3] All the troops in all the ships throughout the British Isles, tense and prepared to launch the long-anticipated landings, were given the order to stand down. Hundreds of ships had already put to sea, including the old merchant vessels that were to be sunk and used as part of the Mulberry breakwater as well as the warships of the bombardment force. A unit of minesweepers did not get the recall order until the ships were only 35 miles from the Normandy coast. They were not spotted by enemy observers in the predawn murk, and went undetected by German radar.

A troop convoy carrying units of the U.S. 4th Infantry Division did not receive the signal at all. The 138 ships were sailing in broad daylight, during mid-morning, making for Utah Beach, and did not respond to any radio messages. A Walrus observation plane finally located the convoy and, after a frantic try, managed to drop a written message on the flagship. (The first note had missed the ship and sunk into the Channel.)

The commander immediately reversed course, and the convoy began its journey back to Weymouth.

When Lieutenant James Murphy got the word that D-Day had been postponed, he knew exactly what had happened: The Germans had somehow found out that they were coming, and the Invasion had to be called off. He had always been afraid that they would find out. No reason had been given for the recall, but Murphy did not need anyone to give him one. Maybe somebody had talked; maybe a German spy managed to get hold of "the secret D-Day plans;" or possibly they had just been able to figure things out for themselves. There was certainly enough evidence that the Invasion was not very far off. "Everything in southern England—every road, every street sign, every little town and village—had something to do with the Invasion."[4] But whatever happened, something had tipped them off. He only hoped that his ship was not torpedoed by E-boats before they could return to port.

General Eisenhower and his commanders were not quite as alarmed or pessimistic as Lieutenant Murphy, but the atmosphere at Southwick House was certainly tense and anxious on the morning of 4 June. Everyone might have felt better about the situation if they had known that the wind and rain were also hindering the Germans. The storm may have been preventing the Allies from unleashing Overlord, but it was also keeping the Germans from finding out as much about Allied preparations as they wanted and needed.

Admiral Ruge complained, "On June 4 the weather changed to rain and stormy westerlies."[5] The weather stopped Luftwaffe reconnaissance flights over southern England even more effectively than Allied fighters. And the E-boats that Lieutenant Murphy dreaded were bottled up in port—they could not negotiate the six-foot waves in the Channel.

Radio reconnaissance units on the Continent maintained their 24-hour watch, however. General Hans Speidel, Rommel's chief of staff, mentioned that, "Code messages were intercepted naming several different dates" for the Invasion "and then reporting postponement of the date of the invasion."[6] Communications Reconnaissance Regiment 5 remained the best source of intelligence, and was not dependent upon fair weather to perform its job.

Colonel Alexis von Roenne was doing his best to keep Hitler and his generals as uninformed as possible, if not altogether misinformed, during the first days of June. As the head of FHW, it was his job to compile regular situation reports for Hitler and OKW. His report dated Sunday, 5 June, mentioned only that the Invasion might come at any time between 5 June and 15 June—which was hardly a blockbuster news bulletin. He said nothing at all about Allied preparations in Britain, although he did say that the enemy's forces had reached the point where they were ready to launch their invasion—another bit of common knowledge. This was deception of omission rather than commission: Von Roenne presented his summary of enemy intentions, which was one of his duties, but gave away absolutely no useful information. Neither Hitler, nor Walter Schellenberg, nor anyone else learned very much about Allied preparations from reading his report.

A typist practicing her technique at the Associated Press (AP) offices in London gave everyone on both sides of the Channel a start. She typed the bulletin "URGENT PRESS ASSOCIATED NYK FLASH EISENHOWER'S HQ ANNOUNCES ALLIED LANDINGS IN FRANCE." It was meant to be nothing more than a keyboard drill, but the exercise was accidentally sent as a genuine news release. The Associated Press retracted the bulletin a few minutes after it had been sent, but it already had been picked up by overseas news services. Both Radio Moscow and Radio Berlin repeated the message.

German intelligence, including Lieutenant Colonel Hellmuth Meyer at Fifteenth Army intelligence, also picked up the AP release. Colonel Meyer correctly concluded that the signal had been either a mistake or a ruse, since there had been no other word from any other source.

SHAEF headquarters shrugged it off. Eisenhower was told about it when he woke up; he had been at Southwick House at 4:15 A.M. for his weather meeting with Group Captain Stagg. His naval aide, Captain Butcher, made light of the incident, noting on 4 June, "The good old AP last night made the oddest bloomer."[7] The premature D-Day announcement did not make a ripple compared with Lord Haw Haw's broadcast concerning the Mulberries off Selsey Bill.

Gwyn Evans, the SD agent code-named Druid, was trying to send something a good deal more substantial than an erroneous report. He was still touring England with his string quartet, giving performances of pop classics at army bases, and still collecting information about the First U.S. Army Group for the SD. Evans had been able to report on some British and American units that he had seen near the south coast—genuine regiments, not part of the Quicksilver deception. He was then asked to explore eastern and northern England to see what he could find there.

Evans arranged a tour of northern England, in the area of Newcastle and York, as well as in Scotland. His string ensemble performed their pop repertoire in training camps and for the crews of ordnance and supply depots; after all this time, they were no more enthusiastic about playing Gilbert and Sullivan overtures than they had been when they first started touring.

The quartet did not perform for any combat units, however, for the simple reason that there were no combat units in the north or in Scotland. Compared with southeastern England, there was nothing at all—certainly no Invasion troops or elements of FUSAG. Evans kept his eyes and ears open, as he had been instructed, and sent word to his contact in Lisbon: He had seen no combat troops in the north. His next job would be to arrange a similar tour of Kent, Sussex, and the southeast.

The German Intelligence Services were about to be played false once again, deprived of vital information that might have proved critical. This time, however, neither Admiral Canaris nor Colonel von Roenne, nor any member of the Schwarze Kapelle, would have anything to do with it. The party involved would be the German meteorological service, which lost several of its Atlantic weather stations, including one in Greenland, earlier in the war. Because they did not have as extensive a network as the British or the Americans, German weather forecasters often were not able to predict as accurately as the Allies.

At about midday on 4 June, Group Captain Stagg examined updated information concerning the various fronts and depressions over the Atlantic. For the first time in days, he was encouraged by what he saw. His charts showed that a cold front was approaching the Channel, followed by a depression that was off Newfoundland at that moment. In between, he saw an "interlude" that would arrive late on Monday, and continue through Tuesday and probably into Wednesday. That interlude indicated that the weather would improve, probably just long enough to allow the paratroops and amphibious assaults of Overlord to land.

That evening, at 9:30, Stagg and Colonel Yates were at Southwick House to report this change. At that hour, it was still raining heavily with a wind of about Force 4. After giving his revised forecast—which was that the conditions on Tuesday and Wednesday would be improved, but by no means ideal—Eisenhower and the other commanders questioned Stagg concerning cloud cover, visibility, and other details. Admiral Ramsay reminded everyone present that he would have to alert his forces within the next half-hour if Overlord was intended to proceed on Tuesday, 6 June. "But," he warned, "if they do restart and have to be canceled again, there can be no question of continuing on Wednesday."[8]

Following a discussion about the effectiveness of bombing through cloud, led by air chief marshals Leigh-Mallory and Tedder, Eisenhower turned to Montgomery and asked if he saw any reason why Overlord should not go on Tuesday? Montgomery's immediate reply was, "I would say—go"[9]

Some further discussion followed, but the decision whether to send Overlord on Tuesday or to postpone was Eisenhower's. He weighed all the possibilities and concluded, "I am quite positive we must give the order. . . . I don't like it, but there it is. . . . I don't see how we can possibly do anything else."[10]

Another weather meeting was held at 4:15 A.M. on Monday, 5 June, to confirm the weather forecast, as well as the "go" decision, of the night before. Stagg told Eisenhower, Montgomery, and the others that "he was even more confident than he had been on the previous night that the improved quieter interlude would indeed come along." With that pronouncement, Stagg remembered that "the joy on the faces of the Supreme Commander and his commanders, after the deep gloom of the preceding days, was a marvel to behold."[11]

Eisenhower's naval aide, Captain Butcher, wrote in his diary on 5 June, "D-Day is now almost irrevocably set for tomorrow morning, about 6:40." The code signal "Halcyon plus 5" was sent to all commands—D-Day would be 6 June.

There was some fear that the Germans would also detect the calm interlude, which might allow them to conclude that the Invasion would come on Tuesday. But this apprehension had absolutely no justification. Because of inherent deficiencies in their network, the German weather had not been able to spot the break in the weather, and had no idea that the storm would dissipate on Tuesday. Ultra decrypts revealed that Luftwaffe meteorologists were predicting that the wind, rain, and poor visibility would extend through the current tidal period.

Where Eisenhower had been given a priceless advantage by the Allied weather services, the SD had been deprived of the same information by their own meteorological bureau. Knowledge that a fair weather system was approaching might have allowed the SD to guess the date of the Invasion—half of the vital where and when puzzle.

But the German intelligence agencies were about to be given another invaluable clue. Now that Overlord was on again, the resistance had to be alerted. The BBC broadcast the prearranged signal: *"Blessent mon coeur d'une langeur monotone."* Listening posts in France picked up the second part of the Verlaine poem, just as they had done with the first part. And just as German intelligence knew that the first half of the fragment, *"Les sanglots longs des violins de l'automne,"* was a general alert for the resistance, they also knew that the second half indicated that the Invasion would be taking place within forty-eight hours.

The signal was apparently sent three times—on 3 June and 4 June to alert the resistance that the Invasion was scheduled for Monday, 5 June, and again on 5 June, after the landings had been postponed and rescheduled. It was received in the office of General Alfred Jodl at OKW headquarters, Berchtesgaden, on 4 June; the intercept had been sent by Major Oscar Reile. The diary of Fifteenth Army records that the signal was logged in at 2115 hours (9:15 P.M.) on 5 June—*"Zweite Hälfte des Spruches 'Blessent mon coeur d'une longeur [sic] monotone' wird durch Nast abgehört*—and goes on to report that it means "Expect Invasion within forty-eight hours, starting 0000 June 6."[12]

In both cases, the message was also sent to von Rundstedt's headquarters at St. Germain-en-Laye, outside Paris, as well as to Colonel von

Roenne's office in Zossen. Major Reile gave German intelligence, as well as the Wehrmacht, the date of the invasion. Because of the role that the tides would play in the amphibious assault, the German defenders knew *exactly* when the Allies would begin landing their first wave—at about 6:30 on the morning of 6 June.

At OKW headquarters, General Jodl's intelligence officer simply noted the message and filed it away. Apparently, he assumed that the signal would be distributed by von Rundstedt to his forces in France, and that FHW would send it to all the intelligence services. This was, at least, a valid assumption. As commander of all forces in the West, von Rundstedt was responsible for alerting all of his unit and, as head of FHW, Colonel von Roenne should have confirmed the signal and alerted all intelligence agencies.

Colonel Wilhelm Meyer-Detring, von Rundstedt's intelligence officer, *did* send the alert. He notified Fifteenth Army; his message was recorded in the log at 9:15 P.M. Lieutenant Colonel Hellmuth Meyer personally alerted Fifteenth Army's commander, General Hans von Salmuth, while the general was in the middle of a bridge game. "The message, the second part," Meyer burst in, "it's here." There was no need to mention which message—von Salmuth knew exactly what Meyer was talking about.[13]

The general ordered Fifteenth Army to go on full alert, and then returned to his card game. He told his three bridge partners, "I'm too old a bunny to get too excited about this"—a minor masterpiece of sangfroid in any situation.[14]

All units of Fifteenth Army went on alert at about 10:15 P.M. on 5 June. It was logical for Colonel Meyer-Detring to give Fifteenth Army the warning, and not Seventh Army. Fifteenth Army was defending the Pas de Calais, which was where Overlord was expected to come ashore. For months, Meyer-Detring—along with every other German intelligence officer in France—had been kept informed of the build-up of First U.S. Army Group by Double-Cross agents, including Dusko Popov (agent Tricycle) and Roman Garby-Czerniawski (Brutus). Thanks to agent Tricycle, intelligence even had FUSAG's complete order of battle, including the 3rd Army, 3rd Army Corps, and twenty-three large formations. All of these reports had been confirmed by FHW. And all those forces attached to FUSAG, or Armeegruppe Patton, were directly across the Channel from Calais. No one had the slightest idea that FUSAG was nothing more than an illusion, or that Colonel von Roenne was actively working for the overthrow of Hitler and his government by the Allies.

Seventh Army, on the other hand, was stationed in Normandy. Evidently, no one at von Rundstedt's headquarters seriously believed that Normandy would be the site of the Invasion. All evidence, as collected by foreign agents and confirmed by FHW, pointed away from Normandy and directly at Calais. In fact, soldiers serving with Fifteenth Army joked that Normandy and the Calvados coast was a good place to go for a rest. Some sort of diversionary attack might come ashore on the Norman beaches, but the real assault would be landing at Calais.

After the Invasion had taken place, and postmortems were conducted into the activities of the defenders, the question of Seventh Army and why its commander, General Friedrich Dollmann, was never notified of the Verlaine passage, has often been asked. The answer is fairly straightforward: Seventh Army was not alerted because the Invasion was thought to be bound for Calais, not Normandy.

The intelligence officer of Army Group B, Colonel Anton Staubwasser, gives his own intriguing slant on the explanation. Staubwasser had been informed of the *"Blessent mon coeur d'une langeur monotone"* signal by telephone. A staff officer at Fifteenth Army told him, and went on to advise him that units in the Pas de Calais area were being alerted independently. Unsure of what he should do—he had heard nothing at all from Colonel von Roenne—Staubwasser asked General Hans Speidel if he should put Seventh Army on alert.

General Speidel was having a dinner party for some friends, including his brother-in-law and writer Ernest Junger, who was also a friend of Rommel's. The party was "virtually a meeting of the Schwarze Kapelle in the West."[15] Ernest Junger had written a draft of an armistice that was to be presented to Britain and the United States and, according to Speidel, had done so at Rommel's request. The main topic of conversation over dinner that night was the twenty-two-page document and its contents.

Speidel listened to what Staubwasser had to say but, instead of answering his question, told him to contact von Rundstedt's headquarters. Staubwasser telephoned St. Germain-en-Laye, as ordered, and spoke with several staff officers who were on duty. In the course of these conversations, he finally received an answer to his question: One of the staff officers told him not to alert Seventh Army. This order, Staubwasser was informed, came directly from Army Group West—von Rundstedt himself. Staubwasser did as he had been ordered, and did not issue a warning to Seventh Army that the Invasion had been predicted for the following day.

Von Rundstedt simply refused to believe Staubwasser's report—or, rather, Major Reile's report—concerning the Verlaine signal. This reaction was based upon his ingrown stubbornness, as well as his deep-seated distrust of the German Intelligence Services. He was still very much under the influence of the Canaris Effect, and refused to believe *anything* he heard from intelligence, including the notion that the BBC would announce the Invasion over the radio. Also, von Rundstedt remained convinced that the landings would come in the Pas de Calais, so what was the point of alerting forces in Normandy? "The Commander in Chief West," Speidel reported, "decided that he would not alert the whole front."[16]

Colonel von Roenne was also sent a teletype from Major Reile regarding the Verlaine signal. But von Roenne did not do anything to alter the message, as he had done with so many other reports he had received. He simply made certain that it was never read by anyone else. He knew exactly what it meant, and realized its importance. He filed the message away, but he did not forget about it—he buried it.

Major Reile had certainly done his job; he sent his warnings by teletype as soon as he intercepted the Verlaine passage. But as determined as he was to alert all units in France, he was stopped by two people who were even more determined: von Roenne and Canaris. Canaris' role in this deception was indirect. By his deliberate and prolonged "inefficiency," he cast grave doubts upon the reliability and efficiency of not only the Abwehr, which had become the Abwehr/SD, but also upon all other intelligence agencies. This was the Canaris Effect.

Von Rundstedt was especially disinclined to take intelligence reports seriously, unless he had confirming information from other sources to back them up. A report that an announcement from the BBC had predicted the time of the Invasion must have struck him as another Canaris-like pipe dream.

Von Roenne, on the other hand, played a very direct, as well as extremely effective, part. Besides failing to pass Major Reile's interception along to other commands, he also convinced every intelligence officer in the West that the main Allied attack would come at Calais. He had confirmed every lie that the Allies told about FUSAG, and now the entire Wehrmacht believed them. FUSAG was as much the brainchild of Colonel von Roenne as it was the creation of the Quicksilver planners.

While the merit of Major Reile's information was being debated, several senior officers attached to Seventh Army were either preparing to leave their commands or had already left them. These officers were on their way to Rennes, in Brittany, to participate in an Invasion exercise, a *kriegsspiel*. In the exercise, which was to be conducted on huge maps, like an elaborate chess match, the enemy landings were to begin with paratroops, followed by an amphibious assault on the beaches.

Among the officers taking part in the *kriegsspiel* were several divisional commanders, including Lieutenant General Wilhelm Falley, commander of the 91st Air landing Division, and General Friedrich Dollmann, Seventh Army's commanding officer. One officer who had not yet left was General Erich Marcks, the commander of 84th Corps. Tuesday, 6 June, would be General Marcks' birthday, members of his staff were giving him a party. After the party, he would also depart for Rennes. Marcks had been assigned the role of the Allies in the exercise, a role that gave him a good deal of amusement.

General Dollmann's chief of staff, Major General Max Pemsel, did not like the idea of all these commanders leaving their units at the same time. Even though he had been assured that Normandy would not be the Invasion site, and no alert had been issued, he still felt uneasy. Pemsel was well aware of the fact that past Allied landings had taken place at daybreak; the fact that all of these officers would be away overnight added to his anxieties. He issued this order by teletype: "Divisional commanders and senior officers participating in the *kriegsspiel* are requested not to leave for Rennes before dawn on 6 June."[17] If the Verlaine signal had been taken seriously, the *kriegsspiel* would have been canceled, and all of the commanders would have been ordered to return to their units.

The commander of Army Group B, Feldmarschall Erwin Rommel, was already in Germany. He had left his headquarters at La Roche-Guyon at about 7 A.M. on Sunday, 4 June, and had been driven to his home in Herrlingen. Rommel knew absolutely nothing about the Verlaine code message. During his drive through France and Germany, his main thoughts were of his wife's birthday on Tuesday, 6 June, and his planned meeting with Hitler.

Rommel was tired, tense, and past due for some home leave. The birthday of his wife, Lucie Maria, gave him the perfect excuse to get away from Army Group B and everything that went with it; he was bringing her a pair of hand-made French shoes as a present. But while he was in Germany, Rommel also was determined to visit Hitler at Berchtesgaden to lobby for more reinforcements for Normandy. Although he did not yet have a definite appointment, Rommel had been well briefed by his staff officers on the defenses in Normandy, and he had his arguments thought out. He was planning to convince Hitler that two Panzer divisions and a mortar unit should be released to him and his direct control. "The most urgent problem is to win the Führer over by personal conversation," he wrote in his diary.[18]

While General Speidel and his other friends in the Schwarze Kapelle were discussing armistice terms to be presented to the Allies, Rommel was planning to see Hitler about reinforcing Seventh Army. Rommel was still riding two horses, and was still waiting for something to happen that would allow him to take direct action against Hitler without—at least in his own mind—acting against Germany.

General Speidel received Army Group B's first report of the Allied landings shortly after 2 A.M. on 6 June (which would have been 1 A.M. on the Continent). "The Chief of Staff of Army Group B," Speidel wrote, referring to himself, "received reports in the first hours of the morning of June 6 that enemy parachute troops had been dropped in the vicinity of Caen and the southeastern area of the Contentin Peninsula."[19] The British 6th Airborne Division had come down near the Caen Canal, and the U.S. 82nd Airborne and 101st Airborne Divisions were scattered several miles southwest of what would become known as Utah Beach.

These first reports were sketchy and confused. No one was absolutely certain if these were "airborne landings in strength," as Speidel called them, or independent units sent to link up with the resistance. To confuse the issue still further, rubber dummies were also being dropped by parachute to divert attention from the actual landing zones. These dummies were dressed in army uniforms and strung with firecrackers; when the dummies touched the ground, the firecrackers began exploding in rapid succession, making it seem as though they had opened fire with automatic weapons.

General Marcks' birthday party ended abruptly when a telephone call from the 716th Division, stationed near Caen, reported: "Enemy paratroopers have landed east of the Orne estuary."[20] General Marcks himself received this call. All thoughts of leaving for the *kriegsspiel* at Rennes also disappeared; now he had more immediate concerns. His intelligence officer thought that this must be the beginning of the Invasion. Marcks' response was, "Let's wait and see."[21]

General Marcks' indecision was understandable. Frantic messages from Normandy were being sent to all commands—the navy, the Luftwaffe, von Rundstedt's headquarters at St. Germain—by troops who had very little idea of what was happening themselves. "Reports came piling in from everywhere—" one writer pointed out, "reports that were often inaccurate, sometimes incomprehensible, and always contradictory."[22]

Major General Max Pemsel, Seventh Army's chief of staff, did not wait for more detailed information before taking action. At 2:15 A.M. (1:15 in France) he placed Seventh Army at readiness—*alarmstruffe II*, maximum alert—and telephoned General Dollmann that the Invasion had begun. This took place four hours after the Verlaine signal had been intercepted—which gave the Allies a decisive four-hour edge.

But von Rundstedt had already made an important decision of his own. His operations officer, General Zimmermann, told Pemsel that "Operations OB West holds that this is not a large-scale airborne operation, all the more because Admiral Channel Coast [Admiral Theodor Krancke, von Rundstedt's naval counterpart] has reported that the enemy has dropped straw dummies."[23] Von Rundstedt refused to believe that the Invasion would come anywhere but Calais, even at this stage.

While British and American paratroops were jumping into their drop zones, Lt. James Murphy was just getting out of his bunk, following a fitful night's sleep. His transport was anchored several miles off the coast of the Cotentin Peninsula. In a few hours, he would be coming ashore on Utah Beach. At Rennes, senior officers were in bed, although some had been awakened by telephone because of the parachute landings. And in Berchtesgaden, Hitler was about to retire after an evening of listening to opera recordings. He had taken one of his sleeping potions. His staff decided that it would be best not to awaken him, at least not until they had more definite information about the situation in Normandy.

No one at Berchtesgaden, or Rennes or any German headquarters anywhere in France or Germany, had any idea that approximately 5,000 Allied ships were approaching Normandy at that very moment. The transports and their escorts had already begun entering the Bay of the Seine; those closest to the shore were about twelve miles away from the invasion beaches. In a few hours, they would begin their long anticipated assault of those five beaches: Gold and Sword beaches for the British, Juno for the Canadians, and Omaha and Utah for the Americans.

The landings at Normandy would come as a complete surprise to von Rundstedt and every other German officer who remained convinced that the landings would come in the Pas de Calais—largely because of Colonel Alexis von Roenne. His fictitious reports on the movements and activities of FUSAG were making the Quicksilver deception into a complete success. Motivated by his resolve to undermine Hitler at every opportunity, he would continue to be one of the Allies' most reliable—and completely unknown—assets.

NOTES

1. Cawthon, p. 53.
2. Miller, *Nothing Less Than Victory*, p. 176.
3. Ibid., p. 183.
4. Author interview.
5. Ruge, p. 169.
6. Speidel, p. 78.
7. Butcher, p. 559.
8. Miller, *Nothing Less Than Victory*, p. 186.
9. Harrison, p. 274.
10. Ibid.
11. "Morning" (video).
12. Ryan, p. 97.
13. Ibid., p. 96.
14. Ibid.
15. Brown, p. 719.
16. Speidel, p. 78.
17. Perrault, p. 228.
18. Carell, p. 7.
19. Speidel, p. 78.

20. Carell, p. 25.
21. Ibid.
22. Ryan, p. 147.
23. Ibid., p. 149.

TEN

"Well, Is It or Isn't It the Invasion?"

Lt. James Murphy could not get over how easy everything had been so far. Up to this point, just about everything connected with the landings had been a disaster—The E-boat attack off Slapton Sands that turned Exercise Tiger into a shambles, the cancellation of the landings on 5 June, the terrifying talk about what the German defenses had in store for them. Murphy had been expecting the worst, but now that he had finally landed on Utah Beach, he was pleasantly surprised that everything was going according to plan. There had been no attacks by E-boats, no problems at all on the run-in to the beach, and practically no German opposition after they landed. Murphy had always considered himself to be a "natural born pessimist!"—proving that the British are not the only masters of understatement—but he was very glad that things did not happen the way he thought they would.[1]

Although German resistance on Utah Beach was light, that was not the case on all of the landing beaches. On Omaha Beach, the U.S. 1st Division was decimated by enemy fire. The area was defended by two complete regiments of the veteran 352nd Division and not, as had been reported, by the inferior 716th Division. The carnage on Omaha was so terrible that it looked as though the survivors would have to be evacuated. On Gold Beach, at the village of Le Hamel, another unit of the 352nd Division inflicted heavy casualties on the Hampshire Regiment. But just a short distance away, the Dorset Regiment and the Green Howards were off the beach and moving inland within an hour of coming ashore.

The same situation existed on both Sword and Juno beaches—determined German resistance in one section and none at all in another. On

Sword, the British 41st Commandos were stopped dead at their first objective, the seaside village of Lion-sur-Mer, and the East York Regiment lost over 150 men as soon as they landed. But on another sector, the Suffolk Regiment had only four casualties. Other units also met with light resistance, and were soon off the beach. The Canadian units that came ashore on Juno Beach had a difficult landing. Artillery fire at St. Aubin-sur-Mer created havoc with both tanks and infantry. After about thirty minutes, however, the Canadian 8th Brigade had fought their way through the coastal defenses and were moving south, away from the coast.

"The landings have gone better than expected," Captain Butcher somewhat tentatively wrote on 6 June. "Every outfit is ashore, but we just had a report that . . . V Corps can't get off one of its beaches because of hostile mortar and artillery fire. This is Omaha Beach."[2] The first official D-Day announcement was given by Radio Berlin at about 6:30 A.M. (British time). Radio stations in Sweden, Switzerland, and Spain picked up the Berlin broadcast and began to spread the news of the Invasion. General Eisenhower did not allow the release of the official SHAEF communiqué until he was satisfied that the landings had been a success. At 9:33 A.M., Eisenhower's press officer announced, "Under the command of General Eisenhower, Allied naval forces, supported by strong air forces, began landing Allied armies this morning on the northern coast of France."[3]

In London, the BBC broadcast the first Invasion bulletin shortly after the SHAEF communiqué: "D-Day has come. Early this morning the Allies began the assault on the northwestern face of Hitler's European fortress."[4] The Eisenhower news flash reached the eastern United States in the middle of the night, at 3:33 A.M. New York time, giving newspaper editors just enough time to replace the front page with a revised D-Day edition. "American, British, and Canadian troops landed on the Normandy coast of France by barge, glider, and parachute today," reported the New York *Journal-American*.[5]

At her chateau outside Periers, Marie-Louise Osmont learned about the Invasion from a much more direct source—the booming of the naval bombardment that supported the landings. The firing, "prolonged but fairly far away," awakened her before dawn. After daybreak, she went across the road to ask one of her tenant farmers, ' "Well! . . . Is this it, this time?' 'Yes,' he says, 'I think so, and I'm really afraid we're in a sector that's going to be attacked; that's going to be something!' " His guess was amazingly perceptive. The first British troops from Sword Beach—"the Tommies," as Madame Osmont always called them—would walk onto her pasture land a few hours later, "submachine guns and machine guns under their arms."[6]

Feldmarschall von Rundstedt also was kept informed of the developing situation in Normandy and now was inclined to agree with Madame Osmont's tenant farmer. His mind had been changed by the information he had been given about the British and American paratroop landings, which seemed to be too numerous and concentrated for a diversion or a link-up with the resistance, and especially by a report from Seventh Army that engine noises had been detected out in the Bay of the Seine. General Max Pemsel, Seventh Army's chief of staff, reported, "Ships are concentrating between the mouths of the Vire and the Orne," the area compromising all of the landing beaches except Utah. "They lead to the conclusion that an enemy landing and large-scale attack against Normandy is imminent."[7]

If such a report had come from the SD or any of its related services, von Rundstedt probably would have dismissed it as more gibberish from those fools in intelligence. But because it had come from one of his own generals, he not only listened to the report but also acted on it. At 4:30 A.M.—while Lieutenant Murphy, along with several thousand other men, were boarding their landing craft—von Rundstedt ordered the 12th SS Panzer and Panzer Lehr Divisions to begin preparations for moving to Normandy. He was sending two veteran tank divisions to the zone that Pemsel had indicated, straight to the landing beaches.

He was fully aware that he did not have the authority to give this order—both divisions remained under Hitler's direct control—but he decided to give it just the same. Von Rundstedt hoped that OKW's chief of operations, General Alfred Jodl, would pass this message along to Hitler as quickly as possible, and would stress its tremendous urgency. The message he sent by teletype was both a request for the release of the two Panzer divisions and an explanation for his request: "If they assemble quickly and get an early start they can enter the battle on the coast during the day."[8]

Von Rundstedt had acted decisively and correctly. He thought that his request to OKW would be nothing more than a formality. As one historian put it, "he could not believe that Hitler would object or countermand the order."[9]

When his teletype arrived at Jodl's headquarters, the general was asleep. The officers on duty decided that it would be better not to wake him up; they were of the opinion that "the situation had not developed sufficiently."[10] But they did notify Hitler's quarters at about 5 A.M. The message was taken by Hitler's naval aide, Admiral Karl Jesko von Puttkamer, who had been awakened by the telephone.

Von Puttkamer was not bowled over by what Jodl's headquarters had to say. Instead of emphasizing the urgency of the conditions in Normandy, as von Rundstedt expected, the caller merely mentioned that there had been "some sort of landings in France" and that "the first messages are extremely vague."[11] It was not exactly "The Enemy Is At The Gates" or even an accurate evaluation.

Everybody at OKW, including General Jodl and his subordinates, had been indoctrinated to believe that the Invasion would come at Calais. As such, any other landings could only be a diversion and, therefore, should not be considered important. The seeds of discontent sown by Admiral Canaris, and the fictions of the First U.S. Army Group planted in the minds of OKW by Colonel von Roenne, were now in full flower.

Because the message from Jodl's headquarters was so lackluster and imprecise, von Puttkamer decided not to awaken Hitler with something that seemed so unimportant: "There wasn't much to tell him, anyway, and . . . if I woke him at this time he might start one of his endless nervous scenes which often led to the wildest decisions."[12] Von Puttkamer went back to bed. When Hitler woke up, and more information was available, he would give him an updated report.

General Jodl woke up at about six o'clock. His deputy, General Walter Warlimont, told him about von Rundstedt's ordering the two Panzer divisions to the Invasion area. "Are you sure that this *is* the invasion?" was Jodl's reaction. "According to the reports I have received it could be a diversionary attack . . . part of a deception plan. OB West has sufficient reserves right now. . . . OB West should endeavour to clean up the attack with forces at their disposal. . . . I do not think that this is the time to release the OKW reserves. We must wait for further clarification of the situation."[13]

The influence of Colonel von Roenne upon General Jodl's thought process is unmistakable. OKW had been given numerous reports from von Roenne and FHW that FUSAG would be carrying the *real* Invasion to France, and that FUSAG would land at Calais. Jodl reasoned that Seventh Army had enough troops to deal with any landing in Normandy, since this was probably nothing more than a diversionary attack.

The operations chief at OKW, Major General Buttlar von Brandenfels, was a good deal less diplomatic about the alerting of the two Panzer divisions. Von Rundstedt's chief of operations, General Bodo Zimmermann, telephoned OKW and spoke with von Brandenfels about the release order. "These divisions are under the direct control of OKW!" he screamed at Zimmermann. "You had no right to alert them without our prior approval. You are to halt the Panzers immediately—nothing is to be done before the Führer makes his decision!" Zimmermann tried to reason with von Brandenfels, but was shouted down. "Do as you are told!" was his reply.[14]

The argument between von Rundstedt's headquarters and OKW continued throughout most of the morning. Von Rundstedt's staff officers spoke with a number of generals at OKW, including Warlimont, von Brandenfels, and Hitler's adjutant, Major General Rudolf Schmundt. The result of each of these conversations was the same. As Zimmermann summed up, "When we warned that if we didn't get the Panzers that the Normandy landings would succeed and that unforeseeable consequences would follow, we were simply told that *we* were in no position to judge—that the main landing was going to come in a different place, anyway."[15] A British writer noted that the Quicksilver deception plan "was dominating the Germans' reactions." [16] Actually, it was Quicksilver complemented by the activities of Colonel von Roenne. Without von Roenne's own deception scheme, Quicksilver would not have misled OKW as completely as it was doing at that critical time.

At 7:30 A.M., General Jodl himself let von Rundstedt know that his release order had been countermanded—the tanks could not be ordered to the Normandy coast without Hitler's personal approval, Jodl informed him. The units of the 12th SS Division that already had started for Normandy were to stop at Lisieux; the Panzer Lehr, which had not yet begun moving, was to stay where it was. These two divisions totalled about 500 tanks, about 40,000 infantrymen (Panzer grenadiers), and approximately 100 self-propelled artillery pieces. Jodl's cancellation of von Rundstedt's order insured that they would not reach the Invasion area any time on D-Day. The only armor available to Seventh Army on 6 June would be 21st Panzer's 146 tanks and 51 assault guns.

A tremendous advantage had been lost. General Zimmerman and everyone else at von Rundstedt's headquarters knew it. All von Rundstedt could do was shake his head in disbelief. Zimmermann observed von Rundstedt "was fuming with rage, red in the face, and his anger made his speech unintelligible."[17] He might have made a personal telephone call to Hitler himself to argue his case, but could not bring himself to speak with "that Bohemian corporal," a man that he held in utter contempt. He probably would not have been able to reverse OKW's judgment, anyway, even if he had managed to get through to Hitler. Admiral Ruge, Rommel's naval aide, did not believe that anyone, including Rommel, could have altered OKW's judgment regarding the Panzer reserves. "It is questionable that Rommel could have changed the situation had he been present at headquarters," Ruge said.[18] Everyone had already made up his mind and had no intention of revising their opinions.

Colonel von Roenne's systematic creation of the FUSAG myth, as well as the FUSAG order of battle, certainly had a lock on the Wehrmacht's collective imagination that morning. No one wanted to commit forces to Normandy for fear that this was not the main landing. Army Group B, with General Speidel acting for Feldmarschall Rommel, went on record in the report for 6 June as being unsure whether or not the Normandy landings were the primary attack. Even OB West, von Rundstedt's headquarters, stated that "at the present time, it is still too early to say whether this is a large-scale diversionary attack or the main effort."[19]

Later in the morning, Colonel von Roenne issued a situation report that put the question to rest—the action in Normandy, he assured every intelligence officer and every commander in the West, was just a diversion. The first sentence of this report, which was sent to OKW, Army Group B, and every headquarters in France, is reminiscent of Admiral Canaris' report on Allied intentions just prior to the Allied landings at Anzio: "While the Anglo-Saxon enemy landing on the coast of Normandy represents a large-scale operation, the forces employed comprise only a relatively small portion of the forces available."

Von Roenne continued in the same manner for several hundred more words. "Of the sixty large formations held in southern Britain, only ten to twelve divisions including airborne troops appear to be participating so far," he went on. But this was not just a simple statement to announce that FUSAG was still poised to attack from southeastern England. Von Roenne also made enough of a case for the Normandy landings to protect himself against some possible future investigation. He emphasized the strength of the Normandy assault, and warned not to underestimate its success. "The enemy has gained a bridge-head [beachhead] which is thirty kilometers wide and in places up to eight kilometers deep," he reported. In other words, "If the Allied attack in Normandy does succeed, don't say that I didn't warn you!"

He did not come to the heart of the matter until the middle of his account. "According to a believable Abwehr report of June 2," von Roenne went on, "the forces in southern England are divided into two army groups, the 21st British Army Group and the 1st U.S. Army Group." He knew all about this believable information that the Abwehr/SD had in its possession, because he had passed it along to them himself. He then explained that the forces that had landed in Normandy came from the 21st British Army Group, commanded by General Montgomery, which was common knowledge.

Near the end of his report, von Roenne finally came to the point. "Not a single unit of the 1st U.S. Army Group, which comprises around twenty-five large formations north and south of the Thames, has so far been committed." Another ten to twelve uncommitted combat formations were stationed in central England and in Scotland. In case anyone missed the significance of this information, von Roenne went on to spell it out for them: "This suggests that the enemy is planning a further large-scale operation in the Channel area, which one would expect to be aimed at a coastal section in the Pas de Calais area."

He finished his discussion by mentioning the Allied air forces—which he described as "the Anglo-Saxon Air Arm"—and warned that strong forces were also being held ready in eastern seaports of the United States.

These forces would be sent directly to France if a "port of sufficient capacity" was captured by the Allies. He had already mentioned that the capture of Cherbourg was one of the primary Allied objectives.[20]

All in all, the situation report was a very thorough document, filled with authentic-sounding details concerning the enemy's strengths and intentions. It contained just enough factual material to sound believable, including the names of actual Allied units—such as the British 6th Airborne and the U.S. 101st Airborne. But the heart of the report was pure fabrication—especially the twenty-five large formations of FUSAG—and its overall message was an outright lie.

But because it came from the head of FHW, who was one of the most important intelligence officers in the West, and because it said what everyone was expecting, the report was believed. It was actually the climax of all the misinformation that von Roenne had been issuing to the SD and to all commands since late winter. All of the made-up regiments, divisions, and formations that Quicksilver had concocted, and that von Roenne had brought to life through his artful misguidance, were now ready to do what they had been created to do—launch a fictitious large-scale operation against Calais. FUSAG, which had been created for this precise moment, was finally becoming an active component of Overlord.

Tank commanders and their crews waited to move to the Normandy coast, expecting the order to come at any time. Officers and men of the 12th SS Panzer and Panzer Lehr had already been alerted and then, a short time later, ordered to stand down. No one knew exactly what was happening. All anyone could do was stand about and wait for something to happen, for someone at headquarters to give them an order.

But at every headquarters, the level of frustration was even more wearing. The enemy had come ashore at Normandy and was fighting his way inland. If a counterattack were launched right away, before the Allies could consolidate their forces, the Invasion could still be stopped at the coast. But no reinforcements could be sent to the Invasion area because intelligence insisted that the *real* Invasion had not yet arrived. Commanders throughout the West awaited orders from OKW, but no orders were forthcoming.

The intelligence officer at Army Group B, Colonel Anton Staubwasser, decided to take matters into his own hands and telephone the army's senior intelligence officer—Colonel Alexis von Roenne. Staubwasser wanted von Roenne to help him convince General Jodl and OKW that the Panzer reserves should be released to the Normandy front immediately. As head of FHW, Staubwasser reasoned that he ought to have at least some influence with the general staff. Von Roenne was not available when Staubwasser telephoned. At about 12 noon, von Roenne returned the telephone call.

But Staubwasser did not get the response that he had expected. Instead, von Roenne told him essentially what he had said in his situation report: A second attack was expected in the Pas de Calais area, and as such, there could be no transferring of troops from Calais to Normandy. He also said that FHW had compiled reliable information relating to the impending Allied landings at Calais, which made him absolutely certain that a second Invasion was not far off. Staubwasser began to argue the issue, but von Roenne would have none of it; no one at Army Group B, including its intelligence officer, was as well informed as FHW, and Staubwasser's opinion was not based upon factual evidence.

Von Roenne won his case, and Staubwasser remained as frustrated as before. And the tank commanders and their crews continued to wait for orders.

But even before von Roenne and Staubwasser had their brief but significant conversation, conditions at Normandy already had begun to change. The low cloud and mist over the landing beaches, which had obscured enemy positions from Allied fighter-bombers, was burnt away by the late morning sun. As soon as this happened, "Allied fighters and bombers ranged from the skies smashing at everything that moved."[21] The movement of the Panzer reserves toward the five Allied landing beaches had now become a much more hazardous undertaking.

Hitler had awakened at nine o'clock (ten o'clock British time). His staff, including his naval aide, Admiral von Puttkamer, had prepared a situation map of the Invasion area for him. Puttkamer also had telephone General Jodl's office for an updated report. When Hitler came out of his and Eva Braun's bedroom, even before he had the chance to get dressed, he was told about the landings at Normandy. Maybe it was because the effects of his sleeping draught had not yet worn off, but Hitler did not, as expected, launch himself into a nervous rage when he heard the news. He listened quietly—some accounts use the word "calmly"—and sent for Feldmarschall Keitel and general Jodl from OKW. He then withdrew to get dressed.

By the time Keitel and Jodl arrived at Hitler's quarters, Hitler was in a highly nervous state. The meeting that followed was "extremely agitated," according to Admiral Puttkamer.[22] Hitler heard reports that an important landing had taken place at Normandy, but also was told that a fully detailed update from von Rundstedt had not yet been sent. He repeated several times, more to himself than to anyone in the room, that this was not the main Allied attack. At one point he blurted out, "Well, is it or isn't it the Invasion?"[23]

A consensus was reached that "the fighting on the Normandy coast was merely an enemy diversionary maneuver" in the words of a German historian, "and that the real Invasion was yet to come in the Calais area."[24] Jodl informed Hitler that he had reversed von Rundstedt's order concerning the two reserve Panzer divisions, and Hitler approved his decision. It was his considered opinion that the Normandy landings were not the main Invasion, and that the strategic reserves should not be committed as yet. Von Roenne's reports regarding FUSAG were clearly in the forefront of his mind.

About fifteen minutes after Hitler woke from his sedated sleep, General Hans Speidel decided that it was time to telephone Feldmarschall Rommel with the news of the landings. As soon as he heard Speidel's information, Rommel had no doubts as to whether or not this was the main attack. He realized that this was no diversion; there would be no other landings, at Calais or anywhere else.

Although much has been made of the fact that Rommel was in Germany on the day of the landings, instead of on duty at La Roche Guyon, there probably would not have been very much that he could have done if he had been at his headquarters that morning. He berated himself— "How stupid of me" was his reaction to the news—and was tense and depressed following Speidel's telephone call. But Hitler and his general staff had become so thoroughly convinced that the main Allied landings were still to come, and that they would take the short route to Calais, that Rommel probably never would have been able to talk them out of the idea during the course of a telephone conversation. Hitler and Jodl were basing their decision upon von Roenne's "factual evidence." Any argument from Rommel, regardless of how forceful that argument might have been, would have met with the same short shrift that Staubwasser got from von Roenne.

Rommel forgot his plans to visit Hitler at Berchtesgaden; there was no point in trying to talk to Hitler at this point. He made arrangements to have himself driven back to La Roche Guyon that afternoon. During the trip to France, Rommel's thoughts were on his Panzer units, on the landings, and on his "friendly enemy" General Montgomery, the overall field commander of the Invasion forces. He also must have given his colleagues in the Schwarze Kapelle some thought, which would have depressed him as much as the landings. The armistice that he and his co-conspirators were planning to present to the Allies was to have been delivered *before* the Invasion, while Germany was still in a position to bargain. Now that the Wehrmacht was on the defensive, they would have to think of something new.

Hitler held his usual noon conference, but at Klessheim Castle instead of OKW headquarters. He was meeting with the dictators of Hungary, Slovakia, and Rumania—respectively Horthy, Tiso, and Antonescu—and preferred the baroque setting of Klessheim for such gatherings. The German staff officers who were present expected that Hitler would make some sort of bold decision regarding the situation in Normandy. But when Hitler entered the conference room, he was in an unexpectedly jolly mood. "So we're off!" he announced in a full Austrian accent, and proceeded to carry on "as if this was the opportunity he had been awaiting so long to settle accounts with his enemy." As General Walter Warlimont, the deputy chief of operations, put it, "Hitler decided to put on an act."[25]

Act or not, he did not make any decisions regarding Normandy or reinforcing the defenses in the Invasion area. He boasted to his guests about the strength of the Wehrmacht, and also made a point of mentioning the secret weapons that, he assured everyone, would soon terrorize England—soon to be known to Londoners as the V-1 flying bomb and the V-2 rocket. Following this short lecture, the party adjourned for lunch, and Hitler had his customary vegetarian meal. He said that he would think about the Panzer reserves over lunch.

On this occasion, at least, Hitler was as good as his word. When his luncheon party ended, he released the 12th SS Panzer and Panzer Lehr divisions to von Rundstedt. Word of this decision did not reach Seventh Army until 2:32 P.M., according to Admiral Ruge. The order was not received by the two tank divisions themselves until nearly four o'clock. "Since both divisions were still far from the battlefield," Admiral Ruge declared, "they could not participate in the fighting on that day."[26] Hitler had forbidden the transfer of any units of Fifteenth Army to Normandy, however; he was still waiting for the First U.S. Army Group at Calais.

Colonel von Roenne had given the Allied armies in Normandy another vital advantage. General Jodl, and then Hitler himself, had decided against releasing the two armored divisions from moving to the Invasion area for more than ten hours—a decision based upon information that von Roenne had given them. The Allied landings called for a swift and crushing response from the defenders. Instead, OKW's response was paralysis and confusion. Von Roenne was directly responsible for the inertia of the Panzers as well as for the muddle of Hitler and his generals.

The consequences of having withheld the Panzer units from Normandy were felt before the day was over. A six-mile-wide gap existed between the Canadian forces on Juno and the British on Sword Beach. The two armies had not yet been able to link up and consolidate their landing areas. Neither the British nor the Canadian commanders knew anything about this gap for several critical hours. But if the German armored units found it, and if they moved fast enough, they were in a position to create a disaster for Overlord. The tanks could reach the coast and attack the British and Canadian units that were still isolated and vulnerable on the beachheads, and "could roll up the British landings."[27]

The 21st Panzer Division, which had been southwest of Caen when the landings began, managed to locate this corridor between the two landing beaches. The tanks had trouble getting to the coast; they could not go through Caen, because an air raid had bombed it into a shambles, so they had to go round it. But thirty-five tanks, under the command of Captain Wilhelm von Gottberg, made their way past the town and through the swarms of refugees until they were in the vicinity of Marie-Louise Osmont's chateau outside Periers. Another twenty-five tanks, led by Colonel Hermann Oppelin-Bronikowski, reached the high ground near Bieville, about two miles southeast of Periers.

General Erich Marcks, who had canceled his trip to the *kriegsspiel* at Rennes, spoke to Bronikowski before he started for Bieville. He told him that "the future of Germany may very well rest on your shoulders. If you don't push the British back into the sea, we've lost the war."[28]

Bronikowski's tanks were stopped outside Bieville; in fifteen minutes, he lost six of his tanks. Captain Gottberg lost ten of his tanks—Madame Osmont could hear the firing—and fell back to wait for reinforcements. But some units were able to reach the coast, near the village of Luc-sur-Mer; the men could actually watch the ships of the Invasion fleet out in the Bay of the Seine.

This was the only German counterattack of D-Day. It came as a complete surprise to both the British and the Canadians, and blunted their drive toward Caen. But by the end of the day, the 21st Division had to withdraw from the corridor. Without support, they would have been wiped out. By 9 P.M., the abortive German attack was over.

Had General Jodl given von Rundstedt the two Panzer divisions he wanted and needed, the drive through the Sword-Juno corridor might have ended quite differently. With a ten-hour head start, these units might have linked up with the 21st. The additional 500 tanks, 40,000 troops, and the self-propelled guns would have caused havoc and high casualties among the troops that were trying to fight their way out of their landing areas. "The failure of the Germans to mount a major counteroffensive on the first day, either against Sword or Omaha, was to cost them dearly in the following weeks."[29] It was not a missed opportunity as much as a thwarted possibility—thwarted by months of inflated numbers, made-up facts, and distorted intelligence.

By the end of the day, "Allied commanders had cause for quiet confidence." Four defensible beachheads had been established in Normandy. The fifth, Omaha, was being reinforced. About 150,000 men had landed by air and by sea. The landings had been a success. General Eisenhower and his commanders were optimistic about the coming campaign in France.

But Lord Louis Mountbatten, one of Overlord's preliminary planners, gave three conditions that are necessary for a successful invasion: "1) getting ashore, no matter what the opposition; 2) staying ashore, no matter what the weather conditions; and 3) stopping the enemy from building up his forces against you quicker than you can—otherwise, he'll throw you back in the sea."[31] In other words, getting ashore and staying ashore are two completely different things. Or, as General Omar Bradley put it, "You can almost always force an invasion, but you can't always make it stick."[32]

Eisenhower and his deputies would not have been nearly as optimistic about the future of Overlord had they known that the operational orders for both the U.S. V Corps (the forces that landed on Omaha Beach) and VII Corps (Utah Beach) had been discovered by the Germans. German intelligence now had a vital insight into the plans and intentions of all the American forces in Normandy.

The VII Corps documents had been found on D-Day itself. Men of the 352nd Division spotted a badly damaged landing craft off the mouth of the River Vire, between Utah and Omaha beaches. When they investigated, they found the bodies of several American officers in the boat; chained to the wrist of one of the officers was a briefcase. The briefcase was sent to headquarters, and was found to contain the plans of the American units in the Utah area. On Wednesday, 7 June, soldiers from another unit of the 352nd found the operational orders of V Corps on the body of another American officer. This discovery took place in the coastal village of Colville, just beyond Omaha Beach; the officer had been killed in the fighting.

These documents were highly classified, and were never to have left Britain. Each was stamped with a warning: "DESTROY BEFORE EM-BARKATION." Now they were in enemy hands, and were quickly sent to senior Wehrmacht commanders, including Feldmarschall von Rundstedt and his chief of staff, Major General Gunter Blumentritt. Blumentritt was suspicious of the documents at first; it seemed to him that they had been obtained a bit too easily for them to have been authentic. But the details in the orders convinced everyone concerned that the papers were not an Allied plant, and that they had just stumbled upon an incredible piece of good luck.

The orders contained a treasure trove of details—how the American armies planned to expand their beachheads, which would create space for assembling and organizing reinforcements, and then to push beyond the beaches into Cherbourg and Brittany. A German writer said that the plans "neatly set out . . . each separate phase from D-Day onwards, with day-by-day objectives on the Cotentin Peninsula."[33] The only saving grace for the Allies was that the documents did not contain any information regarding Quicksilver or any other Fortitude operation. But they did give a complete outline of exactly what the Americans planned to do after they had secured their lodgements on the Normandy coast.

Von Rundstedt had been half-persuaded that the Normandy landings were the long-anticipated Invasion before he knew anything about the American documents. Just from the amount of men and material that had been committed to Normandy, he was already convinced that there would be no second invasion at Calais. These captured orders, which he read on Thursday, 8 June, in summary form, now made him absolutely certain. Other senior officers, including General Erich Marcks and Feld-marschall Rommel, also studied the plans and shared von Rundstedt's opinion.

With these operational plans as evidence to back up his suspicions, von Rundstedt telephoned Hitler's headquarters to request the imme-diate release of all reserves to the Normandy front. Hitler also had been informed of the contents of the captured American documents, although he had not read them. Von Rundstedt's headquarters also contacted OKW with the same request. While Hitler and his High Command mulled over this appeal, a change was made in the German field code. Changes in the code were made periodically and affected all German forces. The change also effectively eliminated a vital source of informa-tion and, from the point of view of Allied intelligence could not have come at a worse time.

Another very strong hint that there would be no landing at Calais came from the head of the fighting French, the egocentric General Charles de Gaulle. De Gaulle was disliked and distrusted by virtually all the Allied leaders. When he visited Eisenhower's headquarters at Southwick House on 4 June, he was received with all due politeness and decorum. De Gaulle was shown every courtesy; Eisenhower himself showed him maps and explained the landing phase of Overlord in broad terms. But de Gaulle was not shown anything of importance, and was told that the landings in Normandy were only a diversion from the main attack at Calais. He was not trusted, and was told the same misleading story that the enemy had been told since winter. That way, if he hap-pened to open his mouth at the wrong time or place, he would be help-ing the Invasion instead of putting it in jeopardy. As it turned out, the mistrust and suspicion with which de Gaulle was treated was thoroughly justified.

At six o'clock on the evening of 6 June, de Gaulle gave a radio address to the French nation. Staff officers at SHAEF had written a speech for him—a safe, understated speech containing no details that might be use-ful to the enemy—but de Gaulle wanted no part of it. Instead, he delivered his own speech, which contained the very information that SHAEF and Allied intelligence were trying to keep from the Germans.

De Gaulle began his address by referring to the Normandy landings as the main battle—"*la bataille supreme est engager*"—and went on to an-nounce that "this is the decisive blow, the blow that we have so much hoped for." He then told the resistance to obey the French government—meaning himself—rather than SHAEF or Eisenhower, and urged the "sons of France" to "fight with all the means at their disposal." He made no mention of any Allied power except France, and referred to the entire operation as "France's battle."[34]

The speech was an insult to the Western Alliance but, far worse than that, was also a message to the enemy that there would be no other landings, at Calais or anywhere else. Colonel Staubwasser, at Seventh Army headquarters, reached this conclusion after hearing de Gaulle's speech. His address, coupled with the information included in the captured American operational orders, provided a clear indication that the threatened invasion by FUSAG was a hoax. The work of months was on the verge of being canceled out by two accidents and an arrogant radio address.

On 7 June, Hitler approved von Rundstedt's request for reinforcements—Seventh Army would have its Panzer divisions, which included more than 1,500 tanks. The code message "Begin Case Three," the signal to release the seventeen divisions being kept for the Calais invasion, was issued. The German Panzer units started for Normandy.

Although the Allied armies were consolidating their beachheads, and were growing stronger with freshly arrived troops and supplies, their position was still precarious, and they would never be able to withstand a counterattack in strength. "Counterattack was what we most feared," Walter Bedell Smith, Eisenhower's chief of staff, commented. "It had been our gravest worry during the planning days in England."[35] If von Rundstedt's forces arrived quickly enough, he would be able to attack the enemy with more men and tanks than the Allies had at their disposal. As Mountbatten warned, the Allied armies would face either withdrawal from the beaches or annihilation.

Ultra detected these moves before they began. Operators in England were able to pick up radio signals sent to individual units, including General Witt's instructions to the 12th SS Panzer Division: "The Division will attack the disembarked enemy together with the 21st Panzer Division and throw him back into the sea."[36] Other orders concerned the 25th and 26th Grenadier Regiments, along with reconnaissance, engineer, and antiaircraft units. Air reconnaissance flights also were made over the Calais region, and they reported the movement of German units toward Normandy.

Eisenhower and his commanders realized the delicate position of the Allied forces in Normandy, and that a forced withdrawal from the beaches was still a distinct possibility. They also realized that the approaching German forces would have to be turned back before they reached the Invasion area. First steps toward distracting them were taken at once. During the evening of 7 June, hundreds of dummy paratroopers—the same kind that had been dropped into the British and American zones on the night of 5–6 June—were released over the area west of St. Lo. This deception had the desired effect: Troops were diverted from their advance toward Normandy and sent to counter this new airborne attack instead. But the dropping of dummies could only be a stopgap measure, at best.

Also on 7 June, Eisenhower ordered the BBC to begin broadcasting *messages personnels* to resistance units in northeastern France and in Belgium. Just as they had done prior to D-Day, announcers in London sent their strange, ominous-sounding messages to the resistance: The roses are in full bloom; summer will be long and hot; Samantha has nine lives. Some of these were signals for individual resistance groups to begin sabotage operations in their own area—against telephone lines, rail lines, roads, and what was termed "general harassment" against targets of opportunity. Some were messages to nonexistent units in the Pas de Calais, sent to give the Germans the impression of a sudden increase in resistance activity—the resistance equivalent of FUSAG.

The broadcasts continued into Thursday, 8 June. Their purpose was to mislead German intelligence into believing that this unexpected burst of radio activity must be an indication of another major Allied operation. The sabotaging of targets throughout the northeast of France had both the Wehrmacht and the SD alarmed, but it was the sheer volume of messages to resistance units, both real and nonexistent, that was at the heart of the deception. The activities themselves were not all that important. What the Germans thought these activities meant—namely, the preparation of another invasion—was the object of this particular game.

Other, more intricate, ruses were also employed. All deception activities in the FUSAG area of England—Kent, Surrey, Sussex, and parts of East Anglia—were stepped up. Traffic in Dover harbor was increased. Naval activity also was escalated, with destroyers and other warships scurrying about in the Straits of Dover in dramatically increased numbers. Radio traffic also intensified—radio talk between ships, between the crews of airplanes, between make-believe units of the First U.S. Army Group—for the eager listeners on the other side of the Channel. It was the same kind of extravagant duplicity that had been employed before D-Day, and it had the same purpose—to convince the enemy that a second landing was pending at Calais.

Not that trickery was the only method being employed. The *maquis* were busy blowing up stretches of rail line, as well as dynamiting roads, to slow the German advance. Allied fighter-bombers—RAF Typhoons and U.S. Army Air Force Thunderbolts—made moving by daylight a deadly risk for any Wehrmacht unit, including the Panzers. And the U.S. Eighth Air Force created bottlenecks along the main routes to Normandy—Montgomery called them choke points—by systematically bombing towns along these routes into piles of rubble.

The first of these saturation bombing attacks was against Caen. It was made by 571 B-24 Liberators, which dropped more than 1,400 tons of high explosives on the town,[37] reducing it to a bomb-created ruin. Other towns that met with a similar fate were St. Lo; the cathedral city of Coutance; Falaise, the birthplace of William the Conqueror; Lisieux, Vire; and Argentan. The four-engined bombers also made low-level strikes against bridges and checkpoints, hindering the movements of German tanks and troop carriers. In addition, the "heavies" dropped arms and ammunition to resistance units, keeping them supplied for their guerilla war against the enemy.

The destruction of the picturesque towns of Normandy was horrific, but it accomplished its aim: the choke points slowed the German advance. Troop trains had to stop miles away from their destinations, and the men continued on foot—rail lines had either been blasted away by bombs, or made impassable by mountains of bricks and fallen masonry.

But the main Allied strategy was not just to hinder the German advance toward Normandy. It was to mislead the High Command into believing—once again—that Normandy was only a diversionary landing, that a much larger invasion would shortly come ashore at Calais, and that the divisions released to von Rundstedt had to be recalled. To accomplish this, Quicksilver had to be resurrected and presented to Hitler and OKW as fact, in spite of de Gaulle and the captured American orders. This would require the efforts of agent Brutus—Captain Roman Garby-Czerniawski—and the Spanish agent Garbo. Their job was now to make Quicksilver believable again.

Brutus was the first to report. The SD still placed a great deal of confidence in him and in the information he sent. SHAEF, and Overlord, were counting on Brutus to deceive German intelligence with another hoax regarding FUSAG. Walter Schellenberg still believed that Brutus, a former Polish serving officer, was serving as a liaison between General Patton's staff and Polish units in Britain.

On 8 June, Brutus informed his contact in Paris that FUSAG was now ready to depart for France. General Patton himself had announced that it was now time to land his army in Calais, because the diversion in Normandy was going so well. Brutus also reported that a number of high-ranking individuals, including Churchill, Eisenhower, and King George, had visited Patton at Dover Castle to say farewell. General George C. Marshall, U.S. Army chief of staff, was scheduled to come and see Patton on either 9 or 10 June, as a parting visit before the army left for France. FUSAG, Brutus added, was made up of a least fifty divisions, including at least five airborne divisions.

Coming from an agent as reliable and dependable as Brutus, this was an eye opener. Hitler was given a copy of the report at once. Second thoughts began to emerge. Maybe those American documents *had* been a plant, after all. As for de Gaulle and his radio address, everyone knew that de Gaulle had an ego that could be matched in size only by his mouth. He was prone to exaggeration, which is what he must have been doing in his *"la bataille supreme"* speech. Either that, or the speech was part of the same cover-up as the too easily obtained American documents.

On the following day, Garbo delivered his own report. His radio message took more than two hours to send. It began with a general listing of all the units that were stationed in southern and southeastern England, both real and fictitious. He also made mention of landing barges that three of his nonexistent subagents had spotted. To enhance the reality of his information, Garbo even went so far as to request Luftwaffe reconnaissance to confirm the presence of these barges—knowing full well that no Luftwaffe reconnaissance aircraft could have survived the Allied fighters sent to intercept.

After giving his news on troop strength in England, Garbo offered his opinion of the Allied landings in Normandy. He came right to the point: "The present operation, though a large-scale assault, is diversionary in character." The Normandy beachhead, Garbo said, had been established only to draw "the maximum of our reserves" into that area "so as to leave another area exposed." That exposed area would then be the target of the enemy's main attack.

Returning to the subject of the Allied forces, Garbo stressed their number and their intended objective. "The fact, however, that the massive concentration of forces in east and southeast England remains inactive suggests that these forces are being held in reserve for other large-scale operations." The constant air bombardment of targets in the Pas de Calais indicated that this was the most logical destination for these forces, Garbo continued, along with the obvious geographical fact that this was the shortest route to the final objective "of the Anglo-American illusions: Berlin."

After addressing the subject of Allied air support for such an operation, noting that enemy air bases in England would be "conveniently close to the battle area," Garbo got down to details. "I learned yesterday at the Ministry of Information that there were seventy-five divisions in this country before the present assault began." This number was based upon the figure that Hitler himself had given to the Japanese ambassador, Baron Hiroshi Oshima, on 28 May. Hitler told Baron Oshima that an estimated force of eighty divisions were in England, waiting for the Invasion. Two days later, Oshima radioed a report of this conversation to Tokyo; Ultra intercepted and decoded Oshima's report. By giving Hitler's own estimate back to him, SHAEF cynically, and correctly, thought that he and OKW would be more willing to accept it.

"Supposing that they were to use twenty to twenty-five divisions in the present assault," Garbo went on, "they would still have fifty divisions available for the second strike."

He concluded his report, which was thorough and persuasive and chock fill of convincing details, with this warning: "I transmit this report with the conviction that the present assault is a trap set with the purpose of making us move all our reserves in a rushed strategic redisposition which we would later regret."[38]

Had the German Intelligence Services been more alert, they might have sensed that Garbo was setting a trap of his own. A two-hour radio transmission from England would have been detected by Britain's radio security service had it been genuine—this was more than enough time to pinpoint the transmitter, and to arrest any German agent foolish enough to transmit for so long. Instead, this very long message was edited down to a much shorter and easily digested version. Copies of this shortened form were sent to von Rundstedt's headquarters, as well as to Hitler's headquarters at Berchtesgaden.

At Berchtesgaden, Garbo's edited report was received by Colonel Friedrich-Adolf Krummacher, Hitler's personal intelligence officer. When he read the message, Krummacher underlined its salient phrases: "diversionary maneuver" and "purpose to entice . . . reserves into a bridgehead in order to then launch decisive assault in another place."[39] Hitler read this copy; so did General Jodl.

Hitler now found himself in a dilemma. He was being given conflicting reports by two different sources. General Pemsel of Seventh Army, as well as von Rundstedt, insisted that the Invasion had already come ashore at Normandy, and that there would be no other landings. But two of the SD's most reliable agents were reporting that Normandy was only a diversion, and that the main Allied attack was still to come.

To make matters even more confusing, Gwyn Evans, agent Druid, was sending yet another report from England. Druid had been told by his contact that OKW did not believe Normandy to be the "main thrust of the Anglo-American Invasion." This opinion was based upon reports by agents in England and Scotland, who had sent full particulars of the fifty FUSAG divisions that were being held in readiness. The real landings would be taking place shortly, probably in the Pas de Calais area.

Druid was astonished by this news, and by the fact that German intelligence had been taken in by what was obviously a very clever Allied hoax. He quickly drafted a warning that the feared Allied invasion of Calais was a fake, and told his contact that the agents who had reported fifty divisions in England should be ignored, since they were working for the enemy. "I have just toured the area," Druid argued. "There are no reserve divisions awaiting orders there. There is no such army as FUSAG." The so-called German agents who sent information about FUSAG were "part of an orchestrated English bluff" to mislead OKW into thinking that Normandy was only a diversion. He emphasized that Normandy was the "real thing," and that FUSAG was a fake.[40]

At this moment, Colonel von Roenne showed his hand. Once again, his intervention turned out to be decisive. He telephoned Colonel Krummacher during the late morning of 9 June, probably just after he heard about Hitler's order releasing Fifteenth Army's reserves to Normandy.

Von Roenne was always nervous and highly strung, but that morning he seemed more nervous than usual. He fully realized that if Hitler believed that the landings in the Pas de Calais were an Allied ruse, then his position would be fatal. He had given his approval to everything that Allies had ever said about FUSAG and Quicksilver. In a "high staccato voice," von Roenne told Krummacher that a radio message from Belgian resistance had just been intercepted. This message indicated that an enemy landing had been planned for the next day, 10 June, probably on the coast of Belgium. This would be the main landing, the invasion led by general Patton's *armeegruppe*.

"To choose this moment, therefore, to move our infantry and armor from the Pas de Calais area and Belgium in order to reinforce the front in Normandy," von Roenne asserted, "would be suicidal madness."

Von Roenne had acted as soon as he heard about Hitler's order, and contacted Krummacher because this was the fastest and most direct route to Hitler. Krummacher's reply was exactly what von Roenne wanted to hear: He was on his way to the noon conference at the Berghoff, and he would present the news of the Belgian radio interception "with all the emphasis at my command."[41]

Before ending the conversation, von Roenne made a point of mentioning the port of Cherbourg, which was one of the American forces' main objectives. He told Krummacher that the dock facilities should be blown up before the Americans captured them. This was a fairly safe thing for von Roenne to tell Hitler's personal intelligence officer, since the destruction of Cherbourg's docks to avoid capture by the enemy was a standing order. He was only trying to make himself look good, playing the part of Loyal German Officer for the benefit of one of Hitler's staff officers.

When Krummacher reached the Berghoff, he reported von Roenne's telephone message to General Jodl. It was Jodl who informed Hitler of the Belgian resistance intercept, along with von Roenne's view of the situation. Hitler listened to what Jodl had to tell him, but would not make any decision about the reserves. He would think it over, he said, and would give his verdict at the midnight conference. The meeting adjourned without any action being taken.

Hitler had a lot to think about. On the one hand, von Rundstedt and all the commanders in Normandy were clamoring for reinforcements against the strengthening enemy beachhead. But there were also the reports of the Allied armies in southeast England to keep in mind. And von Roenne's news about a planned invasion for 10 June was another important consideration.

Von Roenne's opinion was treated with a great deal of respect by Hitler. As head of FHW, von Roenne had been compiling and evaluating information about the Allied forces, as well as their intentions, for the past several months. If he had information about an impending full-scale assault in northern France or Belgium, and was firmly convinced that Fifteenth Army's forces should not be moved from Calais, then this view should be given highest priority.

This latest message from von Roenne did not represent anything new or radical; since late winter, he had been saying that the main Invasion would come at Calais. His recommendation to stop the movement of reserves to Normandy was only a variation on that theme. The only new feature was the report from the Belgian underground.

Another reason—probably the most important reason of all—for Hitler favoring the viewpoint of Calais as the main Invasion site was that it coincided with his own. But this opinion was not Hitler's own. Originally, he had thought that all signs pointed toward Normandy. His mind had been changed by the Allied deception planners, as well as by von Roenne himself—the evaluator of intelligence in whom Hitler placed so much confidence. Von Roenne swore to all the lies, especially Quicksilver, of the Joint Security Control, the London Controlling Section, and all the other deception groups. Now, with the ruse about the Belgian resistance intercept, von Roenne was adding another lie, this one of his own making.

At midnight on 9–10 June, after weighing all the pluses and minuses, Hitler announced his decision: All forces on their way to Normandy from Calais, including the 1,500 Panzers, were to stop their advance. He relayed the decision to General Wilhelm Keitel, chief of staff at OKW; Keitel passed it along to von Rundstedt's headquarters.

For the second time in four days, the dour old *feldmarschall* had been given an order that defied logic; he had not been told about von Roenne and the Belgian resistance intercept, which he would not have believed anyway. And, once again, his orders for strengthening the defenses in Normandy had been countermanded by a man he considered beneath contempt. Von Rundstedt had been dismissed by Hitler in November 1941, for ordering a tactical retreat at Rostov against Hitler's orders, but was reinstated three months later. Now, he was on the verge of resigning his command in the face of this stupid and infuriating order.

Hitler's directive not only halted Fifteenth Army's tanks and infantry; it sent them back to their old positions in Calais. He wanted the Pas de Calais strengthened; the 1,500 Panzers would be needed near the Belgian border. Once again, Colonel von Roenne had given the Allied forces in Normandy a respite, as well as an enormous advantage. Garbo and Brutus had sent their reports, but von Roenne—a serving German officer—had backed them up. Without von Roenne's opinion that reinforcing Normandy at the expense of Calais was "suicidal madness," it is unlikely that Hitler would have issued the recall order.

But even though von Rundstedt considered Hitler's order to be stupid and incomprehensible, it was still an order. When he received Keitel's telephone call, von Rundstedt had no choice but to halt all forces that were making for Normandy. "As a consequence of information which has just been received," the communiqué stated matter-of-factly, "C-in-C West has proclaimed a second degree alert for 15th Army in Belgium and northern France."[42]

All units heading west toward the Invasion area stopped where they were and began to turn back. No explanation was given to the soldiers and officers in the Panzer units and infantry regiments; like von Rundstedt, they saw it as an order to be obeyed. Some of the commanders—especially in the forward units, who had come so far under such adverse conditions—shook their heads in bewilderment. Others shrugged their shoulders in resignation. It did not matter what the reaction was; the result was the same—doubling back to the Calais area, to wait for an invasion that would never come.

The operators at Ultra were focusing their attention on northern France, and had been especially alert since Fifteenth Army's advance from Calais began. Radio traffic between von Rundstedt's headquarters and the Panzer and infantry units, and even between the units themselves, was closely monitored for any clues that could be picked up. Among the items they intercepted was Hitler's recall directive, which was passed along immediately.

General George C. Marshall was visiting the underground war rooms in London's Storey's Gate, along with General Alan Brooke and a number of other British and American dignitaries, on the morning of 10 June. The atmosphere in the large room was anything but confident. Everyone was well aware of the German movements, of "those big red blobs on the war maps moving towards Normandy all the time."[43] There was a good deal of worry on the faces of those present, worry over whether all the bridges over the Seine had been destroyed, and especially over what the Germans would do next. In the middle of a particularly anxious discussion on the situation, a secretary brought a message that she thought would be of interest. The message was the Ultra intercept of Hitler's Case Three cancellation.

The tension and anxiety immediately changed to smiles all around. The head of the London control center, Colonel John Henry Bevan, was as astonished as he was relieved. He had his doubts as to whether or not his deception team would be able to change Hitler's mind. A while later, Churchill came in with the head of British Secret Intelligence (MI-6), General Sir Stewart Graham Menzies. When he heard the news, Churchill said that it was "the crowning achievement of the long and glorious history of the British Secret Service—or something like that."[44]

Churchill did not know it, but it was also a notable achievement of a dedicated and persistent anti-Nazi at work in Hitler's own Intelligence Service. Without the efforts of Colonel von Roenne, the work of Garbo, Brutus, and everyone else concerned with this particular bit of subterfuge would not have been nearly so effective and might not have succeeded at all.

When they were told of the Ultra intercept, General Marshal, Brooke, and the others at Storey's Gate realized that this was a turning point in the battle of Normandy. There would certainly be hard-fought battles to come, but they felt sure that they had won. And when the Germans heard the news, they realized that they had lost. Major General Buttlar von Brandenfels, who had scolded General Zimmermann over the releasing of the Panzer Lehr and 12th SS Panzers to Normandy on D-Day morning, recalled that the Panzer units in the Calais area were the only real prospect of turning back the Allied armies. Twenty years after the event, he gave his own view of Hitler's decision: "Had they been flung into the Normandy battle right away, and not sent back to wait for the assault from southeast England that never came, we might have repelled the invasion. . . . A concentrated attack with 15th Army's SS Panzers and the other armor might conceivable have hurled back the invasion—despite your immense air superiority."[45]

A few weeks after the Normandy landings, Feldmarschall Rommel listed ten reasons behind the success of the landings. The reasons that Rommel gave were:

1. Superannuated divisions, insufficiently equipped; construction of fortifications in arrears; unsatisfactory supply situation.
2. 12th SS Panzer too far back.
3. Panzer Lehr Division too far back.
4. 3rd Antiaircraft Corps not between the Orne and the Vire.
5. The mortar brigade not in the Carentan area as proposed.
6. The Bay of the Seine not mined.
7. Air support less than promised.
8. Naval support less than promised. On the night of the Invasion, the Bay of the Seine was not protected by patrol boats.
9. No organic quartermaster for supplies.
10. Command relations insufficiently regulated.[46]

Of these ten reasons, four can be directly attributed to Colonel von Roenne and his constant efforts to make Quicksilver believable to Hitler and OKW. Points 2 through 5 all occurred because OKW deliberately kept these units away from Normandy to counter FUSAG's threat against Calais. The 12th SS Panzers, Panzer Lehr, 3rd Antiaircraft Corps, and mortar brigade were out of position as the direct result of von Roenne's secret support of Quicksilver's deceptions.

Admiral Ruge expanded on Rommel's listing. Ruge explained that if OKW and Hitler had listened to Rommel's advice, the 12th SS Panzer Division would have been in position to attack the American landing sites, while the 21st Panzer Division would have done the same to the British "and certainly would have destroyed the British paratroopers."[47] But Hitler did not listen to Rommel. He listened to von Roenne, who told him things that he wanted and expected to hear.

The standard explanation for the German failure to counterattack, especially early on, while the Allied position was at its most vulnerable, is to blame Hitler. It is absolutely true that Hitler withheld Panzer units from Normandy on two critical occasions, but that decision was not really his. Hitler gave the orders, but von Roenne was the guiding force behind them. Hitler put his trust in the judgment of an officer with an impeccable background and service record, one who held the key position in his Intelligence Service. He had no idea that this officer was working secretly against the Nazi regime and was doing everything in his power to overthrow the Nazi regime. No one—on either side—had any idea as to Colonel von Roenne's role in the success of Overlord, a role that was both pivotal and vital.

NOTES

1. Author interview.
2. Butcher, p. 565.
3. Eisenhower Library.
4. Longmate, *How We Lived Then*, p. 489.
5. New York *Journal American*, Tuesday, 6 June 1944.
6. Osmont, pp. 40–43.
7. Ryan, p. 183.
8. Ibid., p. 184.
9. Ibid.
10. Ibid.
11. Ibid.
12. Ibid., p. 185.
13. Ibid., p. 255.
14. Ibid., p. 257.
15. Ibid., pp. 257–58.
16. Brown, p. 739.
17. Ryan, p. 256.
18. Ruge, p. 173.

19. Ryan, p. 260.
20. Delmer, p. 170.
21. Harrison, p. 333.
22. Ryan, p. 284.
23. Ibid.
24. Carell, p. 88.
25. Warlimont, p. 427.
26. Ruge, p. 173.
27. Ryan, p. 250.
28. Ibid., p. 297.
29. *Battle of Normandy* (video).
30. Ibid.
31. "Morning" (video).
32. Ellsberg, Preface.
33. Carell, p. 135.
34. *The Times* (London), 7 June 1944, and *I Can Hear It Now* (sound recording).
35. Smith, p. 66.
36. Carell, p. 123.
37. Freeman, p. 163.
38. Delmer, pp. 15–16.
39. Ibid., pp. 188–89.
40. Mosley, *Druid*, p. 212.
41. Delmer, pp. 15–16.
42. Ibid., p. 189.
43. Brown, p. 770.
44. Ibid.
45. Delmer, p. 20.
46. Ruge, p. 174.
47. Ibid., p. 178.

ELEVEN

Clear and Decisive

With the success of the landings at Normandy, and the reinforcement and consolidation of the five Allied beachheads, it began to look at though Quicksilver had outlived its usefulness. The feared German counterattack in strength had not taken place. The two Mulberry harbors had been built, and were transfusing men and supplies into the landing areas in massive numbers. Air strips were being built in the landing zones for British and American fighter-bombers, which made the already formidable Allied air superiority even more overwhelming by bringing it closer to the enemy.

It looked as though the Allied armies were on the verge of pushing out of their coastal lodgements and fighting their way inland. They were inflicting losses which the Germans could not afford, while the British and American forces became stronger with each passing day. Keeping Fifteenth Army at bay with a fictitious First U.S. Army Group was beginning to lose its importance.

But beginning in mid-June, several things happened to change this point of view. The first was the Channel storm that began on 19 June, which was the worst in over forty years. The four-day storm demolished the Mulberry at St. Laurent, seriously damaged or destroyed about 800 ships, and reduced the flow of supplies by about 80 percent. The supply situation, which seemed to have been going so well, was suddenly in serious jeopardy.

The capture of Cherbourg now became more important than ever. The port fell to American troops on 26 June, but the loading and unloading facilities had been thoroughly demolished by the Germans before they surrendered. Three weeks passed before the first supplies were unloaded at the port, which helped to avert an extended supply crisis. It would require months before the facilities could be rebuilt.

But the supply problem helped to precipitate another potential crisis. After Cherbourg surrendered, American forces turned southward across the *bocage* country toward the town of St. Lo, in what would become known as the Battle of the Hedgerows. The *bocage* was a series of hedges and ditches that crisscrossed fields for miles on end, which favored the defending German troops and made any advances by American units very slow and extremely costly. General Walter Bedell Smith, Eisenhower's chief of staff, said that the *bocage* was "where every small field was a fortress, every hedgerow a German strongpoint." [1] In seventeen days, American troops lost about 40,000 men. General Bradley called for reinforcements, but the destruction of the St. Laurent Mulberry made supporting the American offensive slow and difficult. There was a similar problem with ammunition—units were told to conserve rounds because supplies were low.

On the other side of the landing area, British and Canadian forces were not having any better success on their front. The SS units defending Caen had put up a determined resistance, and had been able to prevent all attempts to capture the town. General Montgomery ordered a new effort. Supported by more than four hundred RAF bombers, the attack broke German resistance and forced the SS units to abandon Caen on 9 July. But the Germans did not surrender; they merely withdrew across the River Orne and dug in, blocking any further advances by the Allies.

By this time, Quicksilver had begun to die out, but not through any of SHAEF's plans or designs. Hitler had been kept well apprised of the situation in Normandy, and finally came to the conclusion that the Allied offensive in Normandy was a major operation and not just a small diversionary attack. He decided that an attack in the Pas de Calais was still a very real probability, especially since the V-1 offensive against London was being carried out from Calais. The first flying bomb had been launched on 13 July, and several hundred more had been fired from ramps in Calais since then. But Hitler now believed that the troops fighting in Normandy were the best that the Allies had. Patton's First U.S. Army Group, Hitler decided, was made up of second-rate troops, the units that were not good enough to be sent to Normandy. Because of this, Calais should no longer be considered a major Allied objective, except for the fact that it was the site for the V-1 launching ramps.

During the first week of July, Fifteenth Army was kept on alert—the moon and tide conditions between 6 and 8 July closely resembled the conditions prior to the Normandy landings, a bit too closely for OKW. Heavy air attacks against targets in Calais—including the V-1 launching sites—helped reinforce the impression that some sort of activity might

be expected along that coast. But when these days came and went without any Allied attack, Hitler's thoughts turned to another matter.

On 8 July, Hitler ordered a counterattack against the British and Canadian front at Caen: Operation Luettich. It was the assault that SHAEF
had been fearing and expecting for over a month. Operation Luettich
would consist of an assault by eight Panzer divisions—including Fifteenth Army's reserves. To insure surprise, it would not be preceded by
the usual softening artillery barrage. Luftwaffe units would be scraped
together from all parts of France, as well as from fighter squadrons defending Germany against American bombing attacks, and would include
a number of the new Messerschmitt Me 262 jet fighters. Hitler meant to
drive a wedge between the British and American fronts, and realized
that he would be needing all the armor and air support he could round
up. First units began to move forward for the offensive on 13 July.

Alert Ultra operators picked up the radio signals from the Panzer units
and their headquarters, and passed them along to SHAEF. Eisenhower
and his staff knew exactly what it would mean if Operation Luettich was
sprung upon the stalled units at Caen. At best, it would result in stalemate—if the British and Canadian divisions had not been able to break
through the German lines up to this point, they certainly would not be
able to do it once the lines were reinforced. At worst, it might mean a
German breakthrough, which would precipitate a crisis on the eastern
end of the Normandy front.

Eisenhower asked General Montgomery to draw up plans for an attack
against the Germans—to launch an offensive before the enemy could
begin their counteroffensive. "Ike had been smoldering," his naval aide,
Captain Harry C. Butcher, wrote on 7 July, "and today burst out with a
letter to Monty which, in effect, urges him to avoid having our forces
sealed into a beachhead."[2] Montgomery was well aware of the criticism
he had been under for failing to break out from the Caen perimeter, and
had already made plans for an assault. What he had in mind was a joint
attack by American and British units, a two-pronged attack from each
end of the Normandy lodgement. The British attack against the German
units outside Caen was given the code name Goodwood. After this phase
had been launched and was under way, the Americans would launch
Cobra, an attack on the Panzer and infantry divisions at St. Lo. This one-
two punch was calculated to catch the Germans off guard; if it succeeded, it would result in the trapping of Seventh Army between the
British and American pincers. This offensive was not without its risks,
and was unlike Montgomery and his usual cautious and "tidy" methods.
But it was better than stalemate, or waiting for the Germans to attack
first.

But this offensive, especially the Goodwood phase, would have much
less of a chance if the Panzers of Operation Luettich arrived to reinforce

the units outside Caen. To stop these eight divisions from ever reaching Caen, or possibly from ever starting out, Quicksilver would have to be made believable—yet again. Hitler and OKW would have to be convinced that FUSAG was not only alive and well, but was a thriving army waiting for the right moment to throw its full weight against the Pas de Calais. It was basically the same ploy as before, but with two variations: It was to be run by American officers instead of British, and it would be known by the code name Rosebud.

Apart from these changes, Rosebud was no different from Quicksilver. Its immediate purpose was to prevent Hitler from sending Operation Luettich to Normandy, which meant that he would have to be convinced that Calais was still in peril of attack from FUSAG. Rosebud's objective was to deceive the SD and OKW into believing that FUSAG was a major combat unit, at least the equal of the forces in Normandy. The means of deception were still the same smoke-and-mirrors methods that had been employed by Quicksilver: radio messages sent to resistance units, both real and fictitious, in Calais; signals between nonexistent units in England, to be picked up by eavesdroppers in France and Germany; dummy tanks, vehicles, ships, and aircraft, displayed for the benefit of Luftwaffe reconnaissance aircraft, which would be allowed to take their pictures as long as they did not fly too low. This charade may have begun to wear a bit thin by this time, but there was so much as stake that it had to be tried.

Rosebud also maintained the one overwhelming benefit that Quicksilver had enjoyed since its inception—the secret backing and influence of Colonel Alexis von Roenne and, through him, the entire staff at FHW. Von Roenne's collaboration with the Allied deception planners, whether British or American, made up for any failings that Rosebud may have acquired by this time. He sent the head of Army Group B, Colonel Anton Staubwasser, unrequested updates on the disposition of the First U.S. Army Group at regular intervals; several times each week, von Roenne either reported by telephone or sent highly detailed summaries via teletype. A situation report sent by FHW on 11 June makes mention of the British Second Army Corps and the British 58th Infantry Division, both of which were fictitious, which were stationed in the Scotland. The report went on that a "reliable source" observed that these units were moving southward, and that "it may be assumed that they are about to go into position in southern or eastern England."[3]

The regiments and divisions listed on von Roenne's teleprinted order of battle outnumbered the troops that were actually fighting in Normandy. If Staubwasser became somewhat quizzical about the numbers that were being presented to him—Hitler was not the only one who was beginning to question the number of troops in England, as well as their quality—von Roenne switched on his Head of FHW persona and stated that Army Group B did not have the means or the ability to assess the situation in southeastern England. Only FHW, von Roenne icily stressed, was in the position to judge the number of troops waiting across from the Pas de Calais, as well as the intentions of their commanders. And von Roenne's judgment went hand-in-hand with Rosebud's deception.

But Rosebud was about to lose an important asset; General George S. Patton had been given his own command in France. General Patton had been one of Quicksilver's most convincing decoys—as commander of FUSAG, how could the SD, not to mention Hitler and OKW, *not* believe that Calais would be the objective of a major Allied assault. The general consensus among German officers was that Patton was the best that either the Americans or the British had and that, as such, any unit he led *had* to be the main assault spearhead. But on 6 July, Patton was sent to France, and would be given command of Third Army—a post that Patton himself relished, and that Eisenhower had awarded with some misgiving. But who would command Armeegruppe Patton now that Patton was no longer in England? And what excuse could be given for his reassignment?

As soon as he landed in France, Patton made himself extremely visible, as well as highly audible. Just as he had done while traveling throughout England, he told everyone, "You did not see me," and immediately proceeded to make a colorful speech. (In his arrival speech, Patton referred to Hitler as "that paper-hanging goddamned son-of-a-bitch," a line that even made it into the 1970 George C. Scott film *Patton*.) His quotable remarks very quickly made the rounds, and the word was out—Patton was in France. Soon everybody, including German intelligence, knew it.

Since Patton was no longer in command of FUSAG, some sort of convincing excuse would have to be concocted to explain his reassignment. Otherwise, SHAEF concluded, German intelligence might very well deduce that FUSAG was a sham and rush all troops stationed in Calais to the Normandy front. But given Patton's manner and past history, creating a good excuse was fairly easy—it was given out that Patton had offended SHAEF and, as punishment, had been demoted from commander of First U.S. Army Group to a lesser position in France. In a letter of 10 July, Eisenhower himself said that this story should be leaked to the press: Patton had committed a gross indiscretion, and had been broken to commanding troops in the field.

Within a very short time of this letter, two items presented themselves that very nicely confirmed Eisenhower's story. The first occurred on 12 July, after General Bradley presented Patton with an overview of the coming Cobra offensive. Patton immediately informed his staff, including his public relations officer, about Cobra; the public relations officer very obligingly briefed other Third Army staff officers. "The resulting leak by Patton's public affairs officer was considered a monumentally serious breach of security," wrote one of Patton's biographers, "for which

Patton, as the commander, was ultimately responsible."[4] General Bradley was not happy to hear that Patton had publicized secret operational plans, to put it mildly, and thought about removing him from command. Instead, this indiscretion was used as part of the excuse for Patton's reduction in rank.

The second item was a good deal less serious, but was more colorful and generated a lot more publicity. On 14 July, two black soldiers were found to have taken a young woman to France for "immoral purposes" and were court-martialed. One of the soldiers was found guilty and sentenced to ten years in prison; the other was acquitted. But a story began to circulate that Patton was behind the whole thing, and that he had allowed soldiers to take women across to France. This produced much moral indignation from church groups in the United States, as well as a convenient and timely publicity campaign against General Patton—not quite as virulent as the attention caused by the slapping incident but definitely of the same nature. Eisenhower had his impropriety, and SHAEF had its reason for demoting Patton from commanding FUSAG. His successor was General Leslie J. McNair, a career army officer who was no happier about commanding a make-believe army than his predecessor had been.

FUSAG now had a new commander, but it also needed a publicity campaign of its own to keep the SD satisfied that it was still a threat to Calais. The general outline of the Cobra offensive had been revealed by Patton, but German intelligence could not be certain that this was not a ruse. Double agents, including ever reliable Garbo and Brutus, kept the SD and OKW supplied with up-to-date information on FUSAG. Actual units, such as the U.S. Ninth Army, were included in reports along with invented formations—when soldiers from Ninth Army's elements were taken prisoner, which was inevitable, this would lend credibility to the agents' reports. Brutus even came up with another excuse for Patton's demotion. According to his story, Patton was angry with Eisenhower because FUSAG's best troops were being sent to Normandy, and the resulting quarrel made Eisenhower dismiss Patton and ship him off to France.

The War Department in Washington, D.C., also did their part. They supplied information on bogus units that were about to depart the United States, which was picked up by the American department of Communications Reconnaissance Regiment 5 in Euskirchen, a suburb of Bonn. These messages were sent along to Walter Schellenberg at SD headquarters, as well as to Colonel von Roenne at FHW. And the War Department did not spare any effort—to make their nonexistent contingents seem more authentic, Washington supplied detailed descriptions of badges and insignia for each unit, and even supplied their historical background. Furnishing a regimental history for regiments that did not exist required imagination, but the War Department managed to do it.

Colonel von Roenne also kept deflecting attention away from Normandy. On 13 July, he reported that restriction to British civilians along the Channel coast west of Portsmouth had been lifted. As such, none of the troops still in England would be bound for Normandy—Portsmouth and ports to the west would be the normal jumping-off ports for Normandy. Calais would be the place for the next assault, von Roenne insisted, although he also said that he did not have an exact date for the attack.

All of this activity certainly gave Hitler pause about Operation Luettich, and also about the wisdom of transferring combat units from Calais to Normandy. Von Roenne's opinion, once again, was given a great deal of weight. But before he had the chance to order a recall, Operation Goodwood began.

At 5:30 A.M. on 18 July, more than 1,000 RAF heavy bombers released their loads over the German positions at Caen. "The bombers flew in majestically and with a dreadful, unalterable dignity unloaded and made for home," an observer noted.[5] After the RAF turned for home, 571 "heavies" of the U.S. Eighth Air Force repeated the effort.

The artillery of the British Second Army, which fired more than 40,000 shells, along with the combined fire power of about 800 fighter-bombers, completed the bombardment. Canadian and British units—about a quarter of a million men and 1,500 tanks—began the attack, moving out of their positions and toward the shattered German line. But the tanks became bogged down by the hundreds of bomb craters, which slowed down the advance and allowed the SS Panzer units time to recover. After an advance of about three miles, British armored units were being stopped by antitank guns that had escaped the Allied bombardment.

By 20 July, Canadian troops had taken the remaining districts of Caen from the enemy. But they also lost about 5,000 men and 500 tanks. And the breakthrough that General Montgomery had hoped for had not taken place; the SS divisions had stopped it. "The attempt to burst open the barrier around the bridgehead between the Orne and Dives had once more been foiled," said a German writer. "Goodwood had not been such a good day's racing after all."[6]

Because of the failure of Goodwood, Montgomery came under even more criticism. Although he claimed that he was satisfied with the results of the offensive, no one else at SHAEF had any words of praise for either Montgomery or his offensive. Air Marshal Tedder, deputy supreme commander, was one of Montgomery's harshest critics, along with General Frederick Morgan, one of Overlord's original planners. But Eisenhower was not ready to dismiss his ground commander, and told Monty to stand by to make another effort from Caen.

But the Germans had lost as many men and tanks as the Allies, and could not afford the losses. German commanders realized that another attack would explode somewhere along their front, although no one knew exactly where or when. Feldmarschall Guenther von Kluge—who had replaced von Rundstedt on 2 July, after the latter suggested that the Germans make peace or face disaster—had no real idea where the next Allied offensive would take place. But mainly because he had a much higher opinion of the British and Canadian fighting forces than of American units, von Kluge reasoned that the attack would probably come in the Caen sector.

Colonel von Roenne kept sending his reports and evaluations, which helped to keep von Kluge in the dark. On 21 July, his communiqués began to show signs that he was losing faith in his ability to sustain the myth of the Calais offensive for very much longer. This change of mind was probably brought about by conversations with the increasingly skeptical Colonel Staubwasser. Von Roenne now maintained that FUSAG would *not* attack at Calais, because so many of its troops had been sent to reinforce the Normandy front. But, he went on to say, there was still a very good possibility that FUSAG would attempt a landing north of the River Seine, in the Dieppe-Le Havre area. A landing in that vicinity could either reinforce the British and Canadian forces in Caen, or else could launch an attack on the SS units outside the town. In either case, von Roenne's report gave credence to von Kluge's thoughts about another breakout attempt in the Caen region.

The major offensive that von Kluge and the German commanders were expecting was to come not at Caen, but in the American sector, at St. Lo. Rosebud was put to work giving the impression that Caen was to be the focus of the attack, however, by using the old Quicksilver tricks: naval activity off the Channel coast near Caen, increased activity of the *maquis* in the area, and other deceptions. Once again, Colonel von Roenne also exerted his own influence.

The American offensive at St. Lo was to have begun on 20 July, but had to be postponed twice because of heavy rain, cloud, and poor visibility. On 25 July, the weather finally cleared, and the softening-up bombardment began—for the second time in a week—for another Allied offensive. Over 2,000 bombers, medium and heavy, dropped more than 30,000 tons of bombs into the German positions. Artillery and fighter-bombers added to the havoc. More than 1,000 German troops were killed; almost all the tanks of the Panzer Lehr Division had been destroyed. But several hundred American troops also had been killed when Allied bombers accidentally released over their own positions. Among those killed was General Leslie McNair, Patton's replacement at FUSAG, who was in France as a FUSAG "forward observer."

Operation Cobra itself began at dawn on 26 July with a devastating artillery barrage, followed by an advance by armored and motorized infantry of U.S. First Army. Their initial progress was held up by the bomb craters and debris of the bombardment, as well as by German resistance. But General Bradley was not terribly worried. He told Eisenhower that "it was always slow going in the early phases of such an attack"[7] but that the advance would be more encouraging in the coming days. Eisenhower was satisfied with Bradley's explanation, which turned out to be more than correct.

With the help of 400 medium bombers, which concentrated loads of explosives on enemy strongpoints, the U.S. Second Armored Division managed to break through the German line. Other American units followed Second Armored through the gap. By the evening of 28 July, "packs of American tanks and motorized columns swarmed toward the south along all roads between the Vire and the Atlantic coast," according to one source. "There was no cohesive German line left ahead of them."[8]

During this vital phase, while American forces rushed south toward Avaranches and into Brittany, Colonel Alexis von Roenne was still warning about an attack from FUSAG. On 27 July, he reported that the forces in England "will continue to be held in readiness to attack a German-held coastal sector," in spite of the fact that many of its best units had been transferred to the Normandy front. But he also reported that FU-SAG "will be brought up to its full strength once more by the introduction of fresh drafts from the USA."[9] By insisting that FUSAG still posed a threat to the Channel coast east of Normandy, von Roenne continued to distract OKW, and also prevented von Kluge from sending Fifteenth Army to reinforce Normandy. And at this critical stage, the German units in Normandy, both at Caen and St. Lo, were in desperate need of fresh reinforcements.

But by this time, Rosebud/Quicksilver was finally dying out, and FU-SAG finally was becoming obsolete. The U.S. Fourth Armored Division captured Avaranches on 31 July, and began their advance into Brittany and into the open fields of central France. General Patton, who had chafed under the inactivity of commanding the paper units of FUSAG, began his 400-mile run across France. "Patton was never happier," said an American writer, "it was as if he had been freed from jail."[10] The stalemate, which had kept the Allies bottled up in the Normandy beachhead for nearly two months, had finally ended with "a clear and decisive breakout."[11] After seven weeks of slow progress, and sometimes no progress at all, the tanks and motorized units of the U.S. First and Third armies drove forward with a rush that astonished Allied commanders as much as the Germans. The breakout was succeeding beyond SHAEF's most optimistic predictions.

Hitler decided that the only way to stop this headlong advance was with a counterattack—which was to be code-named Operation Luettich, the same as his earlier attempt at containing the Allies. Hitler finally authorized Feldmarschall von Kluge to draw on Fifteenth Army's units for his attack. But von Kluge wanted to attack right away, before the Allied forces grew any stronger. During the night of 6–7 August, four Panzer units, along with the remnants of Panzer Lehr Division, began moving toward Avaranches.

In order to succeed, von Kluge's offensive needed good luck and bad weather. As it turned out, Operation Luettich got neither. It was held up by determined resistance outside Mortain, on Hill 317, about seven miles from Avaranches, and was then stopped by rocket-firing USAAF Thunderbolts and RAF Typhoons that operated at will without any cloud interference. "With uncanny precision, the rocket-shells of the Typhoons smashed into their targets," a German writer lamented.[12] After forty-eight hours, the Panzers withdrew to their jumping-off positions.

In spite of the fair weather and the unexpected pocket of resistance—and despite the advance warning of the offensive given by Ultra—the attack very nearly succeeded. The American unit in the Mortain area was the 30th Division; its commander, General Hobbs, remarked that the Germans were so close to his positions that they could have driven his men off Hill 317 if they had onion on their breath. The 2nd SS Panzer Division advanced to within a mile of Hobb's command post, and looked as though they would break through to Avaranches.

But besides bad luck and fair weather, Operation Luettich also had the determination of Colonel Alexis von Roenne working against it. Had von Roenne not advised the SD and OKW that FUSAG still posed a real and potent threat, von Kluge's reinforcements from Fifteenth Army at Calais would have arrived long before he needed them for Luettich. General Eisenhower wrote that if the counteroffensive had succeeded—as it nearly did, even without reinforcements from Fifteenth Army—the "results achieved would have undoubtedly been publicly characterized as a lost battle."[13] If Fifteenth Army had not remained bottled up in Calais for so long, these fresh troops might have made all the difference between success and failure for Operation Luettich.

While Operation Luettich was grinding to a halt at Mortain, the Canadian First Army attacked south toward Falaise. About 600 tanks struck von Kluge's right flank and penetrated 3 miles of German-held territory. Generals Montgomery and Bradley, as well as Eisenhower at SHAEF headquarters, saw that the position of Seventh Army was extremely vulnerable. With the Canadians pressing southward, Bradley's and Patton's forces had the chance to outflank the German position, moving east and then circling up toward Falaise to surround the entire Seventh Army. To prevent the enemy from slipping out of the trap, it was decided that another deception move should be employed.

The plan to fool Hitler and OKW into keeping Seventh Army in place was given the unglamorous code name Tactical Operation B. Although the name was plain, the deception itself was another colorful Quicksilver-style ruse: Make the enemy believe that you are going to do something, and then do just the opposite.

SHAEF wanted von Kluge, and Hitler, to believe that the American units at Mortain and Avaranches were about to be withdrawn to Brittany. Agents of Double-Cross Committee, including the unfailing Brutus and Garbo, reported that American commanders of the 4th and 6th Armored Divisions had urgently requested an immediate transfer of men, artillery, and supplies in order to take the ports of Brest, Lorient, St. Nazaire, and St. Malo. General Bradley, the reports continued, was sending at least three divisions to Brittany in response to the emergency, and had ordered Patton to send reinforcements from Third Army, as well. The front at Avaranches, according to Double-Cross communiqués, was being reduced in order to strengthen the American attack in Brittany.

Actually, nothing could have been further from the truth. The capture of the Breton ports had been assigned to Major General Troy Middleton and his VIII Corps. General Bradley's forces were committed to taking up a position on Seventh Army's left flank, while Patton's Third Army kept driving to the east. But a special unit trained in deception methods, given the innocuous name U.S. 23rd Headquarters Special Troops, did move from Avaranches into Brittany. This 1,200-man unit wore shoulder patches of Third Army and First Army divisions, and made noises like entire armored and infantry divisions on the move. While Bradley's and Patton's forces were encircling Seventh Army, the Double-Cross agents and the Special Troops were giving the impression that several American divisions were moving in the opposite direction.

Von Kluge did not agree with Hitler's order for a counteroffensive, and was afraid that the Allies might encircle his forces. But he was a career soldier, and had no choice but to follow orders. Four Panzer divisions—the 2nd, 116th, 1st, and 2nd SS—were moved into position against the American front at Mortain, at the expense of the defenses in the Caen sector.

It must have seemed like a good idea to Hitler—take troops away from Caen and send them to attack the supposedly weakened Mortain/Avaranches front. But sometime during 11 August, Hitler must have taken a look at a situation map of Normandy, and saw for himself the predicament of Seventh Army. Even if the area east of Mortain had been weakened, he realized that the German forces were surrounded on three sides—only a narrow space between Falaise and Argentan prevented Seventh Army from being completely cut off. Because he saw the situation for himself, without prompting from any of his generals, Hitler decided to reverse an order. He gave permission for Seventh Army to withdraw from Mortain/Avaranches.

But by that time, it was too late. American armored units were within sight of Argentan by 13 August. The Canadian First Army launched another attack toward Falaise on 14 August, this time joined by the British Second Army. "The Germans were now confined to a pocket 40 miles long and 13 miles wide shaped like a giant horseshoe, with a 25-mile opening in the east."[14] And this 25-mile gap between the British-Canadian forces and the Americans narrowed with each passing day.

Von Kluge ordered his troops to withdraw to the east, through this gap, on 16 August. But the men and machines of Seventh Army were under almost constant artillery fire, as well as attacks by the seemingly ever present fighter-bombers. The Falaise pocket became known as the Killing Ground. Some Germans referred to it as "the Stalingrad of Normandy."[15] The remnants of tanks, vehicles, and men were scattered along every road; some bodies were so burnt and mangled that they no longer appeared human. "Germans charred coal-black, looking like blackened tree trunks, lay beside smoking vehicles," a Canadian soldier remembered.[16]

General Montgomery has often been criticized for not being aggressive enough in his drive to close the gap and cut off the German retreat. Several thousand German troops did manage to escape through the Falaise pocket, although they had to leave almost all of their equipment behind. (Estimates range between 2,000 and 50,000 men. German figures tend to be higher than Allied estimates.) But if several thousand men got away, an estimated 10,000 had been killed, and another 50,000 were taken prisoner, in addition to 200 tanks that had been destroyed. In focusing on what was not accomplished at Falaise, it is easy to overlook what was achieved—the destruction of Seventh Army as a fighting force.

When the Falaise gap closed, and Seventh Army ceased to exist as a cohesive unit, the Battle of Normandy was over. Among the killed or captured were four corps commanders and twelve division commanders—losses that could never be made good. Tactical Operation B had succeeded long enough to allow Bradley and Montgomery to encircle the German forces in Normandy. By the time Hitler became aware of Seventh Army's predicament and gave permission for a withdrawal, the trap had already begun to close.

Feldmarschall von Kluge was relieved of his command of Army Group B during the Falaise disaster. His replacement was Feldmarschall Walther Model, who was known as "the Führer's fireman" because he had shown an unusual talent on the Eastern Front for taking crisis situations and turning them around. But the situation in Normandy had gone beyond crisis and into catastrophe by the time Model arrived.

After closing the Falaise gap, the Canadian First Army and British Second Army began their long-awaited advance into Calais. By mid-September, the Canadians had captured the ports of Calais, Boulogne, and Dunkirk. Quicksilver had finally become redundant. There was no point in trying to convince Hitler of an impending Allied invasion of territory that was already occupied by the Allies.

Von Kluge's failure to stop the encirclement of Seventh Army was only part of the reason behind his dismissal. Perhaps it was only an excuse. Hitler believed that von Kluge had planned to surrender Seventh Army to the enemy. Hitler thought that von Kluge had the British in mind, but an article in *Time* magazine stated that he intended to hand himself and his command over to the U.S. Third Army. Hitler had mistrusted von Kluge for some time. When he received word that von Kluge failed to show up at a meeting with one of his armored group commanders, General Eberbach, Hitler sent an order to all division commanders to report on von Kluge's whereabouts. Rumors began to circulate that he had gone off for secret surrender talks with the enemy.

This suspicion, as it turned out, has some factual basis; he did plan to meet with American senior officers. There was also another attempt to contact the Western powers in August 1944, through the American embassy in Lisbon. Members of the German general staff proposed that Germany would surrender unconditionally to the Western Allies if the British, French, and Americans agreed to occupy Germany immediately and keep the Russians from entering Germany. These conspirators obviously had no idea of the political realities involving the relationship between the West and the Soviet Union or, for better or worse, the postwar agreements drawn up between Churchill, Roosevelt, and Stalin. There is no record that this proposal ever received a reply of any kind. There is also no evidence that von Kluge had anything to do with this particular incident. But there is testimony that von Kluge went to the front in August 1944 to meet with American officers, but returned to his own lines when he was not able to make contact.

But Hitler did not need evidence to relieve and replace von Kluge. Model was made commander of Army Group B, and von Kluge was ordered back to Germany. He never returned to Germany, however. After writing a letter to Hitler, in which he argued for an end to the war that he saw as hopeless, von Kluge bit into a capsule of potassium cyanide during a stop on the road to Metz. Hitler claimed that the letter was an admission of guilt for the loss of Normandy.

Units of Fifteenth Army had begun to cross the Seine early in August, to join the battle in Normandy and to strengthen Seventh Army. But this move came much too late. Fifteenth Army had been kept in Calais far too long, waiting for the invasion that never came. "Every additional soldier who came into the Normandy area was merely caught up in the catastrophe of defeat," wrote Eisenhower, "without exercising any particular influence on the battle."[17] The Battle of Normandy had been lost by the Germans. Throwing Fifteenth Army into the fighting was only adding to the loss.

In his last letter to Hitler, Feldmarschall von Kluge blamed the loss on the Allied wealth of materiel. He had no way of knowing that one of the most formidable weapons in the enemy arsenal had been the Quicksilver deception, which allowed the British and Americans to use all of their men and materiel to their maximum effect while, at the same time, keeping a significant portion of the Wehrmacht forces in France out of the battle. He also did not suspect that one of the most powerful intelligence officers in the German army was directly responsible for the effectiveness of this deception, or know exactly how Colonel von Roenne had used his power and influence to bring about the absolute defeat of Hitler's forces in Normandy.

NOTES

1. Smith, p. 74.
2. Butcher, p. 605.
3. Delmer, p. 221.
4. D'Este, *Patton*, p. 619.
5. Blumenson, p. 48.
6. Carell, p. 254.
7. Eisenhower, p. 272.
8. Carell, p. 267.
9. Delmer, p. 23.
10. D'Este, *Patton*, p. 626.
11. Eisenhower, p. 276.
12. Carell, p. 278.
13. Eisenhower, p. 276.
14. Blumenson, p. 82.
15. Carell, p. 301.
16. Blumenson, p. 85.
17. Eisenhower, p. 288.

TWELVE

Ironic Endings

A few years following the end of the war, after there had been time to reflect upon what had happened in Normandy, General Dwight D. Eisenhower wrote about the events of June, July, and August 1944. "During the period of the Battle of the Beachhead," he said in his memoirs, "the enemy kept his Fifteenth Army concentrated in the Calais region." The reason for this unusual behavior, he went on, was because the enemy "was convinced that we intended to launch an amphibious attack" against the Calais coast. He also pointed out that the Allies "employed every possible ruse to confirm him in his misconceptions."[1] This was news in 1948, when *Crusade in Europe* was first published; not many people knew anything about Quicksilver or its impact on the Invasion and its aftermath.

But nowhere does Eisenhower mention Colonel Alexis von Roenne, or von Roenne's indispensable part in the deception that misled, and ultimately overcame, the enemy. There was actually a good reason for this omission: Not even Eisenhower was fully aware of von Roenne's vital role in the resounding triumph of Quicksilver. Von Roenne's deceptions affected every phase of the Invasion and the Battle of Normandy: the landings on 6 June, the consolidation and reinforcement of the beachheads, the breakout from the beaches, and the destruction of Seventh Army and resulting Allied sweep across France to the borders of Germany. His deception was directly responsible for their success. But his role in these successes has been completely overlooked. No Allied planner ever gave him any credit for what he did, at the risk of his own life, to make Quicksilver, and later Rosebud, so convincing.

A few writers have acknowledged that von Roenne deliberately passed along misleading information to his superiors. But most also questioned his motives. Sefton Delmer supposed that von Roenne developed the habit "of embroidering the false information planted . . . by the Allies" to impress his superiors.[2] Others suggest that he had been completely taken in by Quicksilver and that he was simply passing along information about FUSAG that he believed to be genuine. Ladislas Farago implied that von Roenne acted out of fear; Hitler and OKW were unhappy about the lack of hard intelligence regarding Overlord, so von Roenne invented some to save his own skin.

Without any knowledge of von Roenne's background, his attitude toward Hitler, or his contacts with Admiral Canaris and the Schwarze Kapelle, these conclusions might seem feasible. But if von Roenne had been passing false information only because of fear, he would have found some way to correct his forged reports somewhere along the way, before someone discovered what he had done. And as far as being fooled by Quicksilver, no one with von Roenne's mind could have been duped so often and for such a length of time.

And von Roenne had no need to put himself in a good light with his superiors. He was already held in high esteem by OKW, and had been decorated with the *Deutches Kreuz* by Hitler himself. It would have been just as easy for him to send unadulterated information along to the SD as it was to tamper with the data and figures involving Allied troop strength in Britain. The reason behind von Roenne's changing these estimates had nothing to do with fear of Hitler, or with building up his reputation.

By the time von Roenne had been appointed head of FHW, he had already become an anti-Nazi conspirator. He had turned against Hitler and his oppressive regime long before his appointment, probably even before the war began. His contacts with Hans von Oster, Admiral Canaris, and other members of the Schwarze Kapelle persuaded von Roenne to do something to back up his convictions. And his way of fighting the Nazi war machine was to inflate estimates of Allied troop strength in England, and convince Hitler and OKW that the main Allied landing would take place in Calais instead of Normandy. Von Roenne realized that he was putting his life on the line. But he also had decided that the end justified the risk. Von Roenne had gone from non-Nazi to dedicated anti-Nazi, with the help of Admiral Canaris, Hans von Oster, and their colleagues in the Schwarze Kapelle. He used his position and his influence to further their anti-Nazi goals, which had now also become his own.

Eisenhower and other Allied leaders were not alone in overlooking von Roenne's deceptions. Neither Hitler, nor the general staff, nor Walter Schellenberg, nor anyone in any of the German intelligence Services, had any idea that the Wehrmacht's senior intelligence officer was secretly working against them. No one could quite understand why German fortunes in France had collapsed, but no one blamed von Roenne. Some blamed bad luck, or poor planning, or—increasingly—Hitler. German writer Paul Carell thought that there must have been a jinx on all German operations. The thought never occurred that the head of FHW, operating from his headquarters in Zossen, outside of Berlin, might be at the bottom of the string of disasters in Normandy.

For more than half a year, von Roenne undermined every German defense against Overlord, and then subverted the Wehrmacht's attempts to block an Allied breakout. And for more than half a year, he got away with it. No one on either side knew about his activities. But in early August, while the U.S. 1st Army was fighting Operation Luettich at Mortain, Colonel von Roenne was arrested for an incident in which he took no active part.

On the afternoon of 20 July, members of the Schwarze Kapelle attempted to assassinate Hitler at his headquarters in East Prussia. This was the culmination of a coup d'etat code-named Plan Valkyrie, which was a plot to kill Hitler, abolish the authority of the Nazi Party, take control of the government, and negotiate an armistice with the Western Allies. Colonel Claus von Stauffenberg, a leader in the conspiracy and an acquaintance of von Roenne and Admiral Canaris, placed a bomb—made of British plastic charges and detonators with an acid time fuse—in his briefcase before leaving to attend a meeting with Hitler at his headquarters. Once inside the conference building, von Stauffenberg set the 10-minute fuse, positioned the explosive-packed briefcase under Hitler's meeting table, and waited for his chance to get away before the bomb went off. While Hitler and the officers present were engrossed with a situation map of the Russian front, von Stauffenberg slipped out of the room unnoticed.

Just after von Stauffenberg stepped out, Colonel Heinz Brandt moved to one side to get a better look at the Russian map. But he found von Stauffenberg's briefcase in the way. He tried to push it to one side with his foot, but it was too heavy. Von Stauffenberg had asked Colonel Brandt to look after the briefcase, because it had secret documents in it. Brandt reached down with one hand and moved the case a few feet away from him, placing it on the far side of a heavy table support. The support stood between the bomb and Hitler, who was seated at the center of the table.

The bomb went off at 12:42 P.M. Colonel von Stauffenberg was waiting not very far away, and saw what happened. He said that the building looked as though it had been hit by a 155 mm howitzer shell. Debris shot high into the air; bodies were blasted out of the open windows. Von Stauffenberg was certain that no one had survived the blast.

He was wrong. Several people had been killed in the explosion—including Colonel Brandt, whose casual act of moving the briefcase had saved Hitler's life and ended his own—and a number of others suffered injuries ranging from slight to fatal. Hitler himself had been injured, but not severely. His eardrums had burst; his trousers had been blown off his legs, which were burnt and lacerated; and his right arm had been temporarily paralyzed. Although he had been badly shaken, he was still alive.

After the initial shock had worn off, first thoughts turned to the cause of the explosion. Hitler thought that a single fighter-bomber might have eluded the antiaircraft defenses and scored a direct hit. General Alfred Jodl, who had been present at the meeting, and was slightly injured by a falling chandelier, had the idea that laborers somehow planted a bomb underneath the building's floor—the bomb blast left a deep crater in the floor, giving the impression that the explosion had come from below. But after an investigation had begun, and the clues were pieced together, what had actually happened became apparent.

Hitler was determined to round up every person who had any connection with the plot to kill him. "The barbarism of the Nazis toward their own fellow Germans reached its zenith," said one historian.[3] Seventeen generals were executed. Hundreds of other German officers, as well as members of their families and other civilians, were tried and convicted for complicity in the failed attempt on Hitler's life. Following a mock trial by the People's Court, which consisted of a torrent of verbal abuse by the Nazi judge and a predetermined guilty verdict, these accused were sentenced to death. Some simply disappeared into Hitler's *Nacht und Nebel*—literally Night and Fog. Wives and children simply vanished after having been arrested. Some of the children were placed in the custody of loyal Nazi families, to be raised as proper Party members. Others were executed without trial, or killed themselves. The total number of those who died in the wake of the failed 20 July plot varies wildly, from several hundred to about 7,000.

Shortly after the bomb went off, Colonel von Stauffenberg telephoned Admiral Canaris to inform him that Hitler had been killed. Canaris pretended to be surprised by the news, just in case the line had been tapped, and asked if the Russians were behind it. Von Stauffenberg did not remain at liberty for long, however. He was one of the first conspirators to be arrested, and one of the first executed. He was shot by a firing squad—unusual, because this was considered an honorable death for a German officer. But most of the other conspirators, and suspected conspirators were hanged—a grisly, torturous death by strangulation.

As the investigation widened, an increasing number of conspirators, most of them members of the Schwarze Kapelle, were arrested. Among them were Colonel Hans von Oster, Admiral Canaris, General von Stuelpnagel, General von Falkenhausen, General Hans Speidel, and

Colonel von Roenne. Reichsführer Heinrich Himmler, head of the SS, used every means at his disposal to hunt down anyone implicated in the assassination plot. Under torture and duress, prisoners talked and gave names of other conspirators.

One of the names that came out of these sessions was Colonel Alexis von Roenne. The Gestapo acted at once, but not in their usual manner. Although they began interviewing von Roenne late in July, they did not actually arrest him. He was interrogated on more than one occasion but was released each time. Possibly the Gestapo hoped that von Roenne would lead them to other suspects in the plot. For whatever reason, von Roenne remained at his post at FHW, and kept sending his situation reports on Allied movements and intentions, including estimates that FUSAG would be brought up to strength by replacement troops from the United States.

Whatever game the Gestapo had been playing, they finally grew bored with it. Von Roenne's last situation report was issued on 8 August, the same date that the first conspirators were hanged at Berlin's Ploetzensee Prison. On the following morning, two officers in the SD, the Nazi Party's intelligence organization, arrived at FHW headquarters to arrest von Roenne. He was driven from his office in Zossen to the Reich Central Security office in Berlin—which had been Reinhard Heydrich's department. Von Roenne's assistant, a Lieutenant Colonel Buerklin, was appointed to replace him as head of the FHW and was promoted to colonel. But von Roenne had done such a convincing job of making FUSAG believable that Colonel Buerklin did not realize that this unit was a fake. Only after the British and Canadian armies had overrun Calais, and information about FUSAG suddenly dried up, did anyone become suspicious. Even then, the doubts were cast on agents in the field, including Garbo and Brutus, and not von Roenne. But by that time, it no longer mattered.

Von Roenne was haled before the People's Court. He was brought before Judge Ronald Freisler, who has been referred to as "a vile, vituperative maniac"[4] and, as had already been determined, was sentenced to death by hanging. Following this humiliation, he was transported to Ploetzensee Prison for the sentence to be carried out.

Hitler wanted no mercy to be shown to any of the conspirators. All were to be hanged like the carcasses of dead animals. His wishes were enforced to the letter.

On the evening of 11 October, von Roenne and nine others were led into a whitewashed cellar underneath Ploetzensee Prison. Among the condemned were a lawyer, a Roman Catholic prelate, and an army officer. They were dressed in prison uniforms, and were lined up single file by the hangman. All were bound hand and foot. The hangman seemed to be enjoying himself hugely through all this. One of the guards in attendance commented that as "he and his assistants slipped a noose around each man's neck, he made comic grimaces and cackled out a long stream of facetious remarks in a broad Berlin dialect."[5]

The prisoners were hanged in order, one man at a time. An iron rail ran the length of the room, just beneath the ceiling; several meat hooks had been hung from the rail. As each man's turn came, the hangman and his assistants lifted him up, caught the noose around one of the hooks, and jerked him down, breaking his neck.

The hanging of the ten men took about twenty-five minutes. The event was filmed by an official camera crew—a sound film, to record the noises of the prisoner's death struggles as well as their visual image. Hitler wanted to see the hanging himself, in every detail. During one viewing of these executions, Propaganda Minister Josef Goebbels had to put his hands over his eyes to keep from fainting.

There has been some conjecture that von Roenne might have been able to avoid this terrible end if he had defended himself against the conspiracy charges. This is not very likely. The Gestapo did not make their arrest until they were certain that von Roenne was implicated in the assassination conspiracy. Von Roenne knew very well that the Gestapo and the SD had enough evidence to hang him. If he thought that he could have talked his way out of his arrest and execution, he most certainly would have done so, or at least would have tried. But when he realized that he was caught, he told his captors that Hitler was a criminal that had to be removed for Germany's good. He realized that his fate had already been decided, and that he had nothing more to lose.

By Hitler's order, none of the condemned were allowed visits by any clergymen, Catholic or Protestant, prior to their execution. But von Roenne did write a last letter to his mother, a devoutly religious letter in which he asked her to take care of his two children, and to raise them "with the same love and loyalty you showed for me." He knew very well that he would be executed very soon—"For the last week I have now been awaiting death day by day"—but wrote that because of his religious faith he was not afraid: "He showed me that the moment of death is the first moment of blessed rest in God's peace." He ended his letter, "I send you my greetings with the whole of my heart and commend you to the power of God and his blessing. . . . Richer and more deep felt love from its mother no child ever enjoyed than—Thine A."[6]

Admiral Canaris did not play as straightforward a role in the success of Quicksilver, and the Allied triumphs in France, as Colonel von Roenne. In keeping with his own manner and personality, Canaris' influence was more subtle and indirect. By his deliberate and repeated failures to give advance warning of the enemy's intentions, especially concerning the invasion of North Africa and Anzio, Canaris had seriously undermined the credibility of all the German Intelligence Services.

Admiral Canaris' seeming incompetence, which was actually an extremely skillful anti-Nazi rebellion, caused Hitler, von Rundstedt, and the entire general staff to disregard information sent by the SD and other agencies. Hitler decided to rely upon his own intuition—and sometimes upon the Churchill/Roosevelt telephone intercepts—instead of his intelligence staff and their reports, in making decisions about the defenses in France. Although Hitler had an excellent espionage and intelligence network, especially his radio reconnaissance units, all of these component parts had been sapped by Canaris.

Besides undermining Hitler's ability to make informed decisions, Canaris' actions also made Colonel von Roenne's own deception more effective. Because von Roenne had done such an outstanding job of appraising British and French intentions at the beginning of the war, Hitler respected his opinions; he was one of the few officers in intelligence who had Hitler's confidence. When von Roenne began to elaborate on the FUSAG figures sent by Brutus, Garbo, and other Double-Cross agents, and later added his own make-believe units to the growing order of battle, Hitler believed him. Other sources, who were sending accurate information on the probability of the main Allied landing taking place at Normandy, including the Welsh agent Druid, were ignored. Hitler paid little or no attention to reports from reliable intelligence sources, but listened to von Roenne's invented information.

Even after he had been dismissed as head of the Abwehr at the beginning of 1944, Canaris carried on with his intelligence guerilla war against Hitler. He continued to send top-quality information to SHAEF about German defenses in northern France, in addition to the Wehrmacht's order of battle. This was a major coup for Canaris, as well as for SHAEF, and served to supplement Colonel von Roenne's deceptions concerning FUSAG and the phony Allied invasion at Calais. While von Roenne supplied OKW with information on fictitious units in Britain, Canaris gave SHAEF accurate figures on the make-up and disposition of the Wehrmacht in northern France.

Because he was no longer being kept under surveillance by Walter Schellenberg, Canaris also was able to carry out other activities. He remained in touch with his Schwarze Kapelle colleagues, as well as with members of British intelligence. MI-6 had a secret organization in northern France; Canaris made contact with one of its directors in the spring of 1944.

This time, however, Canaris was not supplying SHAEF with information. He was communicating with MI-6 to request armistice terms with the Western Allies, an arrangement that would be separate from the Soviet Union. Such a request was impossible—neither the British nor the Americans had any intention of offering any terms at all to Germany, especially terms that would exclude the Russians. Canaris received a letter to this effect, apparently from General Sir Stewart Graham Menzies, the head of MI-6.

Admiral Canaris was disappointed to learn that his armistice proposal had been rejected. But the fact that he had been able to communicate with the chief of British Secret Intelligence, and had received a detailed reply, offers further proof of Canaris' almost supernatural ability to make contact with high-ranking Allied officials. And the fact that he received a reply from Menzies comes as evidence of the esteem in which he was held, both by SHAEF and by the many Allied intelligence services.

In the aftermath of the 20 July assassination plot and the resulting investigation, Canaris' name was mentioned as being one of the conspirators. The man that gave Canaris' name to the Gestapo was probably Colonel Georg Hansen, the director of military intelligence and a subordinate of Walter Schellenberg. Under pressure, the sort of pressure that only the Gestapo knew how to inflict, Colonel Hansen not only implicated Canaris in the assassination conspiracy, but also said that the admiral had been working against the Nazis since the mid-1930s.

The driver of one of the conspirators, a Colonel Werner Schrader, was also interrogated. Colonel Schrader was known to be an associate of Canaris, but had committed suicide following the failed bomb plot. His driver was brought in for questioning and was found to be quite talkative. He said that Colonel Schrader had been entrusted with files that contained highly valuable information, although he did not know exactly what was in them. The Gestapo searched Colonel Schrader's office in Zossen to see if they could find these files.

Inside the colonel's safe, the Gestapo found what they were looking for. Among the documents they discovered were Hitler's medical records from the First World War, which included a report on the effects of his having been gassed, as well as a suggestion that a psychiatrist submit an evaluation on Hitler's sanity. But the most important find, from the Gestapo's point of view, were diaries that had been kept by Admiral Canaris. These took up a number of volumes. Some had red covers; others had black or grey covers. The series documented, in detail, the activities of the Schwarze Kapelle from 1934 onward, including attempts at peace negotiations with the Western Allies. Their contents condemned not only Canaris, but also Hans von Oster, who had persuaded Colonel von Roenne to become an active anti-Nazi.

Canaris had already been taken into custody by this time. He was living in his house in Schlactensee with a Polish cook and an Algerian servant, seemingly waiting for the Gestapo to come and get him. When Walter Schellenberg arrived at his house on the afternoon of 23 July, he said, "Somehow I felt that it would be you."[7] Schellenberg and an SS officer took Canaris away to the SS police school at Furstenberg for questioning.

When they arrived at Furstenberg, Canaris asked Schellenberg if he would be allowed to speak with Heinrich Himmler in person. Apparently, he was counting on using whatever evidence he had against Himmler to prevent being handed over to the People's Court. Schellenberg agreed but also offered Canaris the chance to commit suicide—the "German Chance." Canaris refused. He had not gone through ten years of conspiring against Hitler and the Nazis, of putting his life in peril countless times on numerous occasions, just so that he could blow his brains out in some SS school.

He remained in Furstenberg, under arrest, until he was sent for by SS Obergruppenführer Heinrich Mueller, who headed the investigation of the 20 July plot and had kept Colonel von Roenne under surveillance. Canaris was then taken to Berlin, to Gestapo headquarters, where he was interrogated by Mueller himself. If Mueller thought that he could bully some sort of confession out of Canaris, he very quickly learned that his prisoner was not easily intimidated, and was not as dim-witted as he had been left to believe.

Canaris said that he knew absolutely nothing about the assassination conspiracy, and that he had been as surprised and shocked as everyone else by the news. He knew about earlier plots, he said; he learned about these when he had been Abwehr chief, and knew about all such matters that happened in Germany. Mueller asked his questions; Canaris skillfully sidestepped every one of them.

Canaris was determined not to be trapped. He realized that his back was to the wall and that his life depended on what he said, and the way that he conducted himself, in front of Mueller. But he had no idea that his diaries and all the Schwarze Kapelle files were still in existence. He was under the impression that Colonel Schrader had burned all of the incriminating files and documents. But Schrader had committed suicide without giving a thought to what he was leaving behind.

Canaris still retained his mysterious power over Heinrich Himmler, however. Although Himmler had seen the captured files, and had used them to convict and hang other members of the bomb plot, he did not use this evidence against either Canaris or Hans Oster. These files offered written proof that both of them had been involved in many different treasonable activities, including the forging and altering of military documents, along with Oster's failed attempt to warn the Allies of Hitler's invasion of the Low Countries and France in the spring of 1940. But Himmler chose to do nothing. He ordered the files to be destroyed, and left Canaris and his friend Oster alone.

A great deal of speculation has been offered as to why Himmler acted in such an odd manner. The most likely explanation is that Himmler still feared Canaris' own evidence against him, even at this point in time. Canaris had friends and contacts all over, including Sweden and Switzerland. Himmler was afraid that one or more of these contacts had been given information regarding his own plot to overthrow Hitler, or on his rumored homosexual relationship with Reinhard Heydrich. If Canaris were to be executed by the Gestapo, these reports might somehow find their way to Hitler. Under the circumstances, Himmler thought it best to leave Canaris alone.

Although Canaris was not executed, he was not enjoying a very comfortable existence. He spent most of the winter of 1944–1945 in a cell at Gestapo headquarters. His guards kept the lights turned on in his cell all day and all night. The cell door was also kept open at all times and, because heating for the prisoners was not given a very high priority, he was frequently numb from the cold. None of the prisoners were allowed to speak to one another, but they sometimes had brief whispered conversations on their way to shelter during an air raid.

One bit of good news that made the rounds came on 3 February— Judge Freisler of the People's Court had been killed in a daylight air raid. The same bomb that killed Freisler also destroyed the records of one of Canaris' fellow conspirators, Fabian von Schlabrendorff, and saved his life. Von Schlabrendorff joined Canaris in the cells at Gestapo headquarters.

Admiral Canaris was regularly interrogated by the Gestapo—by agents who specialized in questioning prisoners, and dragging whatever they wanted to know out of their victims. But no one was able to bully or coerce anything out of Canaris. He frequently pretended to be a stupid old man, one of his favorite roles and one that he knew how to play to perfection, and acted as though he did not understand the questions. Or his questioners would ask about one subject, and Canaris would give a rambling response about a completely different matter. Eventually, the Gestapo would give up in frustration.

By an ingenious combination of acting, of sidestepping questions, of distorting the truth, and sometimes of falling back on double-talk and gibberish, Canaris blocked every attempt to find out what he knew about the bomb blot, or about Schwarze Kapelle activities. The Gestapo kept on trying, though. "Yet for months, Canaris baffled them with one ruse after another," von Schlabrendorff recalled with some amazement. "His skill in acting a part, his cunning, his imagination, the ease with which he affected naive stupidity and then emerged into the most subtle reasoning disarmed the security agents who interrogated him."[8]

Even though he was forbidden to talk to anyone, either his guards or his fellow prisoners, Canaris still managed to keep informed of events. His usual method was to trick the guards into telling him things, in spite of themselves and their orders. "I suppose by now we are pushing the Russians back over the Vistula," he would say to one of the SS men.

"Ach, what nonsense!" came the sneering reply. "They are approaching the Oder."[9]

The air raid that killed Judge Freisler also gave Hitler second thoughts about keeping such valuable prisoners in Berlin. He decided to move them out of Berlin for safekeeping—a dead prisoner was of no use to him or to the Gestapo. On 7 February, Canaris was transferred to Flossenburg concentration camp, about a mile from the Czechoslovak border. Other prisoners were sent to Buchenwald and other camps, far away from the paths of enemy bombers. Hans Oster was also brought to Flossenburg, along with his lawyer friend, Dr. Josef Müller from Munich, von Schlabrendorff, and other former members of German intelligence. Prisoners who had no connection with any of the Intelligence Services, including theologian Dietrich Bonhoeffer, were kept in another area, away from Canaris, Oster, and the others.

The cell next to Admiral Canaris was occupied by Lieutenant Colonel H. M. Lunding, the former director of Danish military intelligence. Colonel Lunding was also a political prisoner; he had been arrested for anti-German activities during the Nazi occupation of Denmark. Canaris had met Lunding before the war, and they recognized each other. The two of them began communicating by means of a tapping code, which was the only method of conversation possible at Flossenburg. The messages were usually tapped out at night, when the guards were not as watchful.

After he had been transferred to Flossenburg, Canaris continued to be questioned. Security agents persisted in asking him what he knew about the bomb plot as well as his connection with other treasonable activities. It was basically the same routine as Gestapo headquarters. And the half-truths, duplicity, and play acting that had worked so well for him in Berlin served him equally well in his new surroundings. The Gestapo asked their questions. Canaris answered, but told his interrogators nothing.

At night, when the camp quieted down, Canaris and Colonel Lunding conversed with each other and sometimes compared notes. The alphabet of their simple code was divided into five groups, with the letter 'J' omitted. It looked like this:

	1	2	3	4	5
1	A	F	L	Q	V
2	B	G	M	R	W
3	C	H	N	S	X
4	D	I	O	T	Y
5	E	K	P	U	Z

The first tap indicated the line; the second tap gave the letter on that line.

Throughout February and March, Canaris' questioning went on. A Gestapo commissioner came to the camp to confront the admiral with some sort of new evidence. Colonel Lunding watched through the tiny window that faced the courtyard as the Gestapo man, much heavier and taller than Canaris, spoke in a loud, threatening voice and punctuated his remarks with menacing gestures. Canaris, on the other hand, replied in a conversational tone. As the two walked up and down in the courtyard, the commissioner's voice became louder and angrier, while Canaris remained maddeningly calm. The visiting Gestapo agent had no more success with Canaris than any of his predecessors. He returned to Berlin completely frustrated, and no better informed.

Canaris' morale remained high, in spite of everything. He had succeeded in thwarting every attempt by his captors to trap him. Also, he realized that the war would be ending very soon; the prisoners had heard rumors that American forces were not far off and were heading toward Flossenburg. From his coded conversations with Canaris, Colonel Lunding had the impression that "his neighbor had not lost hope of escaping from the Gestapo noose."[10]

But he had not reckoned with Hitler and his violent outbursts, which were becoming more frequent and increasingly vicious. He was given to periods of hysterical frenzy, alternating with stretches of almost unreal calm. Early in April, during one of his rages, he decided that the prisoners in Flossenburg should be dealt with in the manner usually reserved for traitors against the Reich—given a quick trial and then hanged. Exactly why Hitler chose this particular time is not known. It is possible that he came across a report with their names on it; maybe Canaris' name came up in the course of a daily staff meeting. Whatever the motive, Hitler gave the order on the afternoon of 5 April: Canaris, Oster, Dietrich Bonhoeffer, Dr. Josef Müller, and three others were to be hanged.

Dr. Müller was to have been hanged first. "Now the play is ending," a guard shouted at him. "You will be hanged right after Canaris and Oster."[11] He was taken to the gallows, but he was not hanged. Instead, he was led back to his cell, and then back to the gallows again, where he was left standing. After a while, the SS guards took him back to his cell again, telling him that he had been forgotten for the day.

Admiral Canaris was given his quick trial on 8 April, the same day that Müller was supposed to have been hanged. From all evidence, he was not tried at all but was interrogated under torture. Hitler's order finally allowed the SS to do what they had been wanting to do to Canaris ever since his arrest in July. After he was taken back to his cell, bruised and bleeding, he sent a message in code to Colonel Lunding. "That . . .

will . . . have . . . been . . . the   last . . . I . . . think . . . badly . . . mishandled . . . nose . . . broken." He went on to say, "I die for my Fatherland. I have a clear conscience. I only did my duty to my country when I tried to oppose the criminal folly of Hitler leading Germany to destruction." The final part of his message was a request that his wife and daughters be looked after.[12]

In the early hours of 9 April, a Gestapo official came to von Schlabrendorff and wanted to know if he was Dietrich Bonhoeffer. A short while later, the same man came back to his cell and repeated the question. An SS guard barked the same question at Josef Müller. After daybreak, a perplexed guard came by and removed Müller's handcuffs. "I don't know what's going on," he said. "I was told that you were the leading criminal, and now we don't know what to do with you."[13]

It had been a bizarre night, and a terrifying one. Müller had heard the guards shouting out cell numbers, including Number 22—Canaris' cell—and then "Out! Out!" Colonel Lunding heard Canaris' shackles fall to the ground and heard the order, "Clothes off!" Through a crack in his cell door, he saw Canaris, Oster, and three other prisoners led away to the gallows. (Among the other prisoners that were hanged on 9 April were Dr. Teodore Struenck, Judge Advocate General Karl Sack, a Captain Gehre, and Dietrich Bonhoeffer.)

Von Schlabrendorff was told by one of the guards that Canaris died slowly and horribly. After the war, Dr. Müller said the same thing—Canaris took half an hour to die. An iron collar was placed around his neck before the execution began, and the noose was put over the collar. This was done to prolong Canaris' agony or, as a guard put it, "To give you a foretaste of death."[14] He was hanged with the iron collar, taken down while still alive, and then hanged again. The second time, he was left until he was dead. Von Schlabrendorff wrote that the men who had participated in the execution were given extra rations of sausage and whisky.

The bodies of the executed prisoners were taken outside and cremated on a huge bonfire. Müller remembers someone speaking to him in English through his cell window. Several British agents were also being held at Flossenburg, including two officers named Churchill: Lieutenant Colonel John Churchill and Captain Peter Churchill. The Gestapo and the SD thought they might be of value because of their last name—if they were Churchills, they must be related to the prime minister. The man asked Müller, "Are you one of those top officials to be hanged?"

Müller responded, "Yes, I believe so."

The figure in the window did not think that he would be executed. "Your friends have been hanged already and are now being burned behind their cells."[15]

Müller had smelled the smoke, and had seen flaky bits of ash float through the bars of the open window. It took a minute or two before he understood exactly what was being blown into his cell. He recalled that he "nearly fainted at the sight of shreds of human tissue drifting in the air"—he realised that the light grey flakes were the charred remains of Admiral Canaris, Hans Oster, and the others who had been hanged that morning. The wind was blowing in the direction of the cell block, and the ashes continued to settle all around him.

Both Josef Müller and Fabian von Schlabrendorff survived their stay at Flossenburg. Müller apparently had been lost in a bureaucratic shuffle, and had fallen through the cracks at just the right time—units of Patton's Third Army were only about 100 miles away on 9 April, when Canaris and Oster were executed. The Americans arrived before the SS could decide whether or not they should be hanged.

General Hans Speidel, Rommel's chief of staff, also managed to survive imprisonment at the hands of the Gestapo. He escaped from his prison cell, and was given refuge by a Catholic priest until American troops arrived. His commander, however, was not as fortunate.

Feldmarschall Rommel accomplished virtually nothing in the campaign against Hitler, but ended up receiving more attention than every other member of the Schwarze Kapelle combined. Although he gave his name, his reputation, and his moral support to the Schwarze Kapelle and their activities, he never took any direct action against Hitler or his regime. While Canaris and von Roenne repeatedly risked their lives by relaying false reports to Hitler and OKW regarding the Western Allies and their intentions and, in Canaris' case, sending information to the Allies, Rommel remained commander of Army Group B. To the end, he continued to ride his two horses together—wanting to see Hitler overthrown but unwilling or unable to do anything about it because of his duties as a German officer.

One reason behind Rommel's failure to act—possibly the main reason—was that he never found the opportunity. Colonel von Roenne had his opportunity dropped in his lap—Colonel Michel asked von Roenne to double the estimate of troops that were stationed in Britain, because the SD had been reducing FHW's estimates by half. Von Roenne used this occasion as his springboard. For the next several months, he continued to inflate FHW's figures, and also created a largely fictitious order of battle for FUSAG, which fit very nicely into Quicksilver's deception. Through his activities, he was able to convince Hitler and OKW that Calais, not Normandy, would be the site of Overlord.

Rommel was never offered any similar chance. Also, he did not have either Canaris' or von Roenne's repugnance of the Nazi regime, and he also lacked their dedication. Rommel's entry into the anti-Hitler movement "came as a great surprise to the resistance leaders and was not approved by most of them," wrote author William L. Shirer. Shirer also said that many dedicated anti-Nazis "regarded the 'Desert Fox' as a Nazi and an opportunist who blatantly courted Hitler's favor and was only now deserting him because he knew that the war was lost."[16] Any number of writers and historians share this point of view.

Even after Rommel became involved in the plot to overthrow Hitler, there is no evidence that he actually did anything to back up his new-found convictions. He cautioned against assassinating Hitler on practical grounds. He thought killing Hitler would turn him into a martyr, and might trigger a civil war—a point of view that was proven totally incorrect when Hitler finally committed suicide at the end of April 1945.

There is also no evidence that he ever took part in the 20 July bomb plot. One of his biographers even said that he probably did not even know about it. "But personal participation in the *attentat* [the assassination plot], in murder, was not for Rommel," the biographer noted, "and if he had any 'guilty' knowledge it was imprecise, dubious, and (in his mind) to be deplored."[17]

Rommel's widow, Lucie Maria, insisted that her husband had no part in the 20 July attempt. She made a public statement to the effect that the Feldmarschall did not participate in the preparation of the assassination attempt, or in carrying it out. The romantic myth of the Desert Fox as martyr was just beginning to become well-known at the time of her announcement, which was shortly after the war had ended. In 1950, another writer said that "Frau Rommel begged her husband to go before the court," meaning Judge Freisler's People's Court. "He had never been a party to the killing of Hitler, nor would he ever have agreed to it."[18]

Rommel did not use his position as Army Group B's commanding officer to act against Hitler, as Admiral Canaris and Colonel von Roenne had used their posts and prestige to misinform and deceive the Nazi regime. He could have done, but it was not part of his make-up. He might have sent detailed descriptions of the Normandy coastal defenses; it would have been easy for him to have sent such reports to SHAEF by way of almost any of his Schwarze Kapelle acquaintances. This would not have been absolutely vital to SHAEF, since commandos and the resistance had already submitted so much information regarding the obstacles on the landing beaches. But it would have been reassuring to have this intelligence confirmed by the commander of all German forces in northern France.

There were any number of things that Rommel might have done, if he had the inclination and the resolve. He might have sent a series of Army Group B's order of battle, giving SHAEF the exact number and location of units stationed in Normandy, as well as in Calais. He could even had pulled the best units of Seventh Army out of Normandy entirely. Von Roenne already had given him the perfect excuse for making such a move—FUSAG was gathering its strength just across the Straits of Dover. But Rommel chose to wait and see what might happen, and ended up doing none of these things.

There is no doubt that Rommel was thoroughly disillusioned with Hitler. But this disapproval was based upon Hitler's failure as a military leader, and not on any moral or ethical grounds. Rommel met with Hitler on 17 June and again on 29 June, along with Jodl, von Rundstedt, and other senior officers. At both meetings, Hitler's only idea concerning the impending disaster in Normandy was for all German units to hold their ground "at all costs." When Rommel tried to interject a note of realism, telling Hitler that the entire world was in arms against Germany, and that his hold at all costs strategy was losing the battle, his comments were curtly dismissed. At the 29 June meeting, Hitler told Rommel to deal only with the military situation, and to refrain from mentioning politics. When Rommel persisted, Hitler told him to leave the meeting.

Following these two incidents, Rommel became even more openly critical of Hitler than he had been before. He referred to him as "That damned fool" during a conversation with the head of the local SS. He also said that he had absolutely no confidence in any sort of victory for Germany. "The British are here," he said, gesturing at a map, "the Americans are here, the Russians are here: What is the use of talking about victory?"[19] It is likely that these remarks were passed along to Berlin, and that they wound up on Hitler's desk.

When von Stauffenberg's bomb exploded underneath Hitler's map table, Rommel was in hospital recovering from injuries he had received three days earlier. At about four o'clock on the afternoon of 17 July, Rommel was very nearly killed as he was being driven to his headquarters at La Roche Guyon. Two staff officers were traveling with him, including his aide, Captain Lang, as well as an air sentry, who had the task of keeping a lookout for enemy planes. As the big Mercedes staff car approached the village of Sainte Foy-de-Montgomery, the air sentry shouted that two RAF Typhoons were approaching from behind. The driver, Staff Sergeant Daniel, put on a burst of speed and tried to reach a place where the road was covered by a cluster of trees. But before he could get under cover, the lead aircraft opened fire.

The Mercedes was hit by several 20 mm shells. One of them struck Sergeant Daniel, making him lose control of the car. Rommel had also been hit—as he turned to see the enemy fighters, he was knocked unconscious by flying glass and stone. The car struck a tree stump, skidded across the road, and landed in a ditch. Rommel was thrown from the car, bleeding from his wounds.

Captain Lang and the other staff officer carried Rommel from the road, stopped a passing car, and had the feldmarschall and Sergeant Daniel driven twenty-five miles to the Luftwaffe hospital at Bernay. An examination showed that Rommel's skull had been fractured, his left temple had two fractures, his left cheekbone had been smashed, and his left eye was badly injured. Although his wounds were severe, he had not been hurt as badly as Sergeant Daniel, who died from his injuries.

One of the doctors who attended Rommel did not think he had much of a chance of surviving. But he not only survived; he also recovered from his wounds, and fairly quickly. He had many visitors while in hospital, including Captain Lang, naval aide Admiral Ruge, and his staff from Army Group B. When he was told about the assassination plot of 20 July, Lang thought that Rommel was "deeply shocked" by the news.[20] He continued to criticize Hitler, however, and told his visitors that the war must be brought to an end.

Rommel was driven home to Herrlingen on 8 August, just over three weeks after the strafing attack. He was both saddened and angered when he heard of the fate met by the conspirators in the bomb plot. He was also shaken by the news that Hans Speidel, his friend and former chief of staff, had been arrested by the Gestapo. He wrote a letter of protest to Hitler concerning General Speidel's arrest, but received no reply.

The Gestapo were also watching Rommel. While he was recuperating, they kept his house under almost constant surveillance. Frau Rommel received a telephone call informing her that two suspicious looking men had been seen near the house, apparently looking for a way to get into the grounds. Rommel did not seem either upset or very surprised by this news.

A month after leaving hospital, Rommel received a telephone call from Feldmarschall Keitel: He was to travel to Berlin on 10 October for an important interview, and a special train would be made available for the trip. His doctor advised him not to go, however; it was too far for him to travel, and he was not yet fit enough. He telephoned the head of army personnel, General Burgdorf, to explain that he could not travel in his present state of health. But he later told Admiral Ruge, "I shall not go to Berlin: I would never get there alive." Ruge did not believe this, but Rommel insisted. "I know they would kill me on the way and stage an accident."[21] He also told another visitor, an old army friend, that he was absolutely certain that Hitler wanted to get rid of him.

On the same day that he made this statement, Rommel received a telephone message from General Burgdorf. Burgdorf said that he would be calling on him around noon, and would be bringing another officer from army personnel, a General Maisel, with him. The purpose of the visit was so that the three of them could discuss a new appointment for Rommel, or so Burgdorf stated. But General Maisel had been assigned to the inquiry of the 20 July bomb plot, and was investigating officers suspected of involvement in the assassination attempt.

As he had promised, General Burgdorf arrived at Rommel's house at noon on 14 October, accompanied by General Maisel and two other officers. Following the nominal civilities and introductions, Rommel went into the main sitting room with Burgdorf and Maisel. The three of them remained in the room, with the door shut, for nearly an hour. When they emerged, Rommel went upstairs to his wife's room. The two generals went outside to wait.

Rommel told his wife everything that had happened during the meeting. Generals Burgdorf and Maisel had confronted him with evidence that he had participated in the plot to kill Hitler. Rommel denied having had any part in the plot, but they said that they had statements from von Stuelpnagel, General Speidel, and Colonel Caesar von Hofacker maintaining that Rommel had been involved. All of his protests were brushed aside—Hitler was convinced of his guilt, and was greatly disappointed and upset by his betrayal. But because of his past services, Hitler decided to give Rommel a choice: a trial by the People's Court, or swallowing poison that would require only three seconds to act. Burgdorf had even brought a vial of the poison with him. Rommel had already decided which course of action he planned to take. "In a quarter of an hour I shall be dead," he told her.[22]

His aide-de-camp tried to change Rommel's mind—they could shoot their way out, and he could escape. But Rommel quickly vetoed that idea. The SS and the Gestapo had the house surrounded and the streets blocked, and had even taken over the telephone. Besides, he had his wife and his son, Manfred, to think of; he was promised that if he committed suicide, they would be left alone. Even if he elected to appear before the People's Court, he said, the Gestapo would kill him before he reached Berlin. And there was one other consideration—"I will never let myself be hanged by that man Hitler," he said with conviction.[23]

After saying good-bye to Manfred and Lucie Maria, Rommel left the house and climbed into the back seat of one of the waiting cars. He is usually described as being calm and composed during this time, having resigned himself to what was about to happen. General Burgdorf and Maisel went with him. The car drove off, accompanied by another car that was occupied by men in civilian clothes.

Rommel was driven only a few hundred yards away from the house before the driver pulled over. General Maisel later said that he and the driver were asked to get out of the car by General Burgdorf. Burgdorf and Rommel were alone in the car for about five minutes. Then Burgdorf also got out, and began walking up and down in the road. About five minutes after this, he motioned to Maisel and the driver to come back.

The SS driver found Rommel "doubled up and sobbing but practically unconscious and obviously in his death throes."[24] He sat the feldmarshall upright and put his cap on his head. When General Maisel came over, Rommel was already dead, leaning against the back seat. His death had been a lot quicker and easier than that of either Admiral Canaris or

Colonel von Roenne, or any other member of the Schwarze Kapelle. His family and friends were told that he had died of a cerebral hemorrhage. The public were given the story that he died of wounds he had received in France.

The excuse for killing Rommel was his complicity in the assassination plot, but the real reason was that he had become an outspoken critic of Hitler. He no longer believed that Germany could win the war, and said so to anyone who would listen. In short, he was guilty of defeatism and pessimism, which were unforgivable offenses in someone of Rommel's stature and reputation. Desmond Young wrote that Hitler disposed of Rommel "not so much for being a traitor as for being right when he and Keitel and Jodl were wrong over Africa and again over Normandy."[25]

Rommel *had* been guilty of the crime of conspiracy, however. He had talked about overthrowing Hitler and his Party with Dr. Karl Stroelin and with other members of the Schwarze Kapelle. One of the charges presented by General Burgdorf and General Maisel was that Rommel had been mentioned on one of the conspirator's documents as future president of the Reich—the Schwarze Kapelle did have an idea of asking Rommel to be president if they had succeeded in ousting Hitler.

But Rommel's part in the anti-Hitler conspiracy consisted of nothing more than talk. He met with the conspirators, and agreed with their point of view, but did not take any action against Hitler or his regime. Any evidence against Rommel was hearsay, at best, or else extracted under torture. But even though Rommel played no active role against Hitler, and was actually guilty only of talk, talk and hearsay evidence were more than enough to hang Rommel or anyone else in the final days of Hitler's Germany.

The impact of Admiral Canaris' and Colonel von Roenne's accomplishments are almost beyond evaluation. Without Canaris' undermining of the German intelligence system, and von Roenne's constant activities to persuade Hitler that an Allied army would land at Calais, Overlord might have had a completely different outcome. If Fifteenth Army had been free to reinforce units in Normandy, German forces very well might have prevented the Allies from ever getting off the Normandy beaches, and might have stopped them from ever getting ashore in the first place.

Canaris frustrated Hitler and his strategies from the very outset of the war. He warned Generalissimo Francisco Franco about Hitler and his plans in September 1940, and advised him to avoid entering into any sort of alliance with Germany. As such, Canaris frustrated Hitler's plans to capture and occupy Gibraltar, a major setback that affected the outcome of the war.

Besides stopping Hitler from taking Gibraltar, Canaris also distracted attention away from North Africa just prior to Operation Torch, and misinformed OKW of Allied plans for the invasion of Anzio. And these activities constitute only the highlights of his long and eventful career against the Nazis. As one of the founders of the Schwarze Kapelle, in addition to being one of its leaders, he also conspired to keep the Western Allies informed of German tactics and intentions, and was also highly successful in his attempts to mislead the SD—under both Reinhard Heydrich and Walter Schellenberg. Even after he was dismissed as head of the Abwehr, Canaris still kept in touch with his Schwarze Kapelle colleagues, as well as with his contacts with the Allies and in neutral countries. From his exile, he even managed to send SHAEF the Wehrmacht's order of battle—the disposition of all units in northern France. Not only was Canaris a dedicated anti-Nazi, but he was also an extremely energetic and resourceful conspirator. He probably accomplished more toward the downfall of Hitler than the rest of his Schwarze Kapelle companions combined.

Canaris' most far-reaching achievement, the item that contributed most to Hitler's undoing, was his discrediting the reputation of the Abwehr and creating the Canaris Effect—causing Hitler and OKW to lose all faith in intelligence. Although the German espionage network had been badly compromised by the Double-Cross Committee, the Intelligence Services still were able to learn a great deal more about Allied secrets and intentions than anyone in Washington, D.C., or London realised. But because of Canaris' deliberate failures regarding Anzio, Operation Torch, and Gibraltar, neither Hitler nor von Rundstedt trusted intelligence. Cooperation between OKW and the Intelligence Services, which was indispensable if the German-occupied Continent was to be successfully defended against the gathering Allied forces, had completely broken down because Canaris made Hitler distrust his own intelligence network.

Hitler had listened to intelligence before Canaris had soured his opinion of the service, and would have been much better off if he had paid attention to it more often. In spite of the Double-Cross Committee, the accomplishments of the Intelligence Services were impressive, and sometimes bordered on the spectacular. The SD learned the meaning of the code name Operation Overlord late in 1943, thanks in part to the greed of the valet of the British ambassador in Ankara. Gwyn Evans, agent Druid, remained at large in England throughout the war, and sent his share of information on Allied plans. He reported the date and objective of the Dieppe raid in August 1942, which helped to turn that particular operation into an Allied disaster, and also warned his superiors in Germany about Operation Torch, the invasion of North Africa.[26]

German agents in the United States, including Walter Koehler, as well as agents in neutral countries, also added to the SD's accumulation of data. The Radio Reconnaissance units were probably the most reliable, or at least the most persistent, source of data on activities in both the United States and in Britain, and managed to monitor specific units on both sides of the Atlantic. Through its Intelligence Services, OKW received a steady input of information on Allied movements and objectives. Not all of it was top-quality, but much of it was, and it combined to give a fairly accurate and up-to-date appraisal of the enemy and his intentions.

The Gestapo's penetration of resistance units provided another invaluable source of information. Counterintelligence were able to learn the meaning of the Verlaine "Chanson d'Automne" code by infiltrating resistance groups and turning their members. This gave intelligence the means of determining when the Invasion would take place. Through reports of agents in the field, the location of the Invasion, either Normandy or Calais, might also have been determined.

If Canaris undermined the credibility of intelligence, Alexis von Roenne rendered German information gathering completely useless. By deliberately overestimating the number of troops in England, and making FUSAG seem as real as any genuine army unit, von Roenne convinced Hitler that the Invasion would land at Calais. Hitler trusted von Roenne's conclusions and his doctored reports, and listened to him instead of his agents, his Radio Reconnaissance, and other elements of the Intelligence Services who were suggesting a major landing in Normandy, and lost the war.

"Fortitude was critical to Allied success," as understated by an American historian who commented on the Invasion.[27] The Quicksilver phase of Fortitude was certainly vital to the success of Overlord and the triumph of the Western Allies over Nazi Germany. But without the efforts of Colonel von Roenne, and of Admiral Canaris before him, Quicksilver would certainly not have been the brilliant success that it turned out to be, and might not have succeeded at all. If von Roenne had not altered the figures that had been compiled by FHW, and had not repeatedly confirmed Quicksilver's lies about FUSAG, Hitler probably never would have been persuaded that Calais was the assigned target of Overlord. And if Hitler had suspected that FUSAG was nothing more than a gigantic hoax, he would have guessed that the threatened invasion of Calais was also a fraud. It then would have been only a matter of reinforcing the defenses of the Normandy beaches and waiting for the Allied armies to come.

General Sir Frederick Morgan, one of the original planners of Overlord, was well aware of the risks involved in the operation. "If the Germans obtain as much as forty-eight hours warning of the location of the assault," he wrote, "the chances of success are small. Any longer warning spells certain disaster."[28] Without the success of Quicksilver, the chances of catching the Germans completely off guard would have been next to impossible. And the odds of Quicksilver succeeding without Canaris and von Roenne would have been slim, at best.

Fifty years after he had come ashore on Utah Beach with the U.S. 4th

Division, James Murphy was still astonished by the fact that the Normandy landings had not been detected in advance by the Germans. He felt certain that this must have been because of some super spy that the British or the Americans had in Berlin—he admitted that he liked spy novels, and thought that he must have read several hundred of them in his lifetime. Whoever was responsible for keeping such a gigantic undertaking a secret from the enemy certainly earned every penny that he was paid, Murphy thought. He should also have been awarded a special medal from Congress for doing more toward winning the war and beating Hitler than any other individual, and for saving countless lives—including his own.

NOTES

1. Eisenhower, p. 288.
2. Delmer, p. 224.
3. Shirer, p. 1069.
4. Ibid., p. 1070.
5. Delmer, p. 238.
6. Ibid., pp. 240–41.
7. Schellenberg, p. 410.
8. Colvin, p. 242.
9. Ibid., p. 241.
10. Brissaud, p. 329.
11. Toland, *Last 100 Days*, p. 404.
12. Colvin, p. 248.
13. Toland, *Last 100 Days*, p. 404.
14. Colvin, p. 249.
15. Toland, *Last 100 Days*, p. 404.
16. Shirer, p. 1032.
17. Fraser, p. 549.
18. Young, p. 535.
19. Ibid., p. 232.
20. Fraser, p. 524.
21. Young, p. 234.
22. Ibid., p. 235.
23. Ibid.
24. Ibid., p. 239.
25. Ibid., p. 244.
26. Gwyn Evans' activities after the war remain a mystery. When Germany surrendered in May 1945, he realized that there was no hope of Hitler granting independence to Wales. Evans almost certainly left Britain. There is a good possibility that he wound up in the service of Soviet intelligence, although no records confirm or disprove this.
27. Sulzberger, p. 301.
28. Breuer, p. 144.

Selected Bibliography

The following listing represents the printed books and magazine articles that were quoted and referred to most often in researching this book. In addition to these sources, many editions of British and American newspapers and magazines were consulted, including: *Time, Newsweek, Life, Picture Post*, and *Illustrated London News*. Archives consulted include: Bundesarchiv-Militarchiv, Freiburg; Eisenhower Library, Abilene, Kansas; Public Records Office, Kew, Richmond, Surrey; and National Archives, USA.

BOOKS

Abshagen, Karl Heinz. *Canaris*. London: Hutchinson, 1956.

Ambrose, Stephen E. *D-Day: June 6 1944*. New York: Simon & Schuster, 1994.

Bauer, Lieutenant Colonel Eddy, et al. *Illustrated World War II Encyclopedia*. 24 volumes. Westport, Conn.: H. S. Stuttman, 1966.

Bazna, Elyesa. *I Was Cicero*. New York: Harper & Row, 1962.

Best, S. Payne. *The Venlo Incident*. London: Hutchinson & Co., 1950.

Blumenson, Martin. *Liberation*. Chicago: Time-Life Books, 1978.

Bokun, Branko. *Spy in the Vatican*. New York: Praeger, 1973.

Bonhoeffer, Dietrich. *Letters and Papers from Prison*. London: S.C.M. Press, 1953.

Botting, Douglas. *The D-Day Invasion*. Chicago: Time-Life Books, 1978.

Bradley, Omar. *A Soldier's Story*. New York: Henry Holt, 1951.

Breuer, William B. *Hoodwinking Hitler*. Westport, Conn.: Praeger, 1993.

Brissaud, Andre. *Canaris*. New York: Grosset & Dunlap, 1974.

Bristow, Desmond. *A Game of Moles*. London: Little, Brown, 1993.

Brown, Anthony Cave. *Bodyguard of Lies*. New York: Harper & Row, 1973.

Butcher, Harry C. *My Three Years with Eisenhower*. New York: Simon & Schuster, 1946.

Calvocoressi, Peter. *Top Secret Ultra*. New York: Pantheon, 1980.

Campbell, James. *The Bombing of Nuremburg*. New York: Doubleday, 1974.

Carell, Paul. *Invasion—They're Coming!* New York: Bantam Books, 1964.

Cawthon, Charles. "On Omaha Beach." In *American Heritage* Magazine, October-December 1983.

Charmley, John. *Churchill: The End of Glory*. New York: Harcourt, Brace & Co., 1993.

Churchill, Winston S. *The Second World War*. 6 vols. London: Cassell, 1948–54.

Clark, Mark Wayne. *Calculated Risk*. New York: Harper & Bros., 1950.

Collier, Basil. *The Defence of the United Kingdom*. London: HMSO, 1957.

Collins, Larry and Lapierre, Dominique. *Is Paris Burning?* New York: Simon & Schuster, 1965.

Colvin, Ian. *Chief of Intelligence*. London: Gollancz, 1951.

Deighton, Len. *Blood, Tears and Folly*. New York: Harper-Collins, 1993.

D'Este, Carlo. *Decision In Normandy*. New York: Harper-Collins, 1983.

———. *Patton: A Genius For War*. New York: Harper-Collins, 1993.

Delmer, Sefton. *The Counterfeit Spy*. New York: Harper & Row, 1974.

Doenitz, Karl. *Memoirs: Ten Years and Twenty Days*. New York: World Publishing, 1959.

Eisenhower, Dwight D. *Crusade in Europe*. New York: Doubleday, 1948.

Ellsberg, Edward. *The Far Shore*. New York: Dodd-Mead & Co., 1960.

Essame, Hubert and Belfield, E.M.G. *Normandy Bridgehead*. New York: Ballantine Books, 1970.

Farago, Ladislas. *The Game of the Foxes*. New York: Bantam Books, 1973.

———. *Patton—Ordeal and Triumph*. New York: Obolensky, 1964.

———. *War of Wits*. New York: Paperback Library:1954.

Farrar, R. *Winged Dagger*. London: Collins, 1948.

Fitzgibbon, Constantine. *The Shirt of Nessus*. New York: Norton, 1957.

Fleming, Peter. *Operation Sea Lion*. New York: Simon & Schuster, 1957.

Foote, M.R.D. *S.O.E. in France*. London: H.M.S.O., 1966.

Ford, Corey. *Donovan of O.S.S.* Boston: Little, Brown & Co., 1970.

Ford, Corey and McBain, Alistair. *Cloak and Dagger*. New York: Random House, 1946.

Fraser, David. *Knight's Cross*. New York: Harper-Collins, 1993.

Freeman, Roger. *The Mighty Eighth*. New York: Doubleday, 1970.

Gehlen, Reinhard. *The Service*. New York: World Publishing, 1972.

Goebbels, Joseph. *Diaries, 1942–1943*. New York: Doubleday, 1948.

Greene, Ralph C. and Allen, Oliver E. "What Happened Off Devon." In *American Heritage* Magazine, February-March 1985.

Hagen, Louis. *The Secret War for Europe*. New York: Stein & Day, 1969.

Halder, H. *Hitler as Warlord*. London: G. P. Putnam, 1950.

Harrison, Gordon. *Cross-Channel Attack*. New York: BBB Special Editions, n.d.

Hastings, Max. *Overlord*. New York: Simon & Schuster, 1984.

Hoettl, Wilhelm. *The Secret Front*. New York: Praeger, 1954.

Höhne, Heinz. *Canaris*. New York: Doubleday, 1979.

Ingersoll, Ralph. *Top Secret*. New York: Harcourt, Brace, 1946.

James, Clifton. *I Was Monty's Double*. London: Rider, 1954.

Johnson, David. *V-1/V-2*. New York: Scarborough House, 1991.

Johnson, David Alan. *The Battle of Britain: The American Factor*. Conshohocken, Pa.: Combined Books, 1999.
———. *Germany's Spies and Saboteurs*. Osceola, Wisc.: MBI, 1998.
Kahn, David. *Hitler's Spies*. New York: Macmillan, 1978.
Kramarz, J. *Stauffenberg*. London: Andre Deutsch, 1967.
Lewin, Ronald. *Rommel as Military Commander*. London: Batsford, 1969.
Longmate, Norman. *The G.I.'s*. New York: Scribners, 1975.
———. *How We Lived Then*. London: Hutchinson, 1971.
MacDonald, Callum. *The Killing of SS Obergruppenfuhrer Reinhard Heinrich*. New York: The Free Press, 1989.
MacDonald, Charles B. *The Mighty Endeavor*. New York: Oxford University Press, 1969.
Manvell, Roger and Fraenkel, Heinrich. *The Canaris Conspiracy*. New York: David McKay, 1969.
Mason, Herbert Molloy. *To Kill the Devil*. New York: Norton, 1978.
Masterman, J. C. *The Double-Cross System*. New York: Avon, 1972.
McLachlan, Donald. *Room 39*. New York: Atheneum, 1968.
Middlebrook, Martin. *The Nuremberg Raid*. New York: Morrow, 1974.
Miller, Russell. *Nothing Less Than Victory*. New York: Morrow, 1993.
———. *The Resistance*. Chicago: Time-Life Books, 1979.
Montagu, Ewen. *Beyond Top Secret Ultra*. New York: Coward, McCann & Geoghegan, 1978.
———. *The Man Who Never Was*. New York: Bantam, 1965.
Morgan, Sir Frederick. *Overture to Overlord*. London: Hodder & Stoughton, 1950.
Mosley, Leonard. *Backs to the Wall*. New York: Random House, 1971.
———. *The Druid*. London: Eyre Methuen, 1982.
———. *Dulles*. New York: The Dial Press, 1978.
———. *On Borrowed Time*. New York: Random House, 1969.
Moyzisch, Ludwig. *Operation Cicero*. London: Wingate, 1950.
Osmont, Marie-Louise. *The Normandy Diary of Marie-Louise Osmont*. New York: Random House, 1994.
Padfield, Peter. *Himmler*. New York: Henry Holt, 1990.
Paine, Lauran. *The Abwehr*. London: Robert Hale, 1988.
Panter-Downes, Mollie. *London War Notes*. New York: Farrar, Straus & Giroux, 1971.
Payne, Robert. *The Life and Death of Adolf Hitler*. New York: Praeger, 1973.
Persico, Joseph E. *Piercing the Reich*. New York: Viking Press, 1979.
Perrault, Gilles. *The Final Secret of D-Day*. Boston: Little, Brown & Co., 1965.
Phillips, C. E. Lucas. *Alamein*. Boston: Little, Brown, 1962.
Popov, Dusko. *Spy/Counterspy*. New York: Grosset & Dunlop, 1975.
Preston, Paul. *Franco*. New York: Basic Books, 1994.
Prittie, Terrence. *Germans Against Hitler*. London: Hutchinson, 1964.
Ruge, Friedrich. *Rommel in Normandy*. San Rafael, Calif.: Presidio Press, 1979.
Ryan, Cornelius. *The Longest Day*. New York: Simon & Schuster, 1959.
Schellenberg, Walter. *The Schellenberg Memoirs*. London: Andre Deutsch, 1956.
Schneider, Peter. "Saving Konrad Latte." In *The New York Times Magazine*, February 13, 2000.

Shirer, William L. *The Rise and Fall of the Third Reich*. New York: Simon & Schuster, 1960.

Shulman, Milton. *Defeat in the West*. London: Secker & Warburg, 1947.

Smith, Walter Bedell. *Ike's Six Great Decisions, 1944–1945*. New York: Longmans Green, 1956.

Snyder, Louis L. *Hitler's German Enemies*. New York: Hippocrene, 1990.

Speer, Albert. *Inside the Third Reich*. London: Weidenfeld & Nicolson & Co., 1970.

Speidel, Hans. *Invasion 1944*. Chicago: Henry Regnery, 1950.

Stagg, J. M. *Forecast for Overlord*. New York: Norton, 1972.

Stanford, Alfred Boller. *Force Mulberry*. New York: Morrow, 1951.

Sulzberger, C. L. and Ambrose, Stephen E. *The American Heritage New History of World War II*. New York: Viking, 1997.

Toland, John. *Adolf Hitler*. New York: Doubleday, 1976.

———. *The Last 100 Days*. New York: Bantam, 1967.

Waller, John. *The Unseen War in Europe*. New York: Random House, 1996.

Warlimont, Walter. *Inside Hitler's Headquarters*. New York: Praeger, 1964.

West, Nigel. *MI-5*. London: The Bodley Head, 1981.

Wheal, Elizabeth-Anne, Pope, Stephen, and Taylor, James. *Encyclopedia of the Second World War*. Edison, N.J.: Castle Press, 1989.

Whitehead, Donald. *The FBI Story*. New York: Random House, 1956.

Whiting, Charles. *Patton*. New York: Ballantine, 1971.

Wiener, Jan. *The Assassination of Heydrich*. New York: Grossman, 1969.

Wighton, Charles and Peis, Gunter. *They Spied on England*. London: Odhams, 1958.

Winterbotham, Frederick. *The Ultra Secret*. New York: Dell, 1974.

Young, Desmond. *The Desert Fox*. London: Collins, 1950.

VIDEOS

Battle of Normandy, The. Polygram International, 1994.

D-Day. WGBH Educational Foundation, 1994, 1998.

World At War, The. Thames Television. Vol. 14, "Morning."

World War II Battleforce. La Mancha Productions, 1998. "Erwin Rommel."

Index

About the Author

DAVID ALAN JOHNSON has written extensively about the Second World War for more than 20 years. In addition to several books on various aspects of the conflict, he has also done nearly two dozen magazine articles, a television script, and has appeared on The History Channel. This is his seventh book.